THE BEGINNER'S GUIDE TO

Colour Pencils

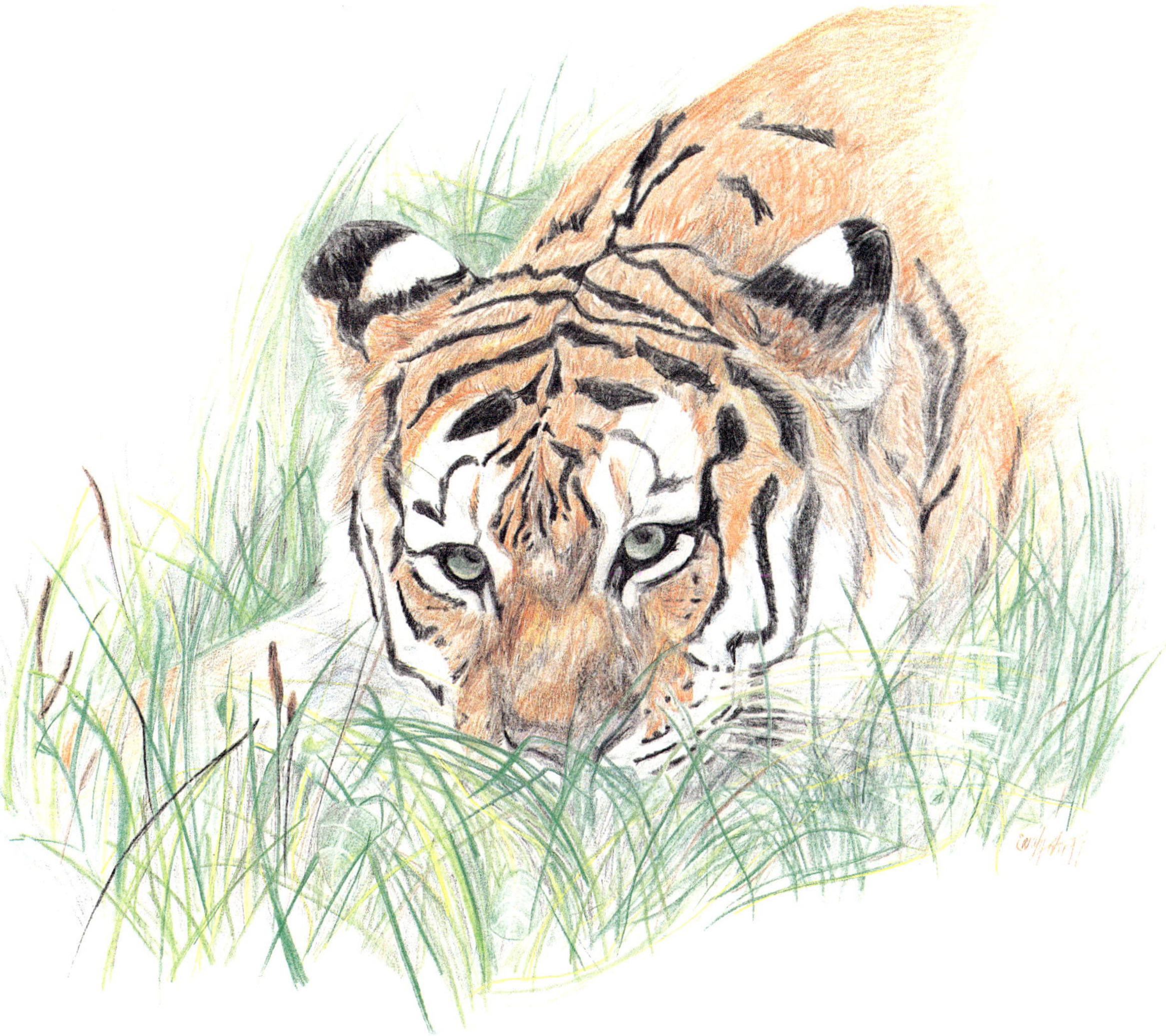

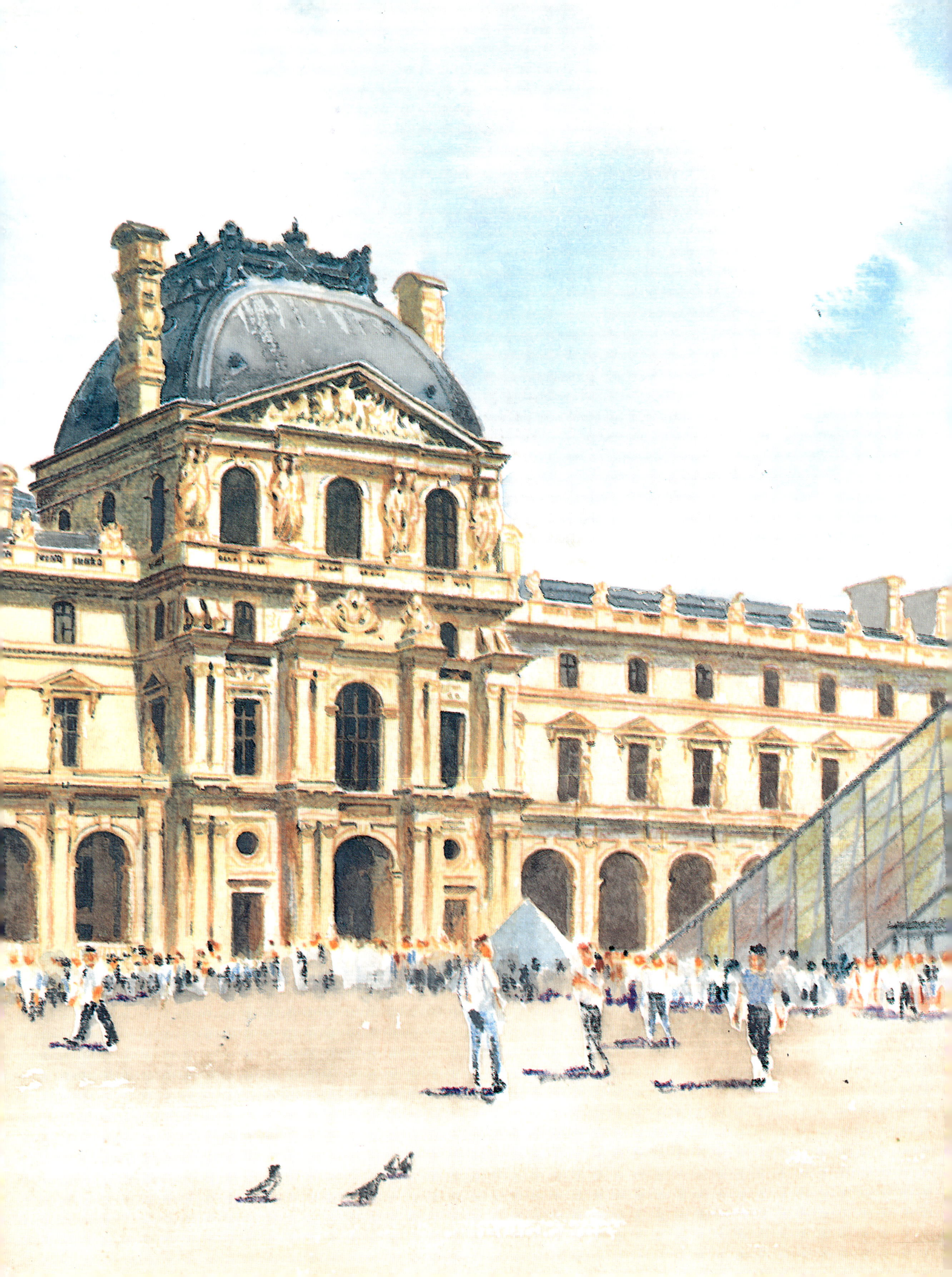

THE BEGINNER'S GUIDE TO

Colour Pencils

Dave Pether

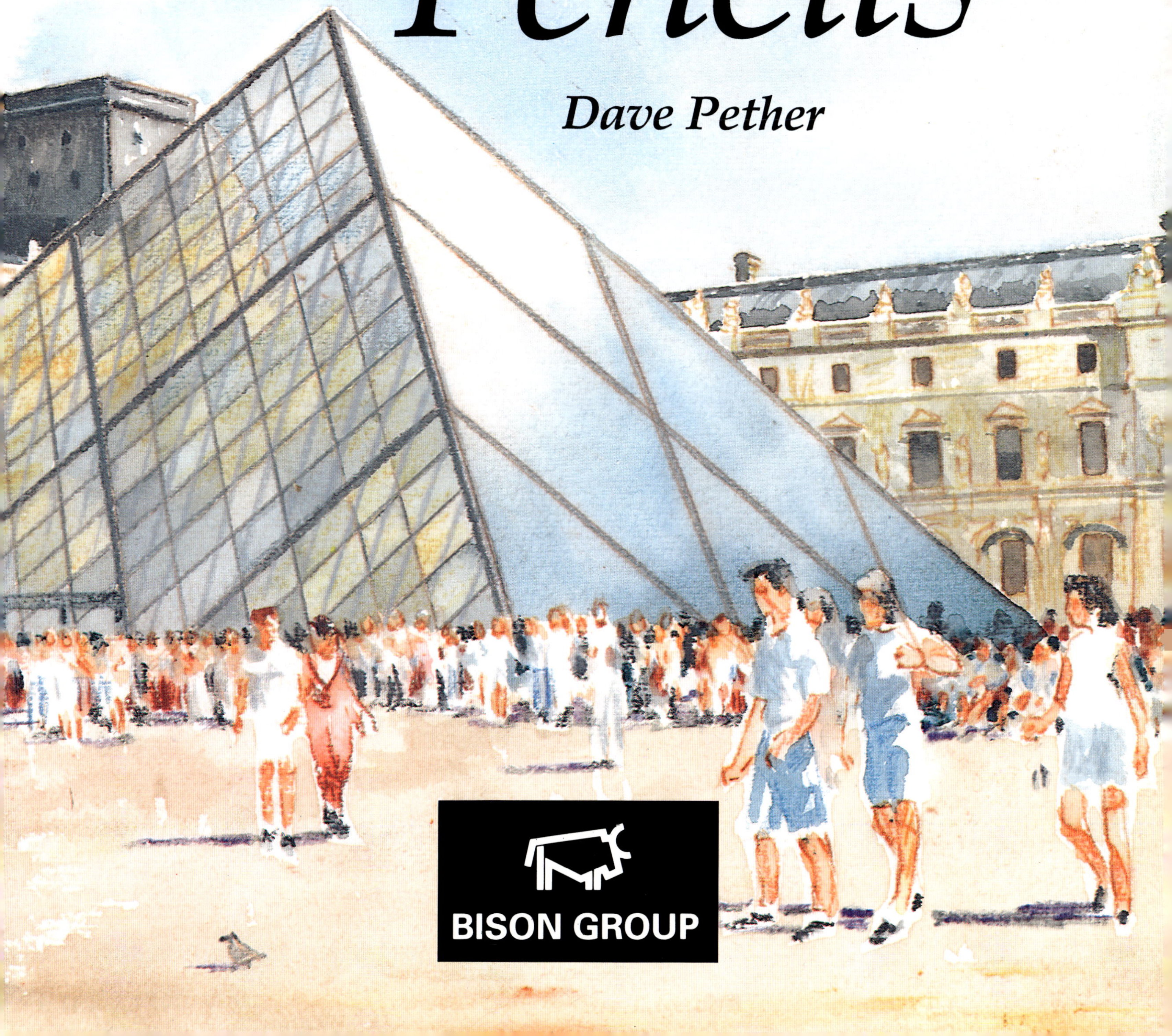

BISON GROUP

First published in 1995 by
Bison Books Ltd
Kimbolton House
117A Fulham Road
London SW3 6RL

ISBN 1-85841-154-8

Printed in Slovenia

All artwork is by the author unless otherwise stated.

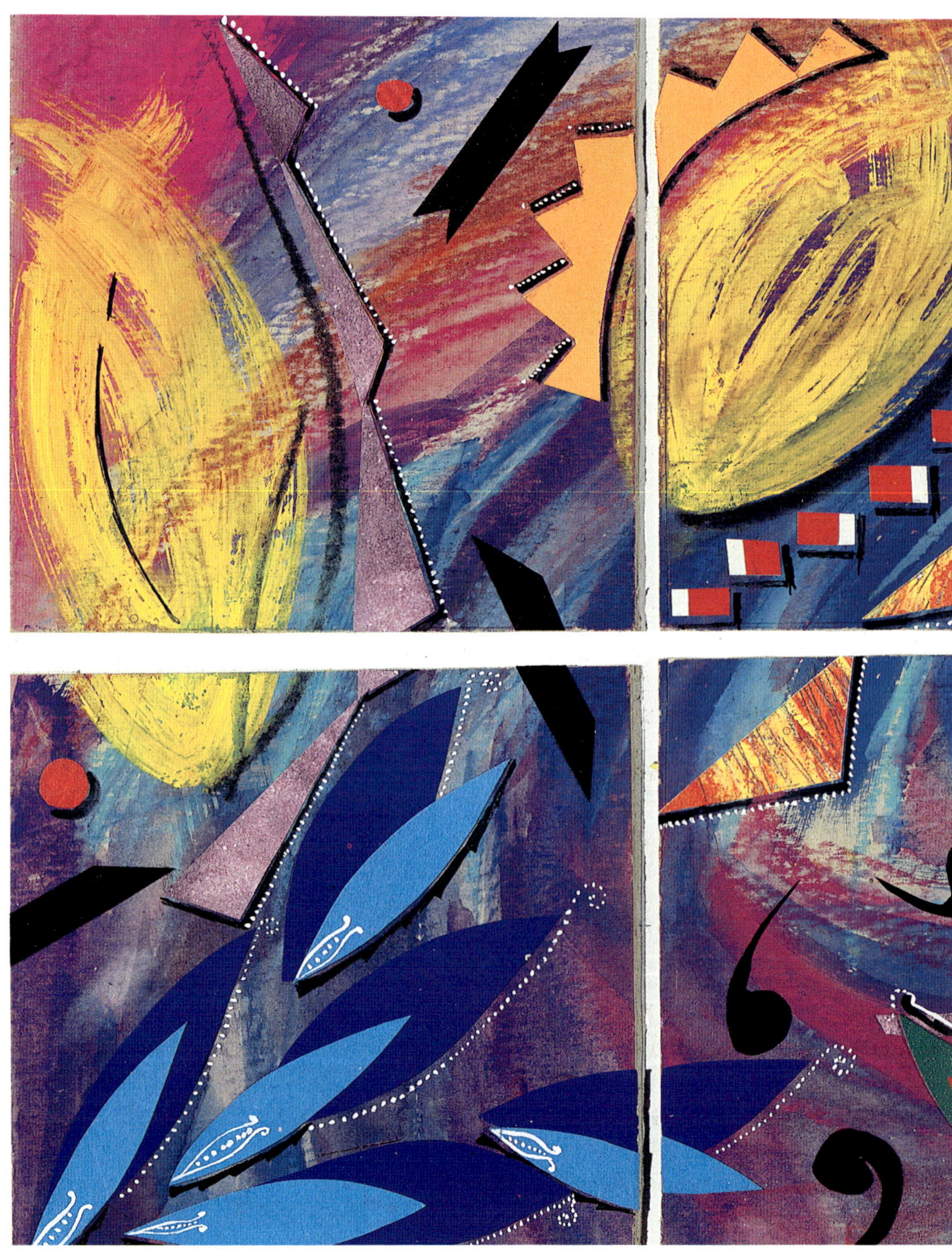

PAGE 1
Sarah Parker
Tiger

PAGES 2/3
The Louvre Pyramid

RIGHT
Devayani Khakria
Underwater Garden

Contents

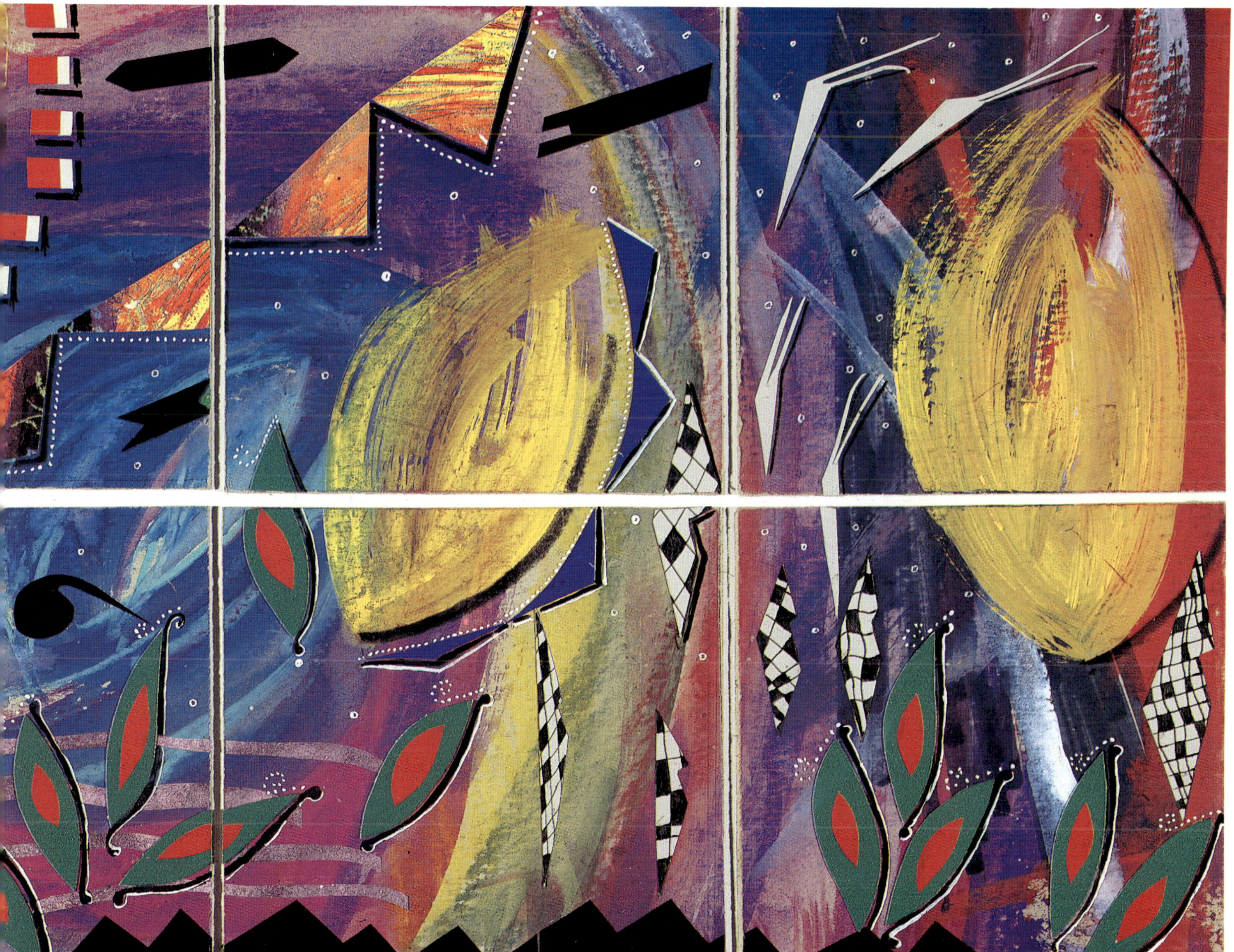

Introduction

If this were a book about oil painting or watercolor technique, there would be a whole range of gallery art, old and new, to illustrate the different methods and approaches. We probably all have an idea of what an oil painting should look like, even though there is a huge range of styles to choose from. Similarly, if the subject of this book was drawing, painting or printmaking, the different approaches would all be reasonably well mapped out, and most of us would have a rough idea of what to expect.

A book on colored pencils, however, is a different proposition. These materials seem to cross the borders between drawing and painting. By using three types of colored pencil, we can explore simple drawing pigment, soluble pigment and soft, heat-sensitive, soluble pigment. We can investigate the qualities in translucent pigment and thick opaque pigment, all described as colored pencils.

Few would anticipate just how versatile this medium has become. If you look through this book, I am sure that some of the more adventurous images will surprise you. My earliest memories of colored pencils come from my schooldays, along with crayons, chalk and bottles of paint. As adults we may come across them in the office, for spotlighting or coding business schedules. These 'new' colored pencils are a different thing from the cruder versions we may remember.

The special nature of this new material gives me an opportunity to address a readership of perhaps mixed artistic abilities. In one sense, we are all beginners with such new materials. To readers with some art experience, I wish to show a range of artists'

The different characteristics offered by the pencils: (below) a broad study using soft, soluble pencils; (bottom left) soluble pencils and a wet brush give almost a watercolor effect; (bottom right) a closely observed drawing using the simple color pencil and cross-hatching.

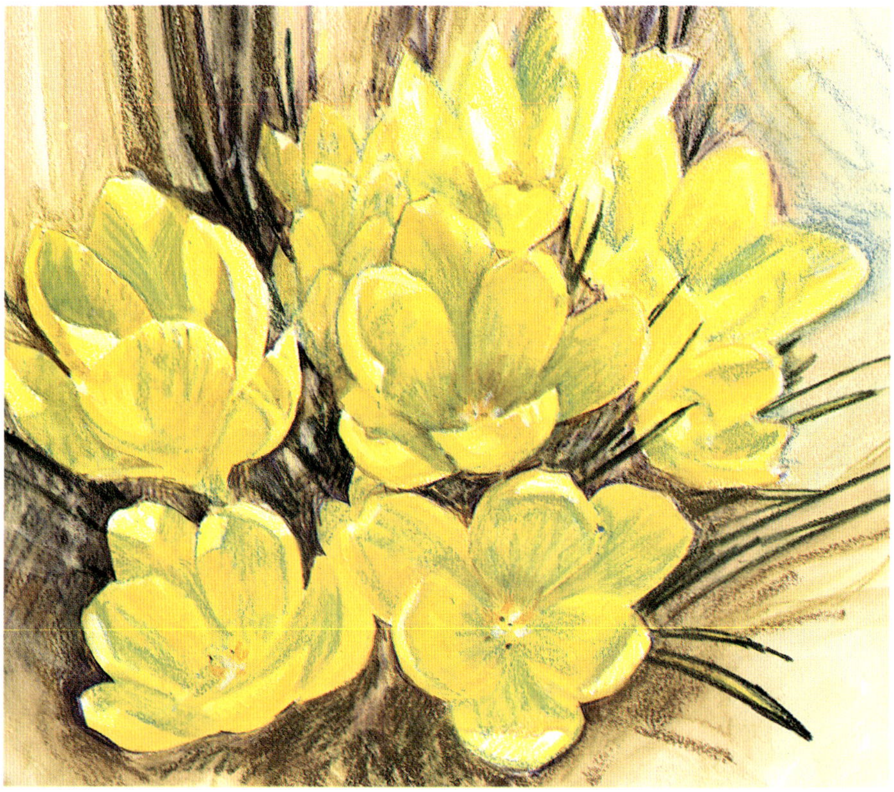

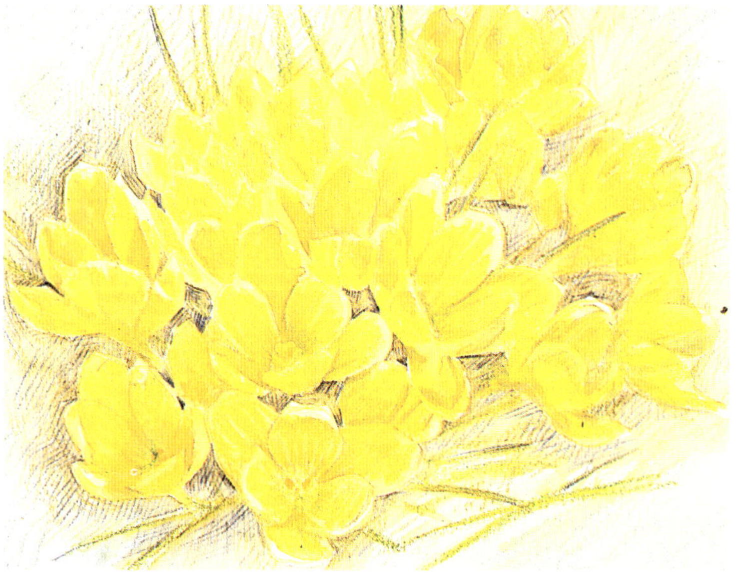

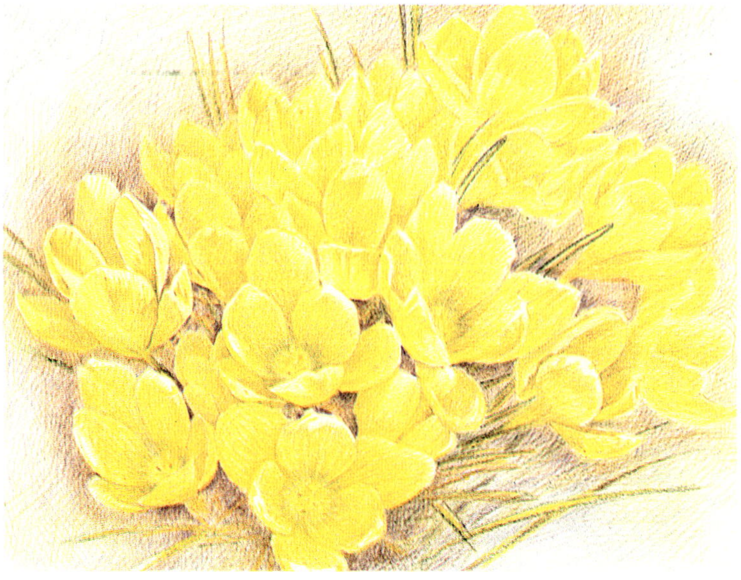

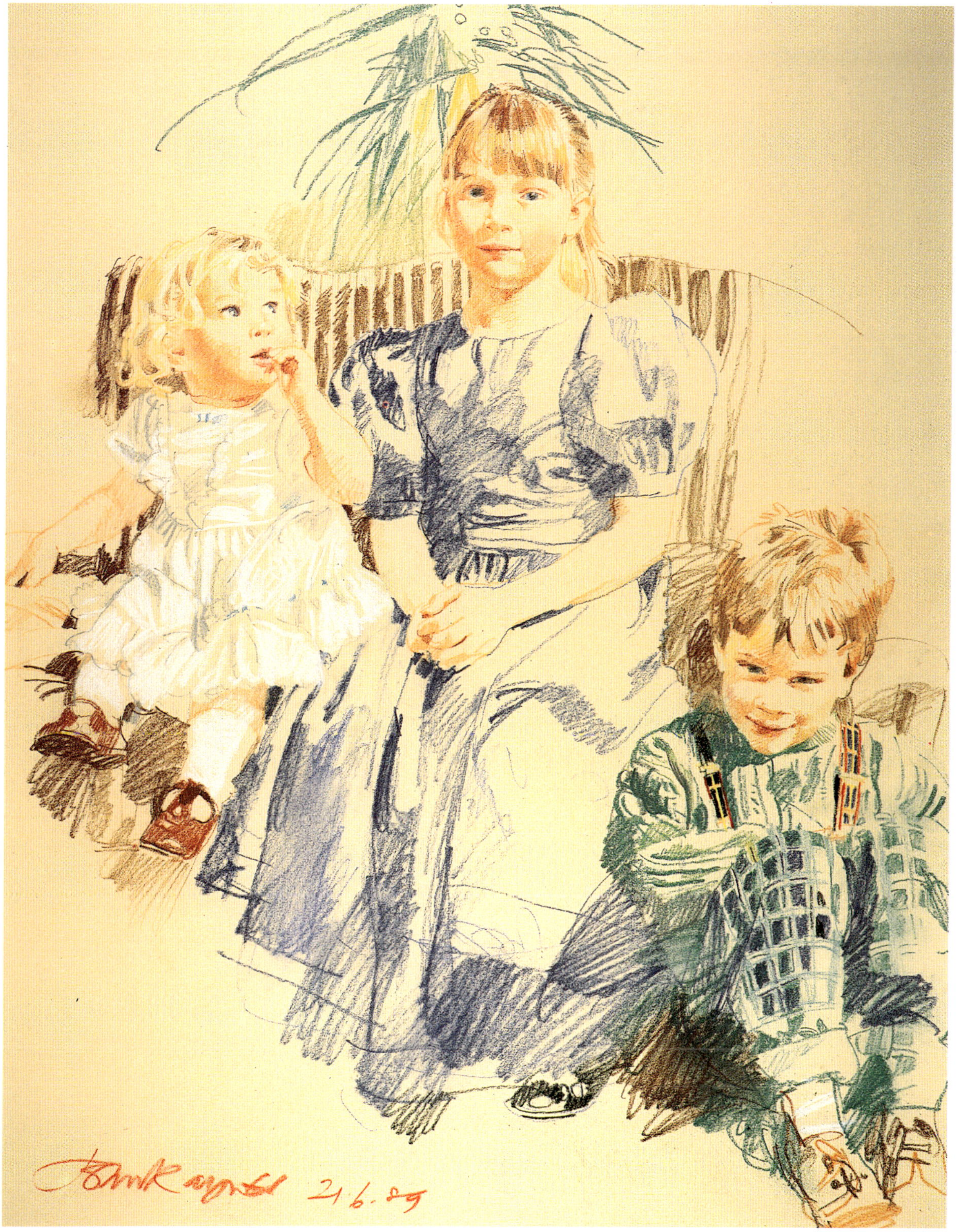

LEFT
John Raynes
Family Group
Using a skilful and vigorous line on a colored support, the artist has made his image by using simple pattern and shadow to describe the form.

work and tested examples that I hope will open up some new possibilities.

For interested readers who may be quite new to art, I have included examples that can also be attempted as exercises. These are designed both to show you the nature of the material and to introduce the basic elements and skills involved in making art. My hope is that these experiences will serve as a guide to a continuing development toward your own visual 'language,' whatever your special areas of interest might be.

Artists' quality colored pencils are comparatively new, and they do not yet have that long history of craft and available imagery that is common to the older, more traditional materials. These pencils, especially the soluble type, cross the divide between drawing and painting. While there is a huge range available, I want to concentrate on the simple color drawing pencil; its soluble companion – identical except in its ability to mix with water; and the large soft, heat-sensitive type recently made available. These colored pencils can offer a really exciting challenge for a relatively low cost, perfect for a home studio, and are very portable. They have the precise control of pencils, coupled with the looser qualities usually found in watercolor. The soft pencil that we shall look at can make marks very similar to thick paint, as well as more crayon-type marks. Within this medium, we now have a larger range of performance and possibilities, and this for me is its great potential.

There can be an unfortunate tendency for people enjoying art through one specific medium to learn blindly and obey a set of craft rules in order for their work to be considered 'good.' A book like this might set out a whole set of exercises and rules that the student could learn and imitate, and eventually feel confident that she or he had mastered their craft. While this process has some virtue, it can also reduce a beginner's willingness to experiment, and there is sometimes a tendency to rely on tried and tested skills and effects, which may become worn-out and meaningless.

I think it is far better to see these 'rules' as a set of guidelines that, with practice and experiment, can build an appetite and taste for picture making that is wholly yours – a personal visual language. The proper question to ask might be whether YOU like what you have made? Does it mean anything to YOU? And do not worry about what the 'rules' tell you to do.

Fortunately, with a new material like this there has not yet been time for a traditional set of techniques to form. It also seems that this material, by its very nature, is resistant to rules and, in the spirit of this age, open to personal experiment.

When we make pictures others may judge them by all sorts of criteria, some appropriate and some not. In this book, along with an investigation of the material, I also want to look at the way in which your imagination can be expressed through the materials. This may form part of how you will eventually judge your work: essentially you must do this from a personal point of view. We will look at how some contemporary artists have worked with colored pencils and hear their views on the success or otherwise of their work.

Your task, hopefully enjoyable, is to work toward an understanding of the materials and how you might use them for your purposes. Art practice is surely about actively seeing and enjoying the materials; it is about letting materials work for you, about play and, hopefully, surprise and delight.

BELOW
Three typres of color pencil. From the left: 12 soft soluble heat-sensitive pencils; 12 soluble pencils; 12 simple color pencils.

RIGHT
Devayani Khakhria
Aztec Gold
Devi makes marvelous images and designs for all sorts of surfaces, from fabrics to ceramics. This piece is made mostly with soft soluble pigment; using high-energy, contrasting colors, she has achieved a rich balance.

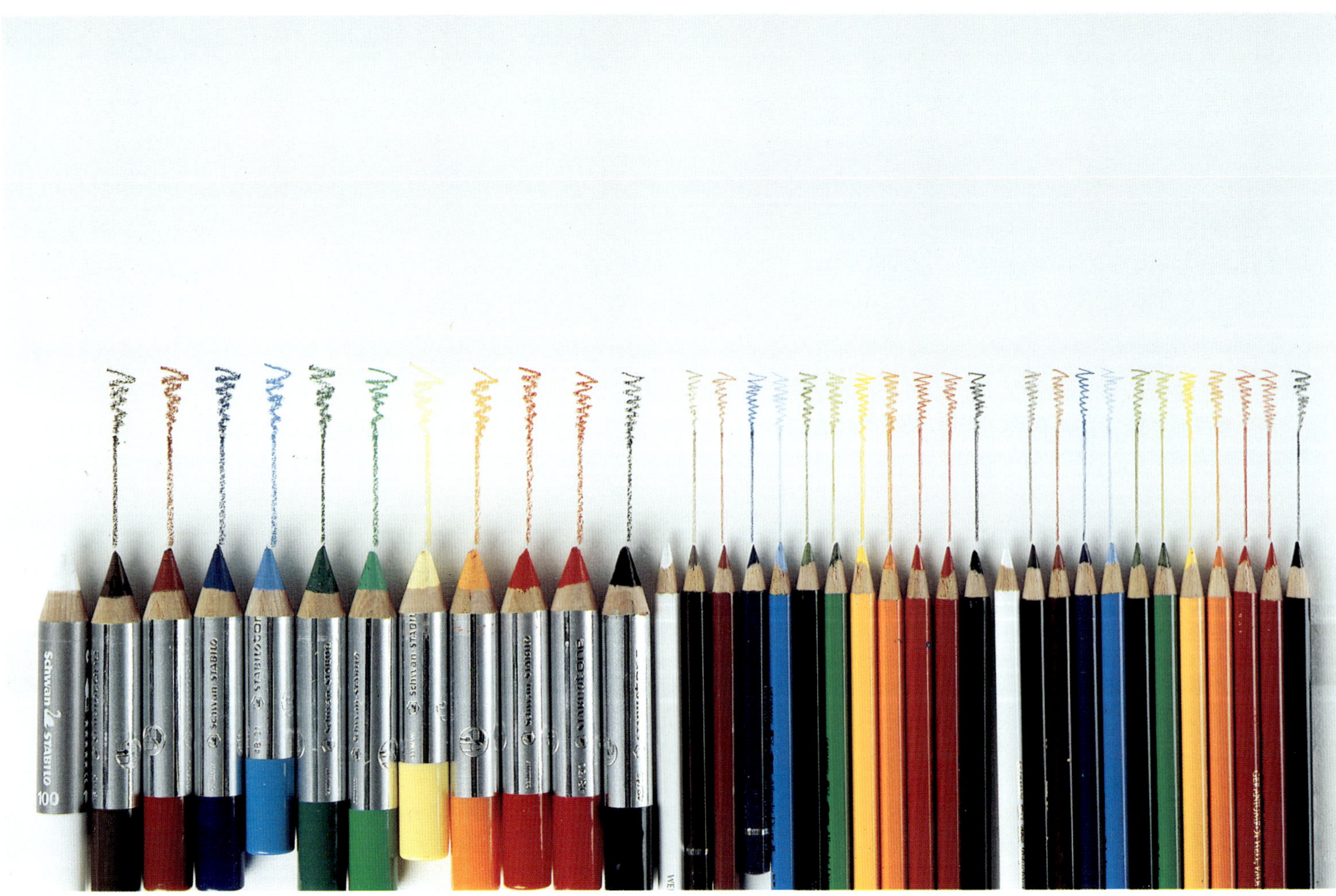

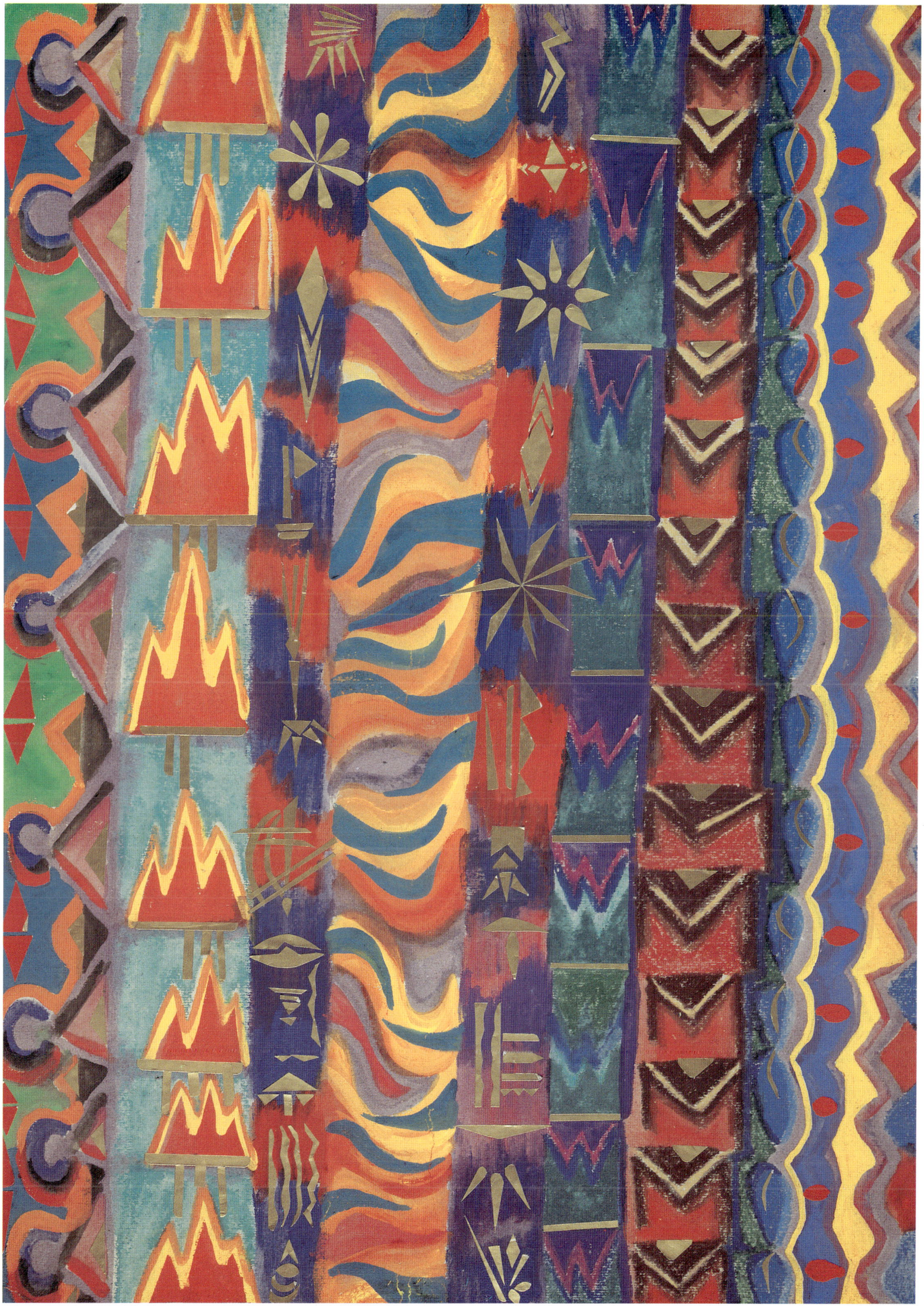

1. History

There is a 500-year-old guide for apprentice artists, written in fifteenth-century Florence by Cennino d'Andrea Cennini and entitled *Il Libro dell'Arte*, 'The Craftsman's Handbook.' In this fascinating book you can get a glimpse of the difficulties surrounding the production of pictures, and how different the experience of materials was then to that of the modern enthusiast. In the fifteenth and earlier centuries, artists made practically everything they needed from crude raw material. We can find references to charcoal, chalk, ink and the earth pigments that artists have used since prehistoric times. But we can also find a bewildering array of 'secret' ingredients and processes that show how far the craft had come.

A fifteenth-century artist's workshop would have looked and smelled like a sorcerer's kitchen, with animal remains, boiling oils, skins of parchment, pestle, mortar and porphyry slabs, all jostling for attention with jars of raw pigment yet to be ground and mixed into real paint. Some of these pigments might be bought from alchemists (early chemists) as a lump or rock, but the actual process of turning raw material into tempered pigment would be part of the artist's craft.

In all this paraphernalia we would not find one pencil, nor is there a reference to pencils in the handbook, although there was a tiny brush that was called a pencil, which much later probably gave its name to the modern graphite pencil. The drawing materials we would find are chalk, slender charcoal, assorted quill pens, and an implement called a 'style.' The style was a pointed metal device that could be tipped with an alloy of tin and lead, or even silver. This was intended for really detailed work. It left a thin track of metal pigment, faint at first, and only later as it tarnished did it achieve the lasting darker quality we associate with silverpoint or leaden style. Drawing with a metal point was similar in some ways to drawing with a modern pencil – we still call the core of a modern pencil a lead, even though it is now made of graphite. But the techniques involved in metal-point drawing were quite different and time-consuming.

Apart from the difficulty involved with the changes of tone, from almost invisible silver-gray to dark brown, silverpoint drawing has the added, perhaps worse, problem of the actual drawing surface. At a time when paper production was still in its infancy, the artist needed to make his own surfaces, and for metal drawing this needed to be abrasive, like fine sandpaper.

If we look once more at Cennini's handbook, we can trace the process of laying a suitable ground, or surface. It was said that bonemeal was the best abrasive for this surface, and the wing bones of a capon (chicken) were preferred above any. The

BELOW
Michelangelo
Ideal Head, c.1520
Red chalk, 8 × 6½ inches (20.5 × 16.5 cm)
Here is drawing as a finished piece in its own right.

RIGHT
Leonardo da Vinci
A Horse in Profile to its Right and its Forelegs, c.1497
Silverpoint on blue prepared paper, 8½ × 6¼ inches (21.4 × 16 cm)
This shows us drawing as part of a process toward some other, more finished, piece of work.

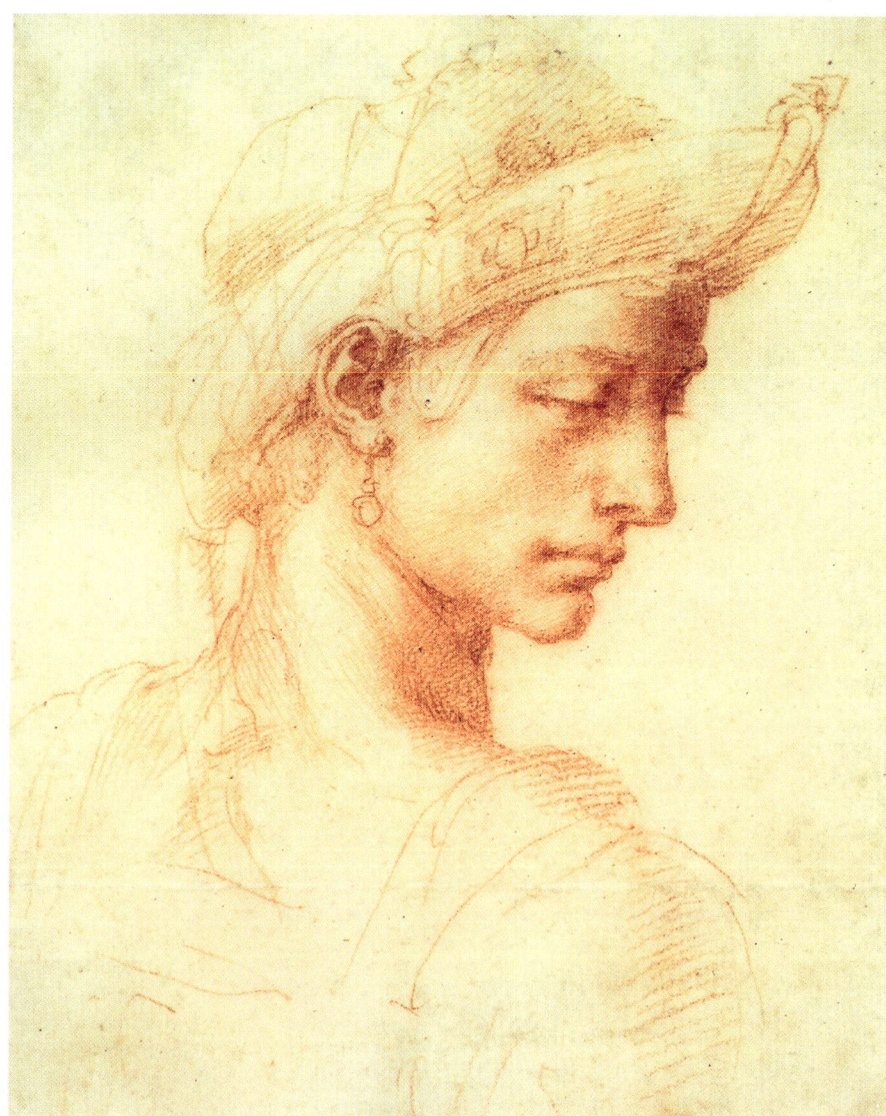

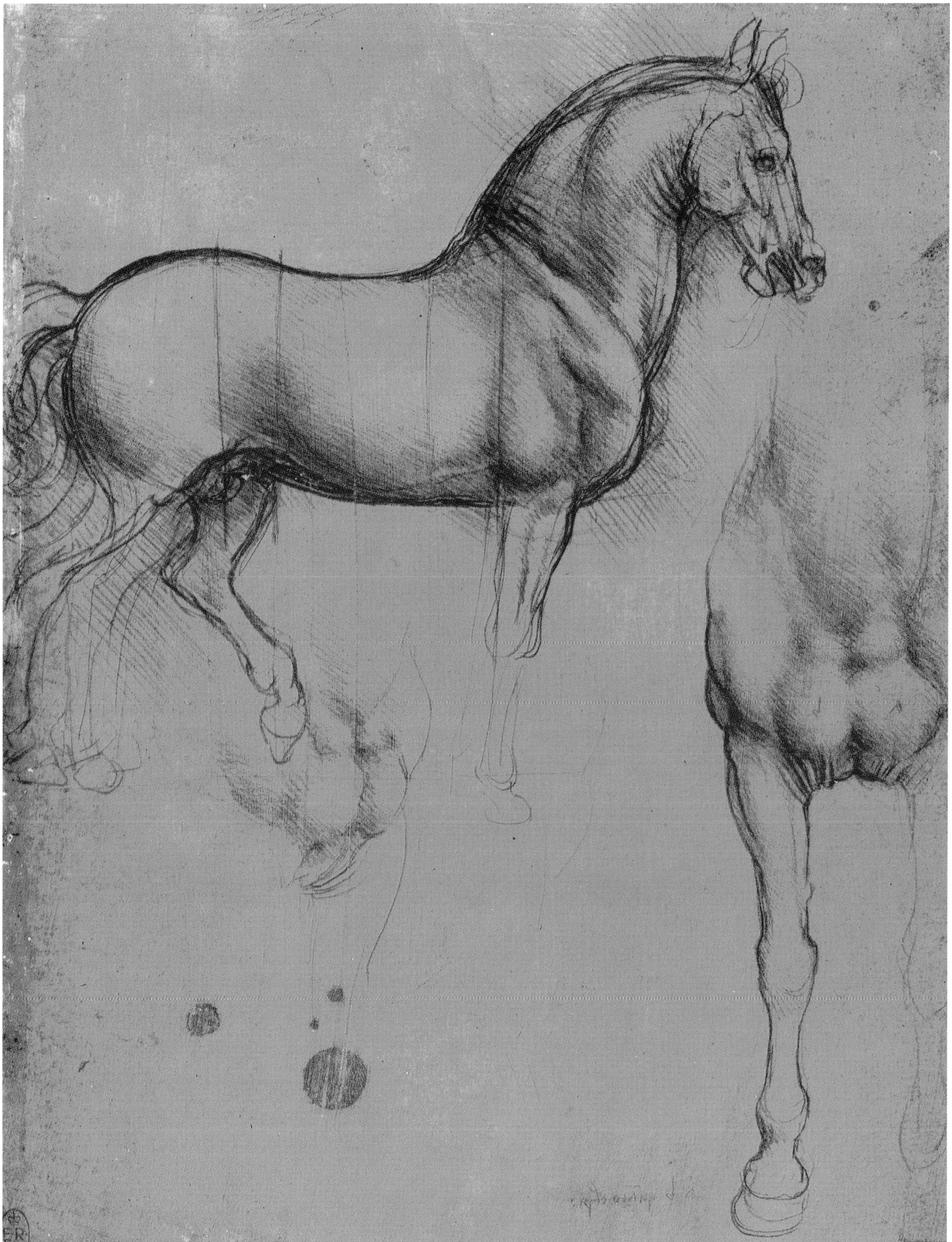

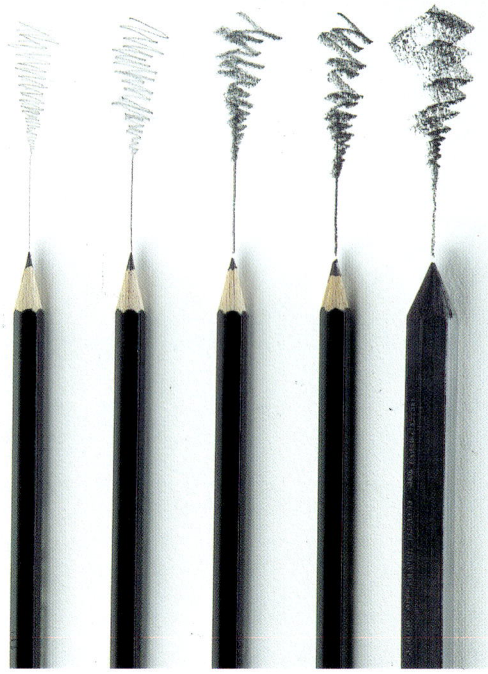

LEFT
A range of graphite pencils with their marks.

bones were heated until they bleached and could be ground to a very fine powder. This powder was applied to parchment, and enough of the abrasive remained in the pores to cause the metal pigment to rub off. On paper or wooden panels, the bone ash needed to be applied with a solution of glue.

I have simplified this process, but by looking at what was done, I wish to make the point that at a time of great art, architecture and scholarship, the means of providing suitable materials to make detailed working drawings were both difficult and time-consuming. Pen and ink provided detail, but once drawn were difficult to erase; chalks and charcoal were wonderfully erasable but lacked the detail. The silverpoint was the best option available and it involved a lot of craftwork. All this work was for predominantly private study or preliminary work, which was never intended for prestigious public art. It is the excellence of these drawings and their historical interest that brings them into galleries in relatively modern times.

By the sixteenth century we can see the beginnings of the graphite pencil. The armaments industries were hungry for ingredients with which to make their explosives; among these substances was raw graphite, which is a naturally occurring form of crystalline carbon. In Britain there was a huge natural deposit of graphite in Cumberland. This was quarried vigorously by poorly-paid laborers who lived near the site. A workman could smuggle a pocketful of 'wad' (raw graphite) and keep his family for a month. But most importantly for us, the stuff was marvelous to draw with. As precise as silverpoint and as erasable as charcoal, this substance can draw on almost anything, sliding over itself and other surfaces almost like a liquid. Better still, it is easily manipulated and leaves a fine residue that is both reasonably permanent and erasable.

There was soon a subsidiary cottage industry formed around sources of graphite, making much-needed graphite styles or pencils. The first pencils were sticks of raw graphite reinforced by wood or ivory. What we would recognize as a pencil was soon to be made from powdered graphite mixed with clay, rolled and fired into a ceramic rod, and encased in cedar wood. The raw graphite on its own makes a consistent metallic black mark, and the different tones are determined by the proportion of graphite to clay mix. A hard silver-gray mark comes from a pencil made mostly from clay, and a soft sooty black from one of pure graphite. This is the simplest and most versatile drawing instrument available, and can be used for the most mundane scrawl or the most

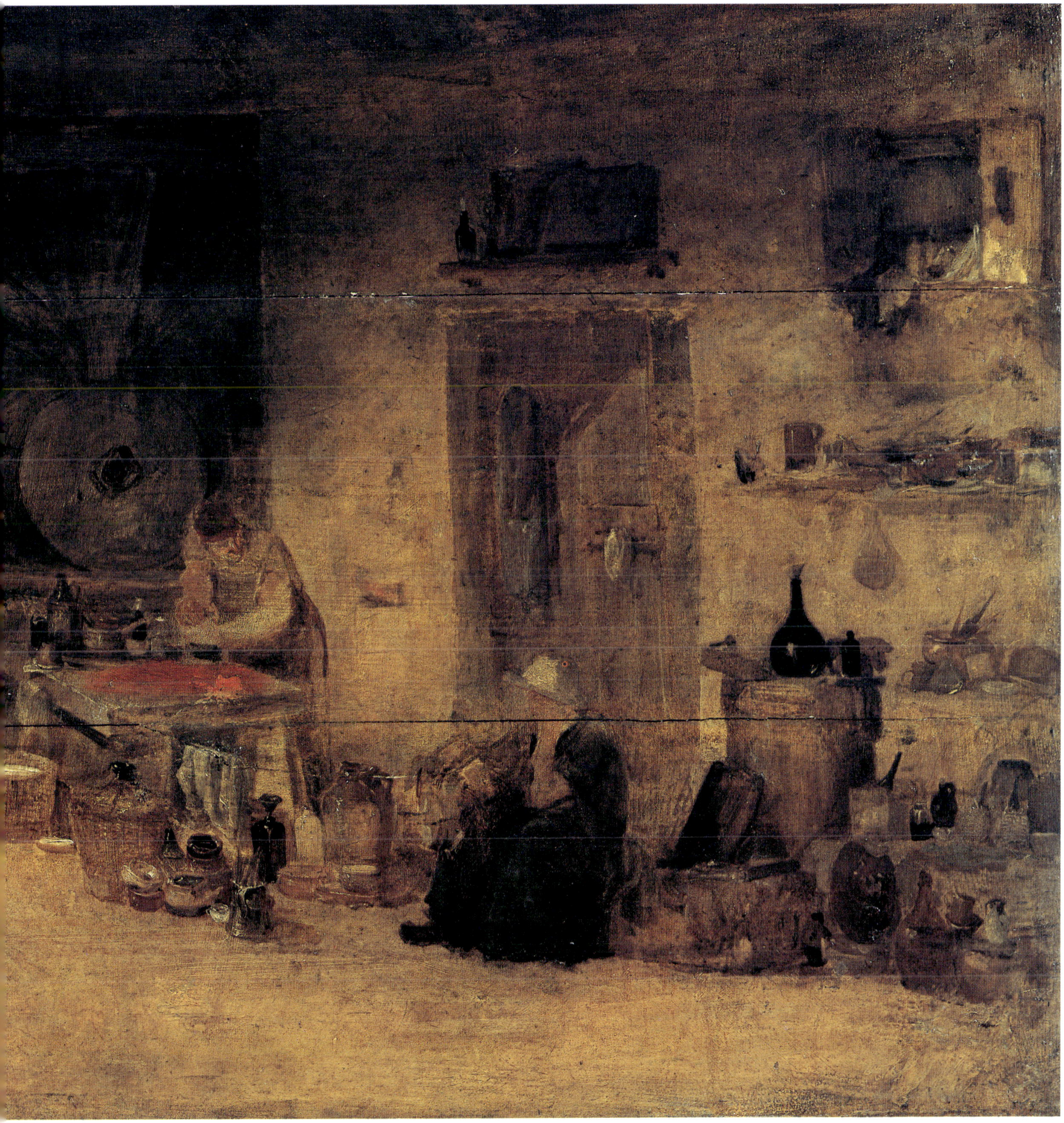

BELOW
J. M. W. Turner
An Artist's Colourman's Workshop
Although in a poor condition, this painting can still show us the beginnings of the separate craft of artist's colorman; here the craftsman appears to be mixing powdered pigment and binders on a marble slab.

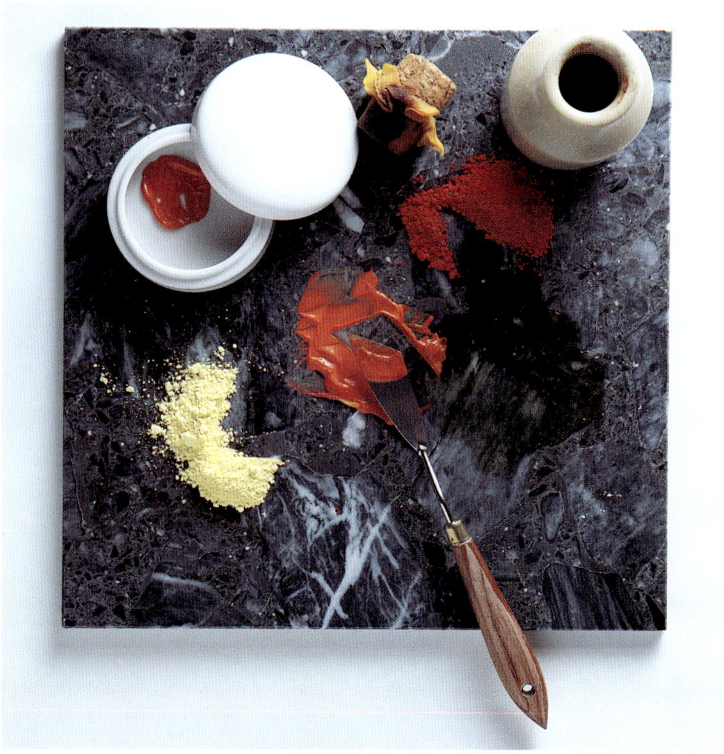

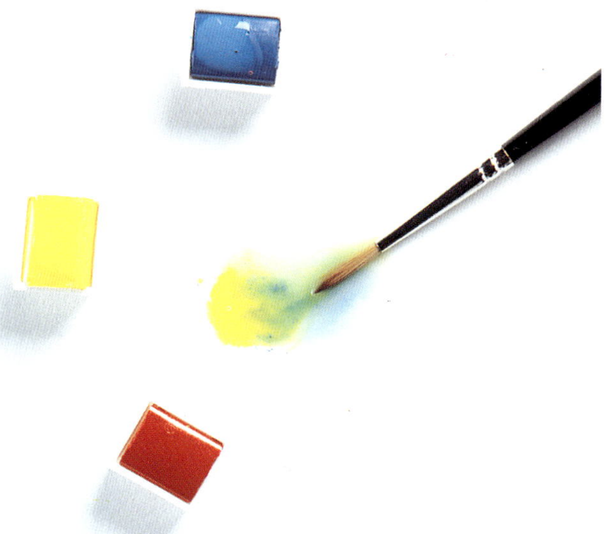

sophisticated finished work on most surfaces. Practically everything that is made is designed; designers and artists need drawing materials that are controllable and correctable. The pencil had arrived.

Paint-making begins with raw pigment. We still to this day use chalk, charcoal, and earth pigments like ocher. Perhaps science and art both began when primitive man noticed that ocher, instead of being consumed to a charcoal black or bone-ash white, magically transformed itself in fire from yellow to red. The ancient Chinese performed alchemic 'magic' on black mercuric sulphide, turning it to the red vermilion we still use. As Cennini tells us, an artist's workshop would contain a large range of these pigments, some gathered raw from the earth, others distilled from animal carcasses and plants. Other pigments were the products of alchemy. Some of these were unstable and could change character and color, some were fugitive and might discolor the surrounding areas.

Throughout the Middle Ages and the Renaissance, the grinding and mixing of paint was the traditional duty of artists' apprentices working from guarded recipes. By the middle of the eighteenth century there emerged the separate craft of the colorman, supplier of paint and materials to the artistic community. By the early nineteenth century the trade was supplying a growing, almost worldwide, demand for art materials. The chemical industry was producing more and more potential pigment.

This range of paints was huge compared to that of Cennini, but it was largely untested. With a growing demand for portable paint, manufacturers began to test, select and grade pigments. The search was for permanence and purity, together with a consistently reliable quality of paint. The most successful result of this exercise was probably in the production of watercolor. By the 1840s pigments had been perfected which were then ground to a fine powder, mixed with gum binders and glycerine moisteners, rolled into a kind of dough, and cut into the small cakes that we see today in a box of watercolors. These were extremely popular with both amateurs and professionals, as a perfect material for sketching from nature. The promise was obvious: a similar color dough could be rolled into leads and existing pencil-making technology could be used to obtain a similarly good range of soluble color pencils.

There was, however, a problem. The mark-making qualities of these early attempts at color pencils were poor, and the 'lead' was weak. This could be improved by the addition of waxes and oils, but at the expense of some color intensity, erasability and solubility. Compared, for example, to the excellence of pastels, the colored pencil was not in the same league. As recently as the 1960s, these early color pencils were being described in various manuals as unpleasant in consistency and effect, adequate for taking notes in sketchbooks, but with nowhere near the beauty of erasable colors.

ABOVE LEFT
Powder pigment mixed with oil binders to make paint.

ABOVE RIGHT
Finely ground pigment mixed with soluble gums and made into cakes, the precursor to color pencil pigment.

RIGHT
Henri de Toulouse-Lautrec
The Seated Clowness – Madamoiselle Cha-U-Kao, 1896
Crayon, brush and splatter lithograph
Toward the end of the nineteenth century, advances in printing, particularly lithography, allowed the viewer to see the artist's hand-drawn marks directly as he drew them on the printing stone.

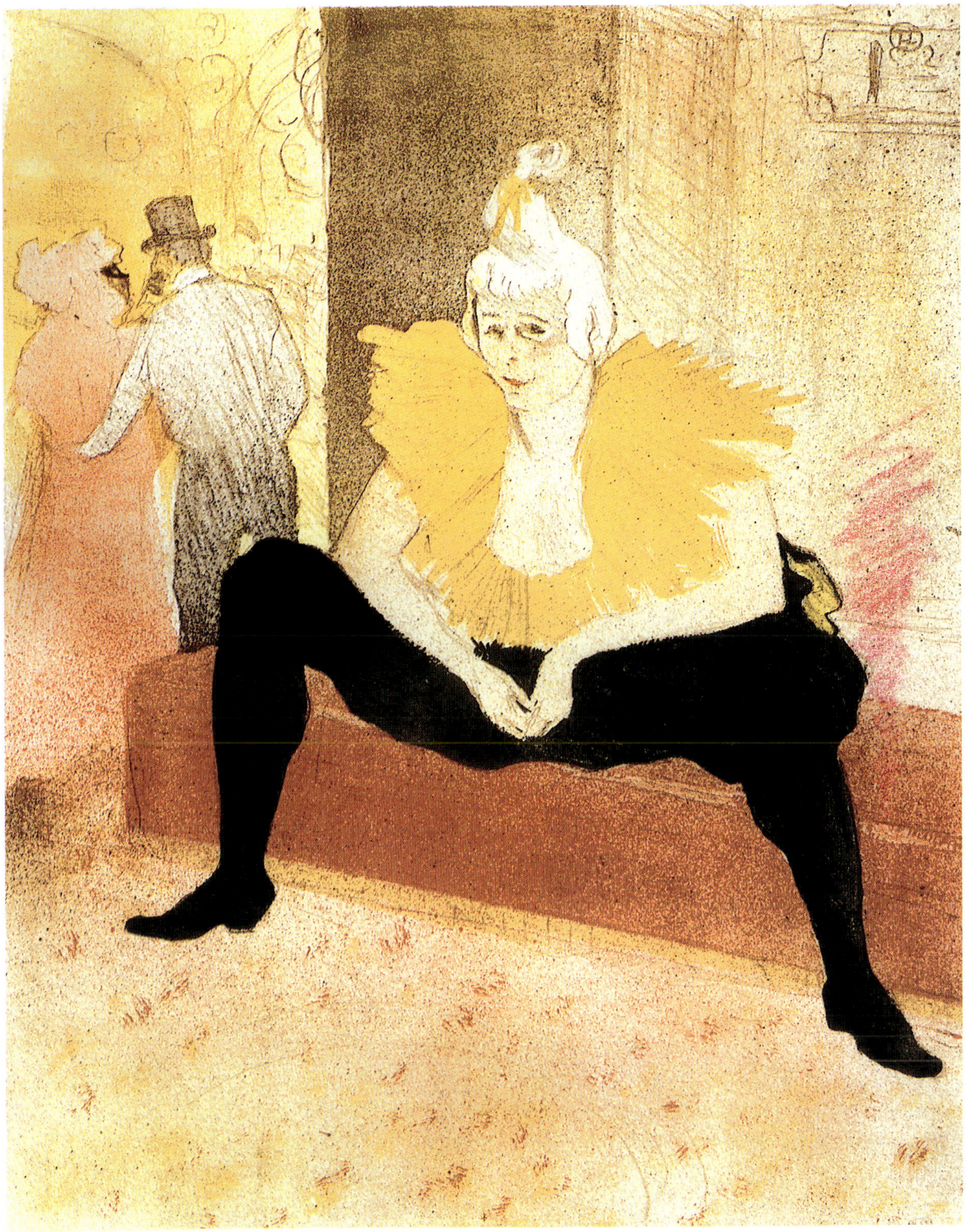

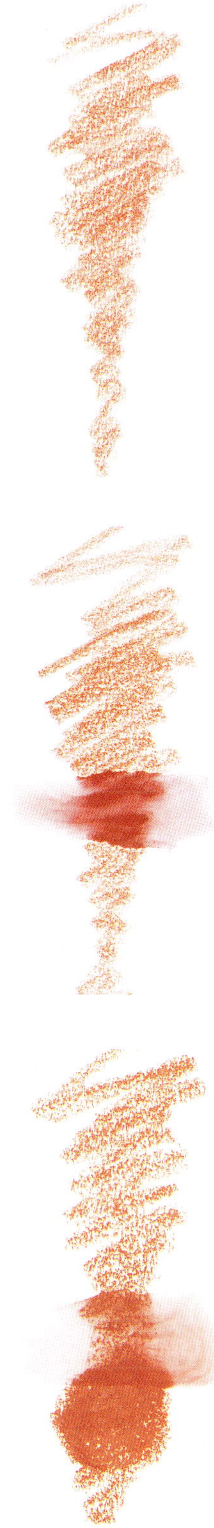

ABOVE
Marks made by (from top) simple color pencil; soluble color pencil; and soft, soluble, heat-sensitive color pencil.

In the last few years new sorts of waxes and binders have been developed that finally seem to have solved the problems inherent in the manufacture and use of color pencils. These waxes have also increased the potential of the medium in three main ways, and it is these three basic groups of qualities which I am going to examine in this book. Although the medium is new, the strategies that the art world has developed, right back to Cennini and beyond, are there to help us.

The first set of qualities belongs to the simple color pencil, offering the entire range of mark-making from controlled drawing to expressive drawing. The next inquiry addresses the ambiguous nature of a pencil that can deliver paint similar to watercolor. The third takes a look at the brand-new qualities of soft pencils that, as well as being soluble, are also heat-sensitive. This pigment can range from translucent watercolor to thick opaque body color. While we may not have the material knowledge and expertise that the old mastercraftsmen attained, we can acquire a similar depth of experience about the way these materials behave on paper.

2. Equipment and Materials

Basic Starter Kit

- A place to work
- Suitable light source, natural and artificial
- A5 cartridge sketchbook
- Range of colored paper
- A2 drawing board
- Board clips and thumbtacks
- Masking tape
- Paper parcel tape
- Range of artist's color drawing pencils
- Range of artist's soluble color drawing pencils
- Range of artist's soft, soluble heat-sensitive color pencils
- Range of graphite pencils: 6B, HB, 3H
- Water jars
- Fine sandpaper
- Sharpening blades
- Burnisher/stump
- Erasers
- Sable brush, size 2
- Decorator's 1″ brush
- Tube of designer's white gouache
- Domestic candle and/or children's wax crayons
- Safe place to store drawings

A Place to Work

A studio is just the place where an artist works, it does not have to be the wizard's kitchen of the Renaissance, nor yet the romantic attic of nineteenth-century Paris. The kitchen table or a corner of the bedroom will do, at least for the early days. It does need to be somewhere where you will not be disturbed and where your equipment is to hand. Suddenly stopping a train of thought to search for something is infuriating. Resist the temptation to go out and spend lots of money before you have working experience of what you need.

Common sense tells us we need good light, whether it is daylight or artificial light. Avoid intense pools of light falling on your drawing area, and also avoid casting a shadow over the drawing. If you can afford it, an adjustable desk light with a white light bulb is perfect. There are also some cooler light elements on the market which can be more comfortable to work with. You need a chair or stool that is both comfortable and allows you freedom of movement; a cramped position often produces cramped drawing.

You need a bit of desk space to lay out your materials to hand, and always keep your materials, and coffee, on your working side. If you are right-handed, keep them on the right; if you are left-handed, keep them on the left. This helps to prevent you stretching over your work, with the possibility of

BELOW
This drawing was made with soft soluble pencils on a clear plastic sheet. Without the texture of paper, the pigment smears in a manner similar to painted marks.

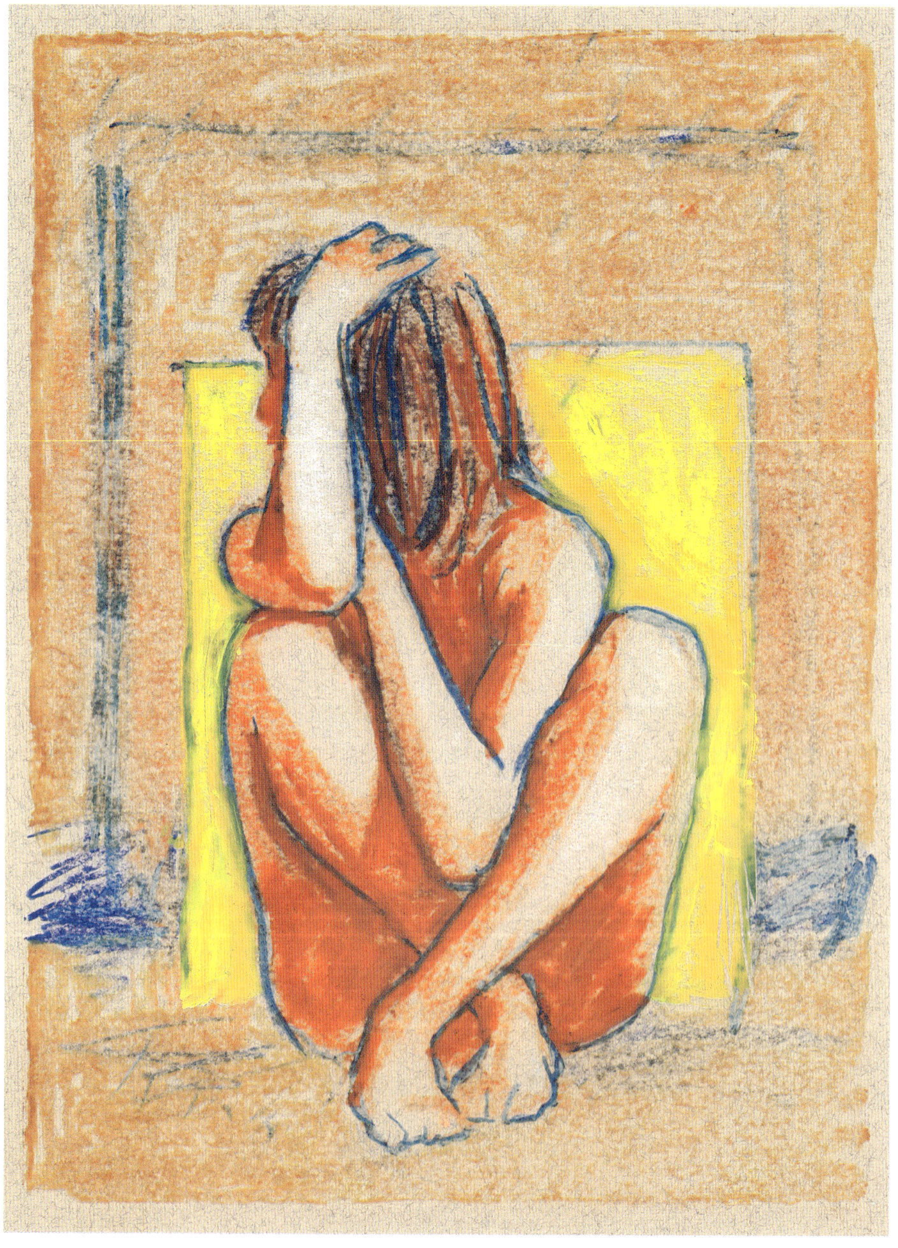

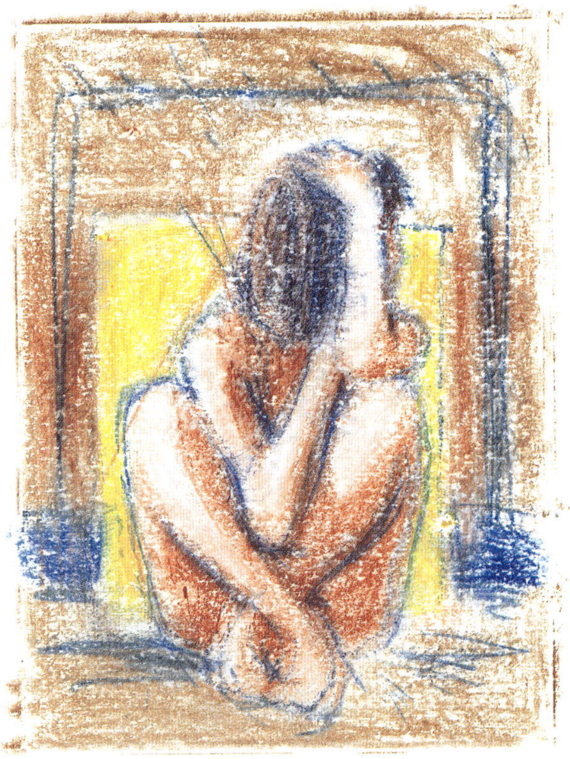

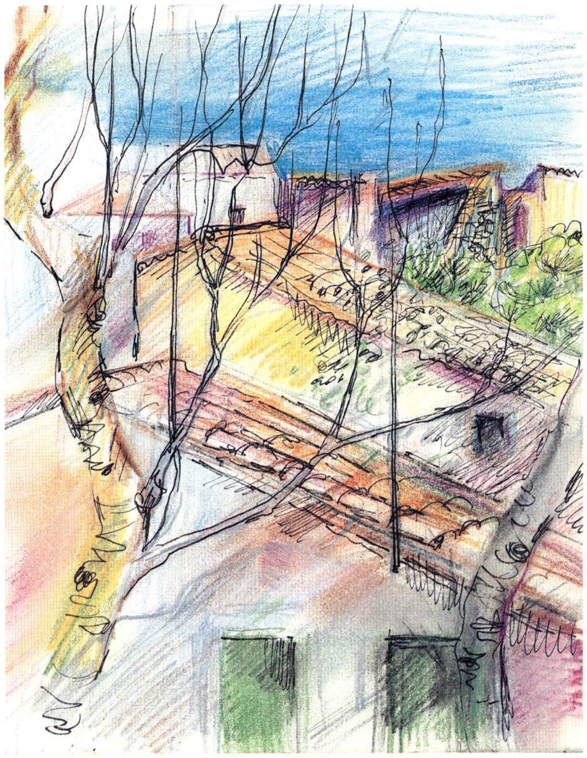

FAR LEFT
This is a surface print of the drawing on page 16, made by laying a sheet of dampened paper directly onto the pigment, heating it with a hairdryer and rubbing it with the back of a warmed spoon. The pigment is thus transferred to the paper surface, adding all sorts of qualities.

LEFT
Oliver McLarnon
Sketchbook study
The soluble colored pencils are beautifully direct; a few lines and a wet thumb can lay in impressions very speedily.

BELOW
The basic starter kit, as listed in the text, far left.

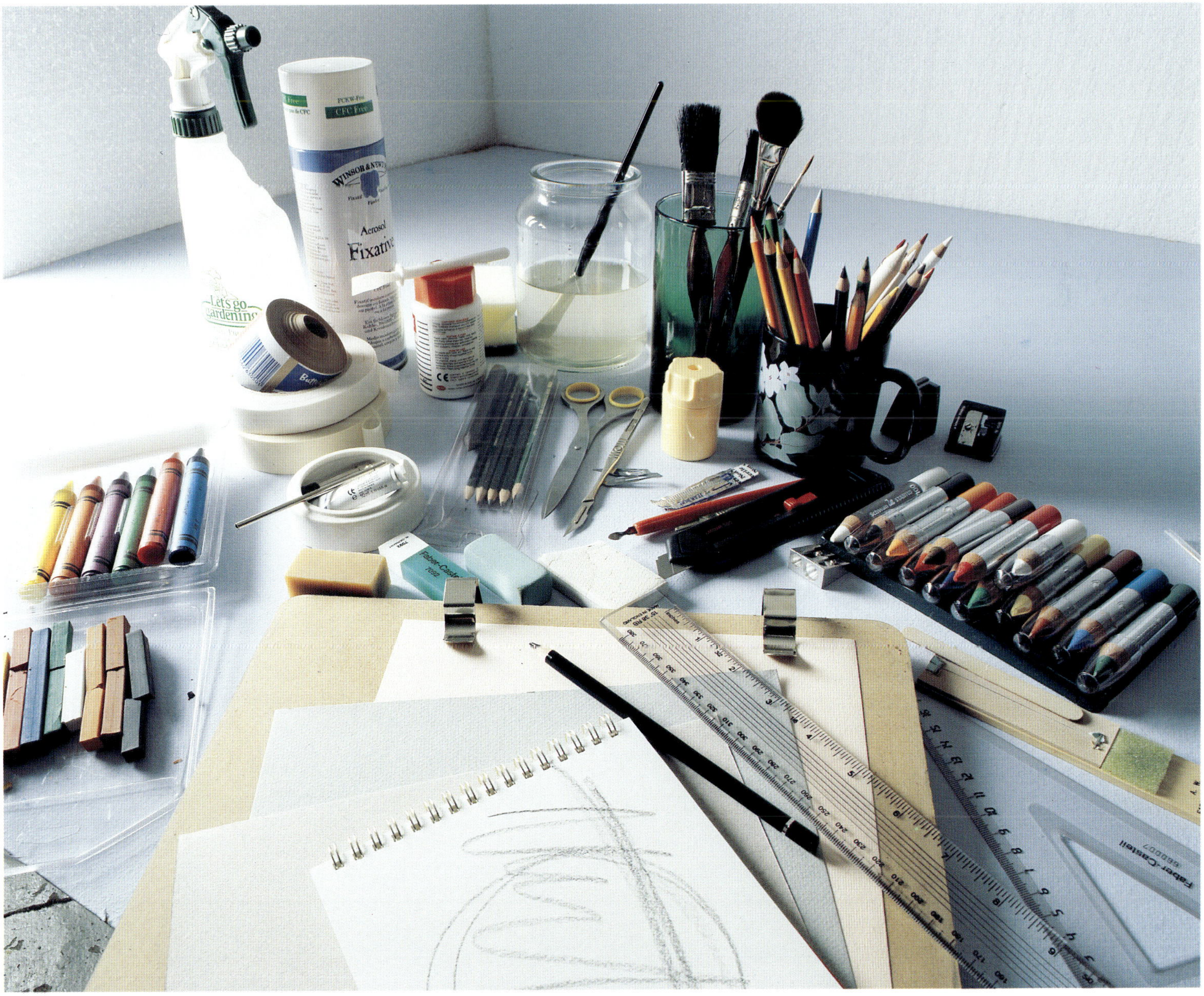

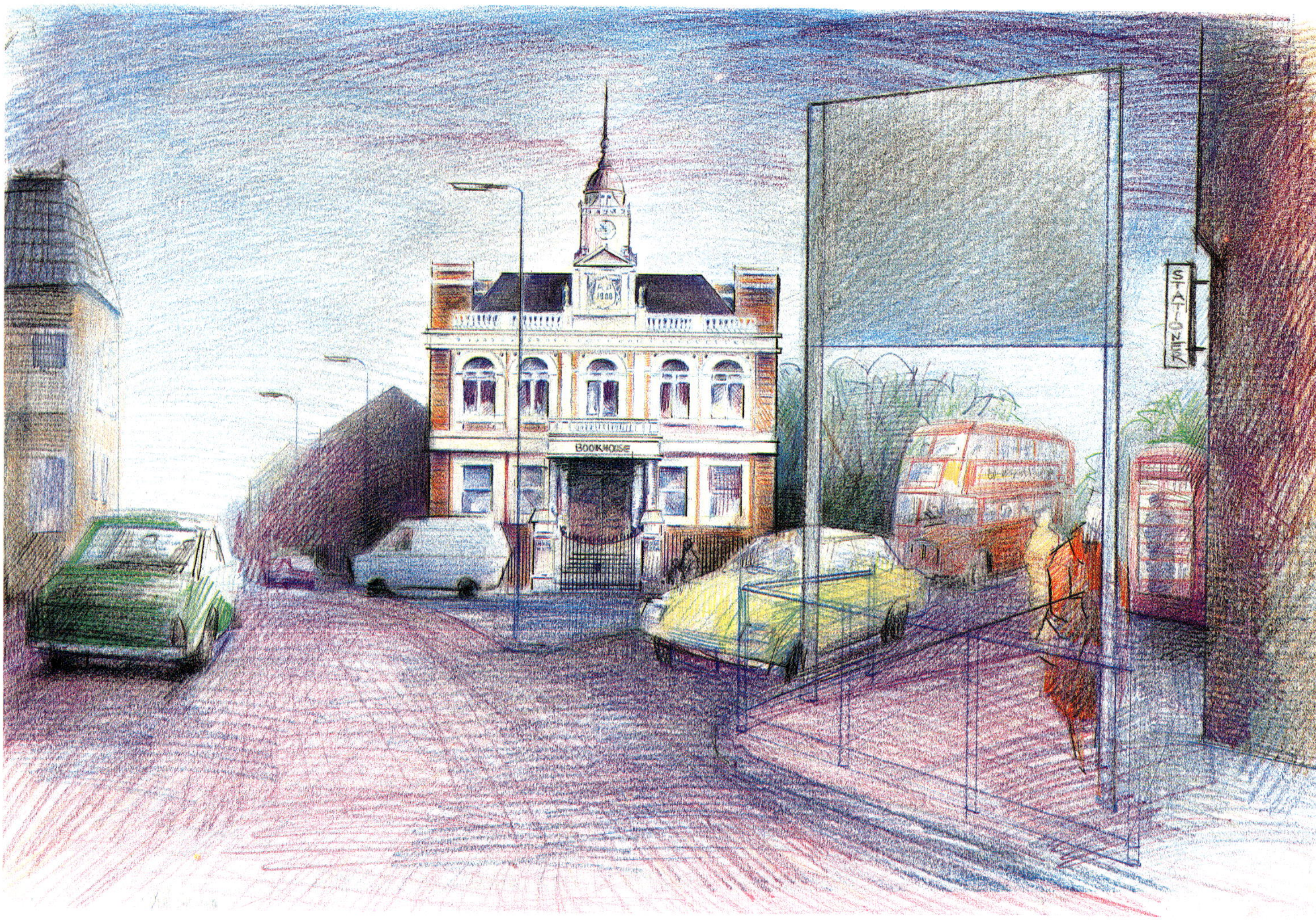

ruining hours of work by smudging the surface or spilling your coffee.

Drawing and sketching easels are designed to hold your drawing board at a convenient angle and height for you to work, whether indoors or out. Although there are good lightweight collapsible easels on the market, I would not advise buying at this stage. Wait until you know what sort of work you want to do, and have some experience of the materials. A simple drawing board propped up at a slight angle on a table is perfectly adequate. Outdoors, the board can rest on your knees.

You will also need somewhere to store your drawings, as they can multiply at an alarming rate. Favorite places are cardboard portfolios under the bed, or a large drawer which can also hold a small stock of papers.

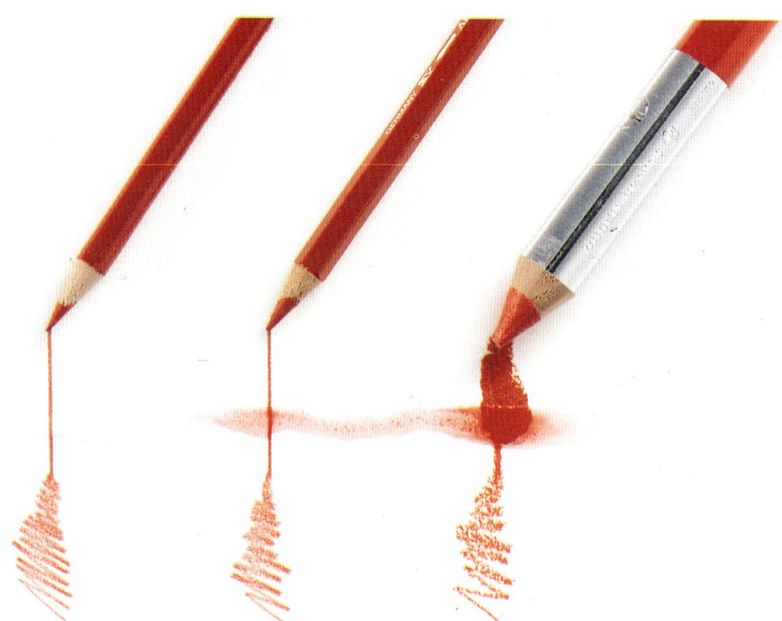

Artist's Quality Materials

Always buy materials that are labeled or described as 'artist's quality.' They are very dependable and consistent in the way they perform.

Sable brushes are best when working with wetter pigment. They can be very expensive, especially the larger brushes. Start with a number two size. Art stores frequently supply a jar of water to test a brush before you buy. A wet, loaded brush should form a perfect point in one shake. If it splits, do not buy it. Once you have a good brush, wash it out well after use, and work it back to a point with a little soap. Kept properly, it will give long service.

TOP
Madeleine Baker
Book House, Wandsworth
This shows how overlaid color pencil can create a sense of movement.

ABOVE
Three basic types of color pencil (left to right): simple color pencil; soluble color pencil; soft and soluble color pencil.

A small decorator's brush is cheap and perfectly usable for wetting and painting large areas. Later, when you are more familiar with the soft, heat-sensitive pigments, you may like to experiment with a stiffer hog-hair oil-painting brush. But it is not necessary at this stage.

There is a huge range of colored drawing materials now available. Pigments of all sorts now come as sticks of pure pigment as well as in pencil form. The range we are looking at can have as many as a hundred colors. But small tins of about twelve colors make a good starting kit.

There are three forms of colored pencil for our work. Try and buy these three types in one manufacturer's range. The color selection will be the same across the three types.

Color drawing pencils These are simple drawing pencils, about the hardness of an HB graphite pencil. Not soluble in water.

Soluble color drawing pencils These are similar to the first type, but slightly softer.

Soft, soluble, heat-sensitive color pencils These are more akin to crayons but provide a wet pigment that ranges from a sort of transparent watercolor to a thicker impasto.

Supports/Paper

A support is what artists call the surface on which they work. This will mostly be paper, which comes in an amazing range. The most popular papers also come bonded on board for professional use. These are expensive, and stretched paper is just as good to work on (see below).

Artist's papers can be confusing, but basically they fall into two groups, handmade and machine-made. Most are machine-made and these will be called 'hot-pressed' (HP); 'not,' meaning literally not hot-pressed; and 'rough.' Hot-pressed paper is fairly smooth, 'not' paper has a moderate texture or tooth, and rough is what it says; it has a rich coarse texture that is great for traditional watercolor and expressive drawings. To test your materials it is advisable to have the three sorts of paper available, HP, NOT, and ROUGH.

ABOVE
A simple range of machine-made papers (from left): hot-pressed (HP): not hot-pressed (NOT); rough.

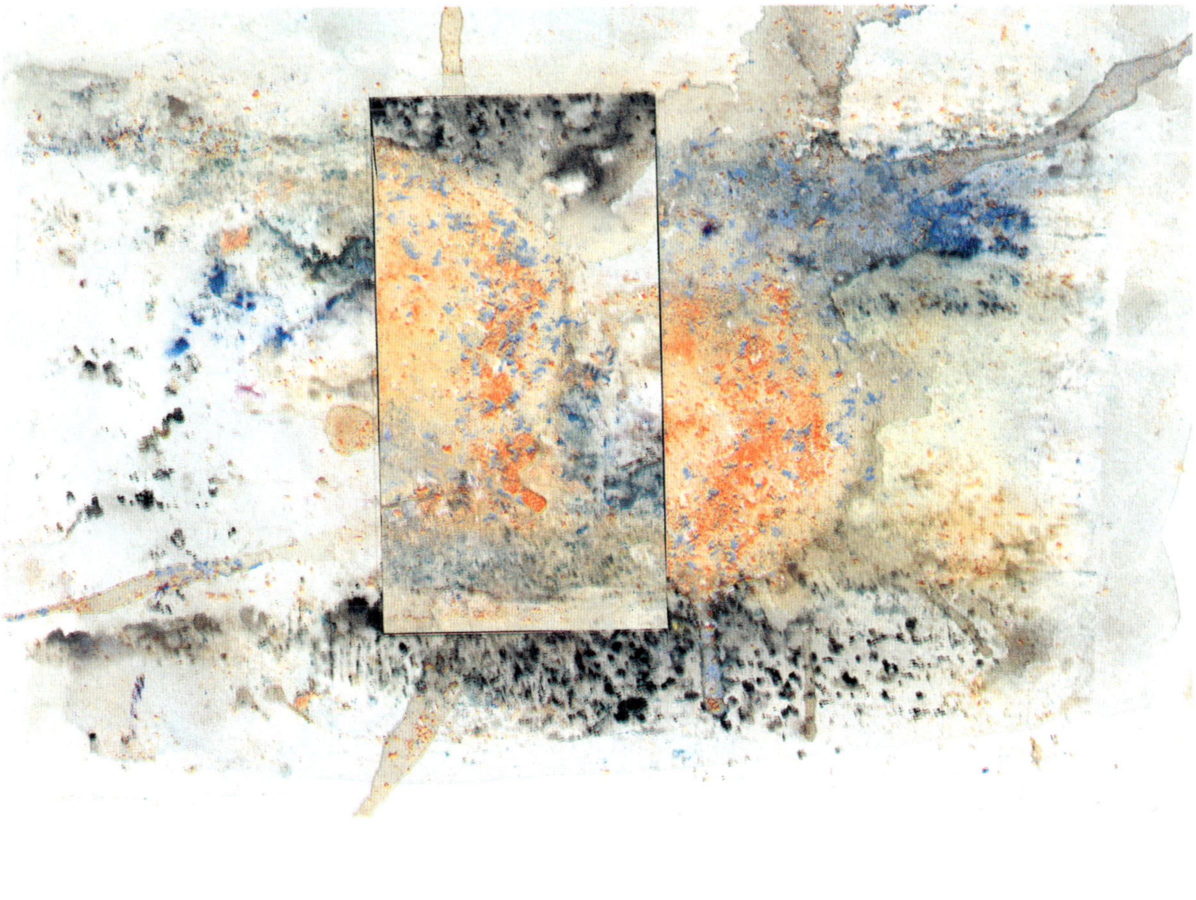

BELOW LEFT
A composition using scraped pencil pigment on wet paper. The rectangle is 'drawn' simply by cutting it out and turning it upside down.

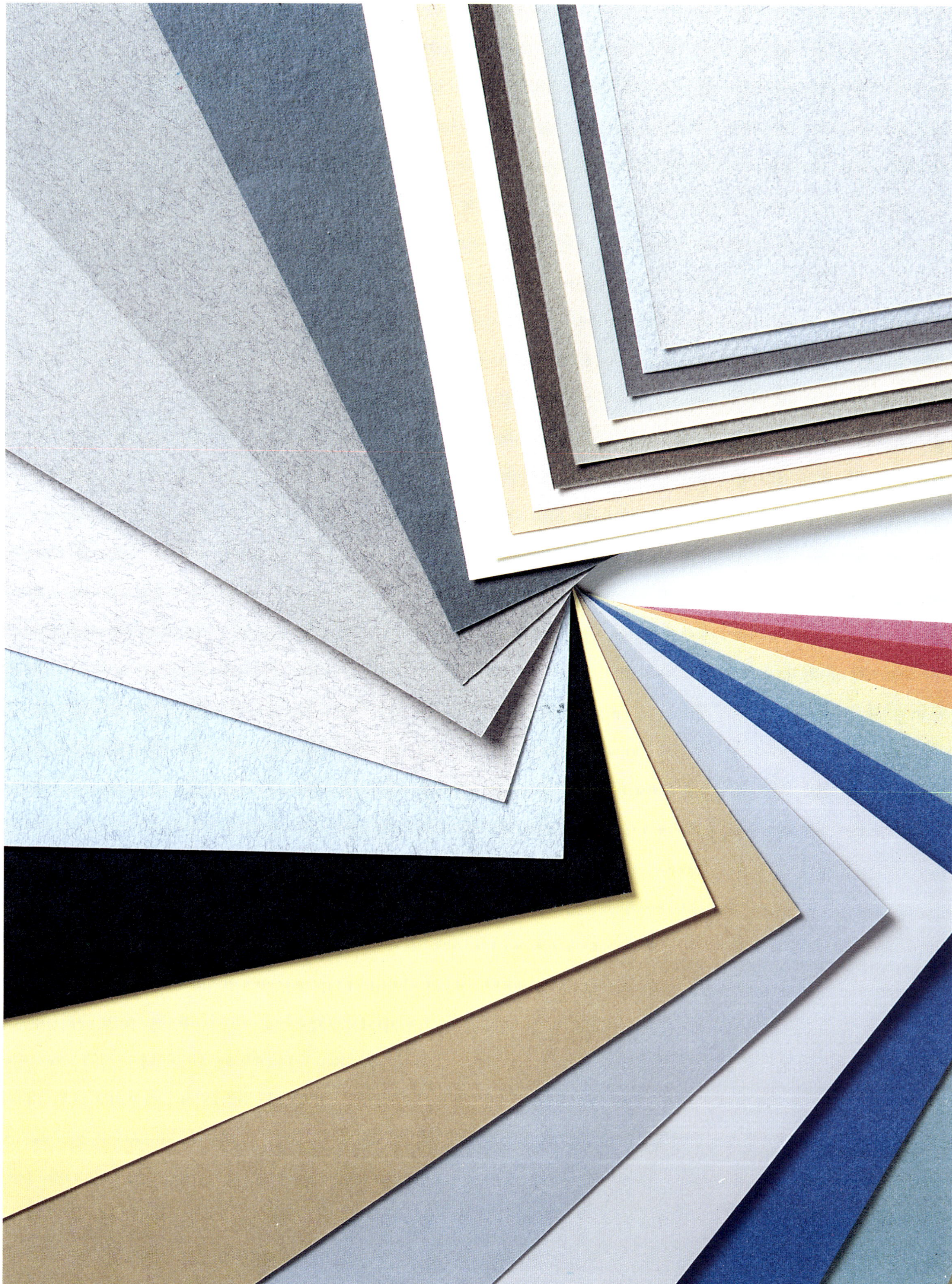

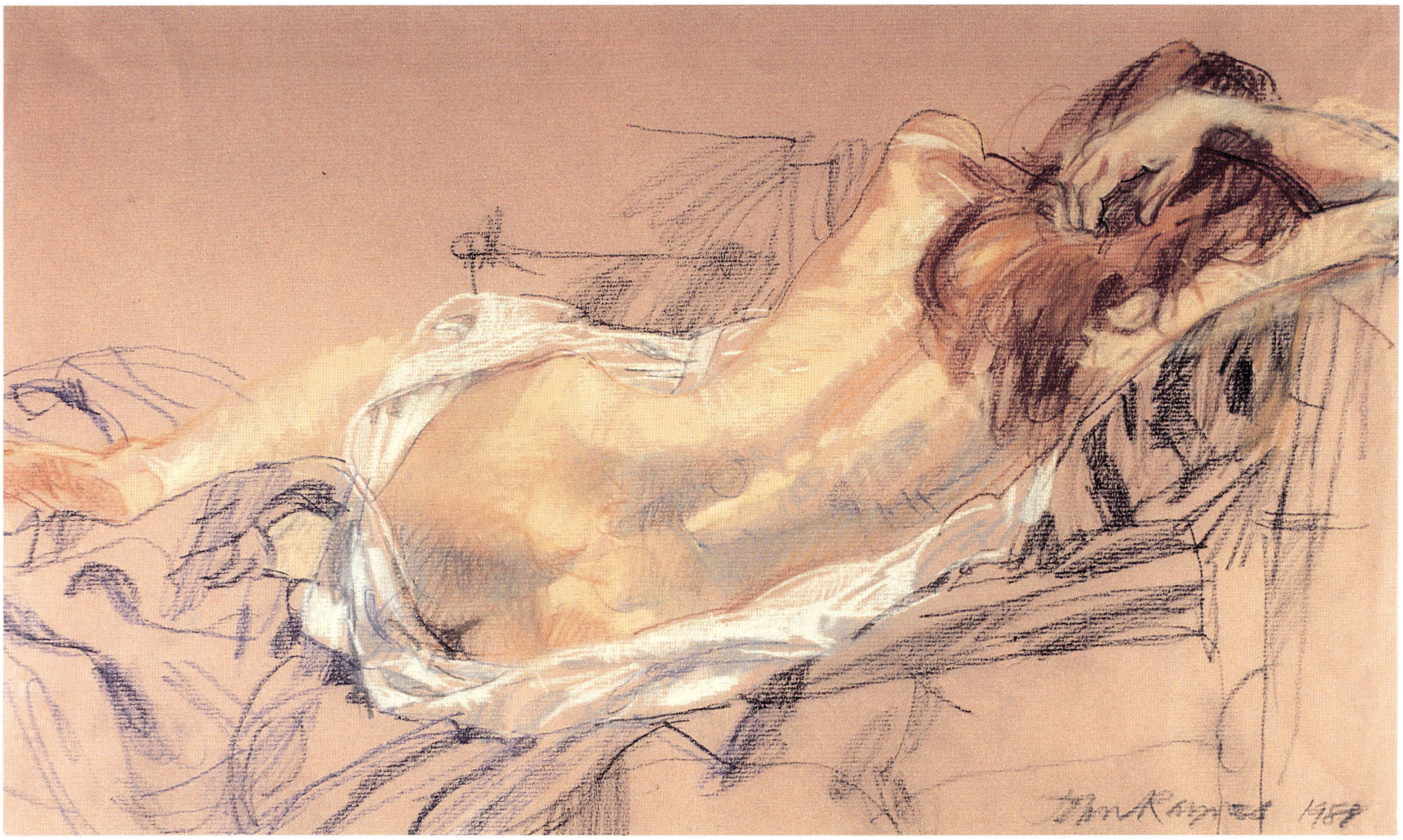

Hand-made papers are expensive, and should be reserved for special projects once you have a feel for the subject. They are usually made from pure linen and have one side only that is treated with size. If you can see the watermark and it is the right way round, you have the right side. If you cannot see a mark, touch the surfaces gently with a moistened lip; the right side will feel slightly sticky and will gently pull on your lip.

All papers, depending on how they were made, have a right side and a wrong side. If they are heavily textured, the more textured side is the proper side for drawing. With more moderate textures, if you hold the paper curving in front of a light surface, you should be able to pick out the texture on the right side. With sugar papers and light cartridge it does not really matter which side you work on, and it is not advisable to stretch these cheaper, lighter papers, as they will probably disintegrate.

Cartridge paper is the normal support for all sorts of work. It is cheap, has a slight tooth, and comes in a range of sizes bound as sketchbooks. For this project an A5 sketchbook will be perfectly suitable. Colored and toned paper also comes in extensive ranges of quality and texture. For us a few pieces of tinted sugar paper will do; the colors are subtle and muted and they are cheap, a fact well known art students.

Paper is bought by name and weight, which for our purpose is really its thickness. The weight quoted for paper is the weight per ream, which is 480 sheets. A lot of the terminology in art and allied trades harks back to historical names. 60-pound paper is relatively thin. 140-pound paper is thick. The thinner papers distort and buckle when worked on with water, and the thicker heavier sheets are more resistant. To be sure of its durability, it is often better to stretch the paper (see below). For the examples and exercises in this book we will not need to stretch paper.

Paper sizes used to be sold with archaic names such as imperial, crown and elephant. These days there is an international convention replacing this system, so that most papers can be bought in what is termed 'A' sizes. All the 'A' sizes have the same proportion of length to width.

'A' sizes

A0 = 1188 × 840 mm
A1 = 840 × 594 mm
A2 = 594 × 420 mm
A3 = 420 × 297 mm
A4 = 297 × 210 mm
A5 = 210 × 148.5 mm

Adhesive Tape

There are two types of tape that you will need. Masking tape, sometimes called pres-

FAR LEFT
A range of colored papers. The lighter tones are valuable in making a color harmony by exploiting the transparent nature of the pencils.

ABOVE
John Raynes
Reclining Nude
This drawing makes good use of a colored paper support, with open drawing at first, and then building up brighter, more opaque blocks of color to describe the form.

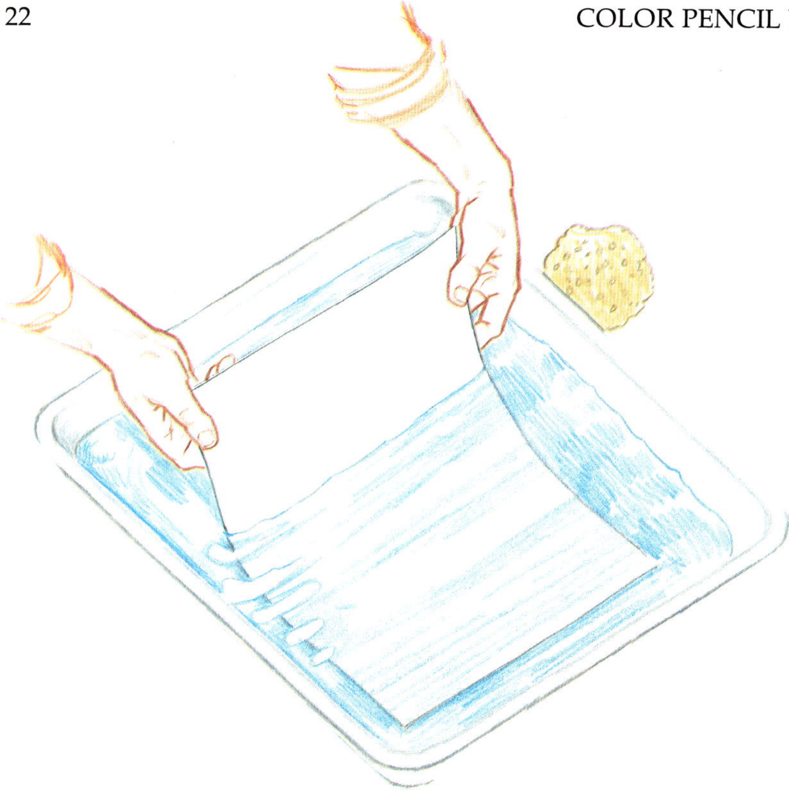

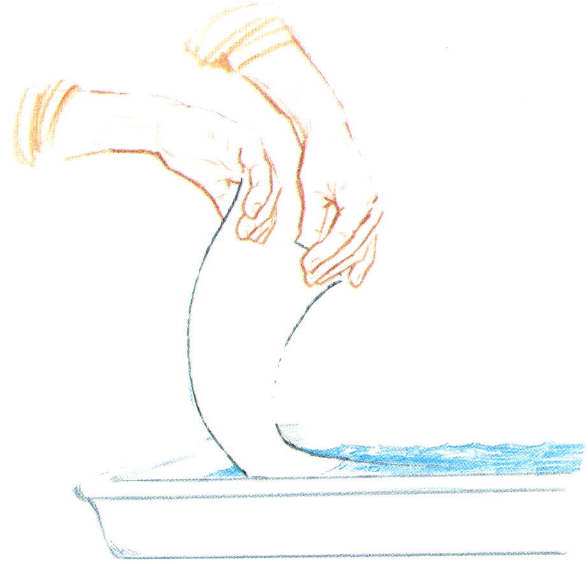

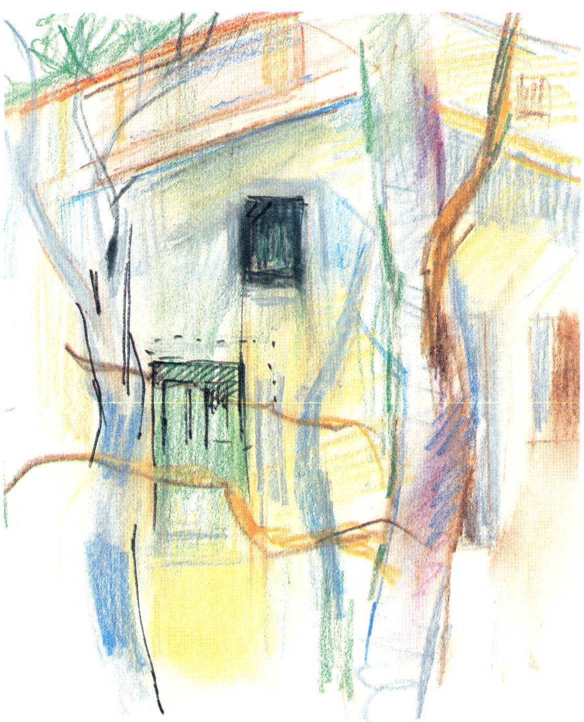

sure-sensitive or low-tack tape, is the one you need for the exercises that follow. It is specially designed to adhere to paper and to be removed without damaging the surface. It can be used to keep the margins clear of paint or to mask designated areas from a wash of color.

The other, stronger tape is useful for later studies, when you stretch paper on a board. Old-fashioned paper parcel tape is ideal for this job, but make sure it has a water-soluble gum.

Stretching Paper

1. Find the right side of the paper, as described above. Remember it, or if you prefer, mark it indelibly at the edge which will ultimately be removed.
2. Lay the paper the right side up on a flat surface, in a sink, a tray, or even the bath if the paper is large.
3. Soak it for about 15 minutes. If you are working on a tray, keep applying water with a sponge or rag.
4. Gently lift the paper and let surplus water drain off.
5. Lay the paper right side up on the drawing board, gently smooth it with a sponge or rag to remove any large air bubbles, and pin the corners,
6. With suitable lengths of moistened gummed paper, stick the edges of the paper to the drawing board. You may need to overlap the strips to make sure you have at least one inch of gummed paper in contact with the wet paper, and a similar amount on the drawing board. These surfaces have to hold firm as the paper dries and shrinks.
7. Let the paper dry naturally, in a flat position to help it dry evenly. It may take twelve hours to dry, so it makes sense to prepare a number of sheets in advance.

Once the paper is dry, it should feel as taut as a drumskin, and be able to take washes and heavy work without distorting.

ABOVE LEFT AND RIGHT
The stages in stretching paper, as described left.

FAR LEFT
Olivier McLarnon
Sketchbook study using soluble color pencils.

FAR RIGHT
Fixatives; a spray can and a simple blow-pipe diffuser.

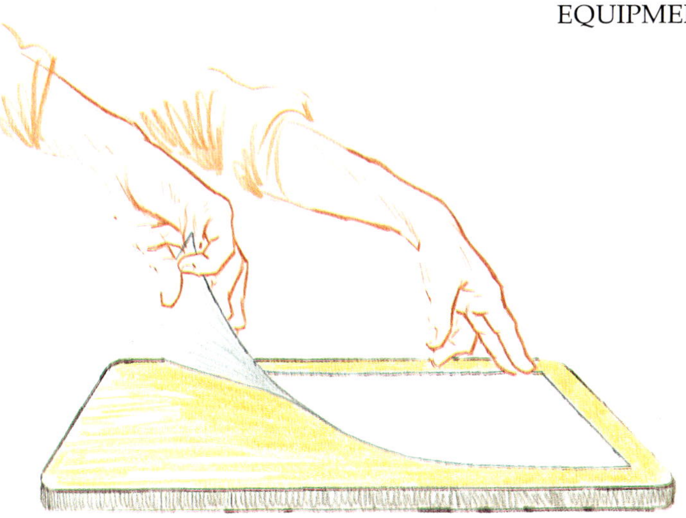

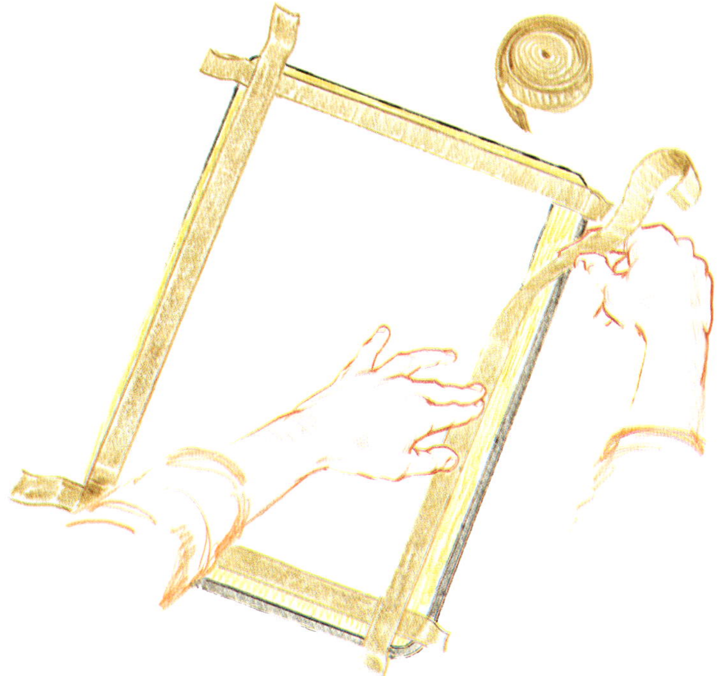

Fixatives

Many pencil pigments and pigments without binders, like charcoal and pastel, need to be fixed once the work is completed. In effect, you are adding a binding agent after the event. Historically, the most universal fixative was made from a two percent solution of shellac in alcohol. Shellac is a mixture of a wax derived from insects and tree resin. This solution can be sprayed onto the pigment, and the alcohol evaporates, leaving a binding coat of shellac. Generally, it is the softer pigments that are in danger of being smudged, but it is probably best to fix all drawings to increase their durability.

Modern fixatives work on a similar principle. As they produce a fine spray of binder in solution, always work in a well-ventilated room, or even outside if possible. If you read and obey the directions carefully, these are relatively easy to use. Fixative is available in aerosols, or bottles which supply a spray by means of a mouth diffuser. Both, if used incorrectly, can overload the pigment, and in some cases change the color balance, so experiment first on a test piece that is not important, and again, read the directions.

The golden rule here is a repeated light and even spray, which is much better than a heavy uneven spray. The blow-pipe diffuser takes a little skill to use, but can produce as good a surface cover as the aerosol, with the added advantages of lower cost and fewer fumes. There are an increasing number of different aerosols now available; be careful that you buy an appropriate fixative, not, for example, picture varnish. If in doubt, ask for assistance.

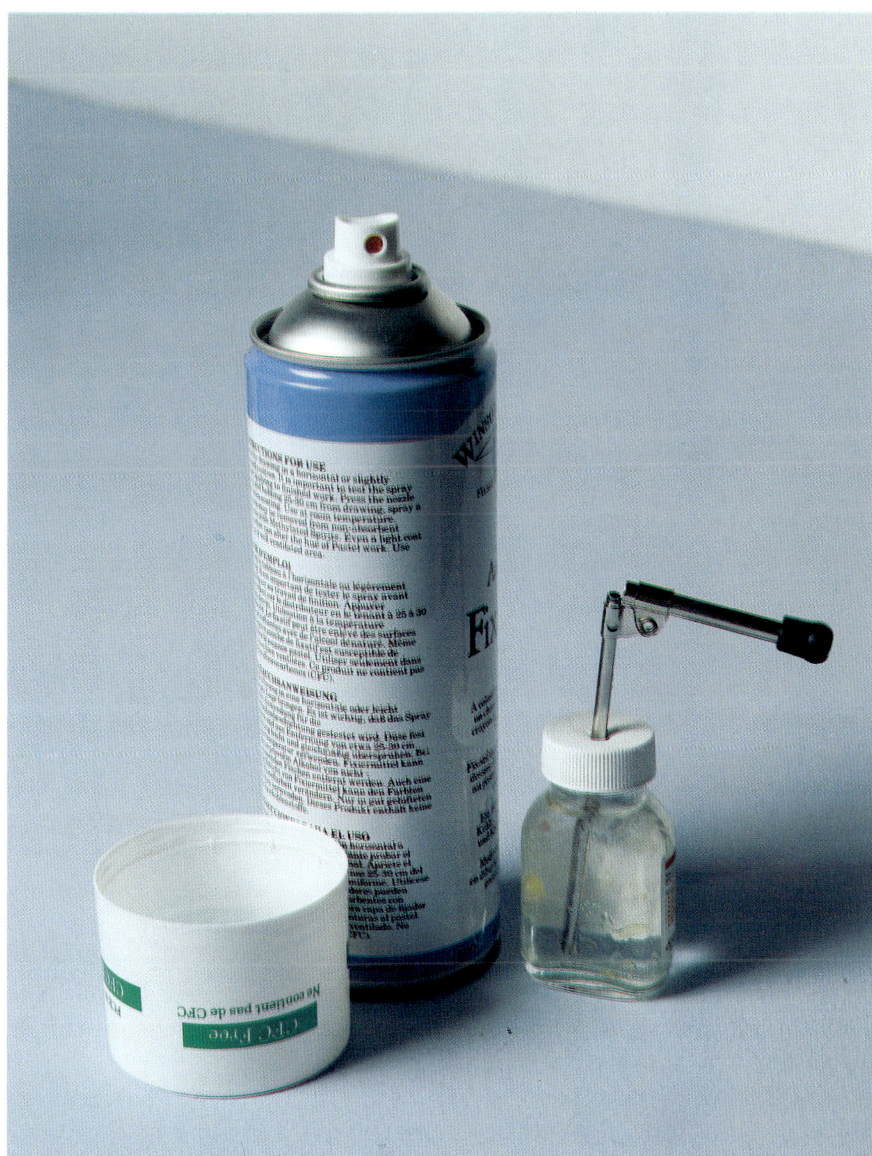

Blades and Sharpeners

When you sharpen a pencil, the shape you cut obviously determines the shape and scope of the possible marks you can make.

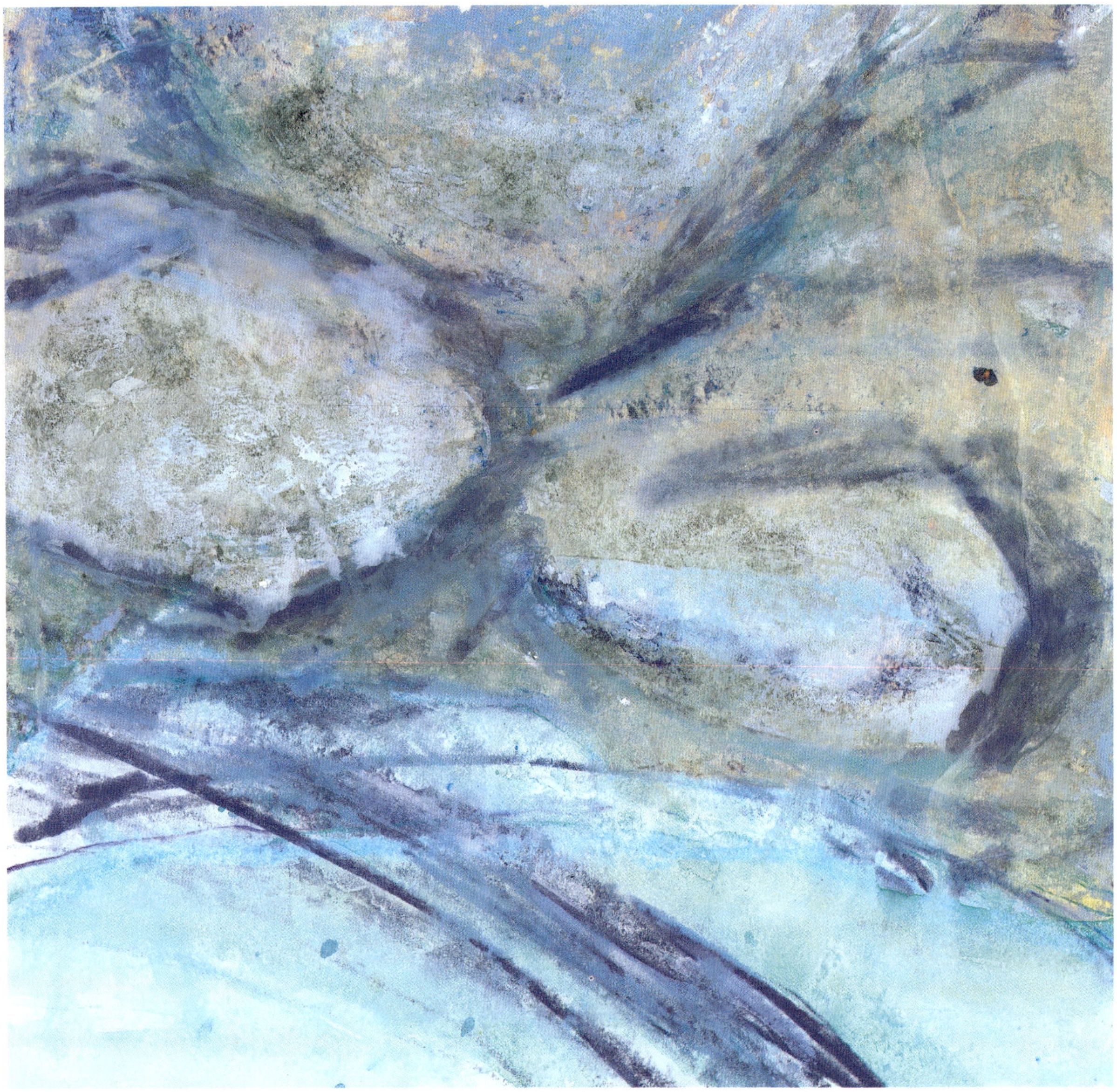

LEFT
Water and Stones 1
This is an experimental piece, loosely based on drawings from the edge of a river and using the whole range of pigments. It was drawn, washed with water, sprinkled with scraped pigment, blotted, and worked with melted color.

RIGHT
Sharpening and shaping the pencil 'lead'.

The pencils come from the manufacturers ready sharpened, beautiful for presentation, but almost useless for drawing. If you sharpen them with a fixed-blade twist sharpener you can get a perfect cone of wood and pigment, but this should be seen as the beginning of sharpening not the end. This cone limits the use of the pencil, in that it only exposes the point of the pigment and a very small area of shaft. By using a blade for sharpening, more wood can be removed so that you can make the pigment any shape you wish.

Try a long sharp lead, which can allow you to draw with the side as well as the point. Try a chisel shape, which makes both a needle-thin mark and a broad stroke. Experiment to get a feel for the possibilities. As far as the actual knives are concerned, it is really a question of finding a knife that is comfortable and sharp enough for the job. I personally prefer a scalpel. They are incredibly sharp, and when the blade blunts I can use it for other purposes. One blade will start its life cutting paper or sharpening pencils, and end as a scraper for removing pigment.

It may seem a simple task but some people have difficulty sharpening a pencil, especially these softer color pigments. I recommend the following method. Rather than push the blade, gently pull back the pencil. If you hold the knife almost against the wood, your thumb can support the back of the knife. Holding the pencil in your other hand, with your thumb at the top, the knife and pencil can come together so that the pencil thumb rests on the knife thumb. By pushing gently with the pencil thumb and holding the knife almost flat, the pencil will slide back, allowing a sliver of wood to be removed from the pigment. Some of these 'leads' can be quite crumbly and difficult.

Once you have created the point you want, it can be finished by stroking it gently on a fine sandpaper block. The cutting texture of the sandpaper can maintain the shape, and can keep it consistent. The

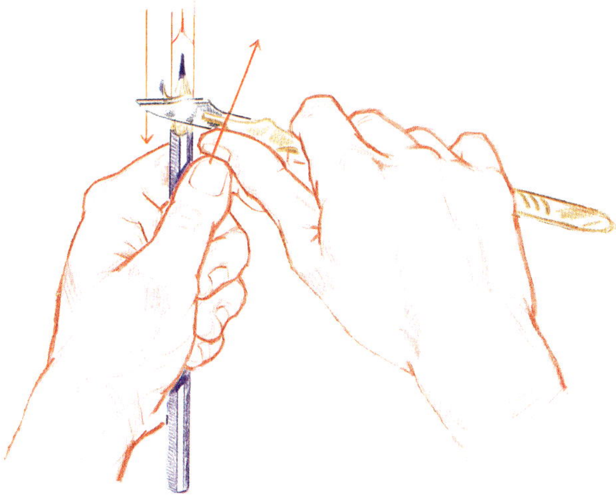

character of the marks can change as the pencil becomes blunt. Sanding pads can be bought or made; a fine grade is best for this purpose, and is also a good way to collect raw pigment.

Erasers and Burnishers

When you draw there comes a time when you need to remove some of the pigment, perhaps to correct an error or to create some surface effect. The main concern here is to erase pigment without disturbing the paper surface. A range of erasers is probably best. A general rule would be hard erasers on hard surfaces, and soft on soft. Starting with the hardest you are likely to need, the old-fashioned ink eraser is fine for radical use. Beware the cheaper colored plastic erasers, as they can leave traces of their own color. However, there are some fine plastic combination erasers, hard and soft, that I would recommend. These can be used in a very controlled manner, particularly with a stencil, or when cut to a point.

Soft-pencil erasers are good all round, although they were intended for graphite pencils. Gum erasers are particularly good for large areas and for blending and reducing color. So is the kneadable putty eraser, which can be shaped and even pulled to pieces. There are now erasers in a pencil form which are in the middle of the hardness range and very good for controlled, clean work, as the contaminated point can be sliced away. This is an important point; because of the nature of the pigments, erasers can become contaminated, and should be cleaned by rubbing on spare paper.

It is worth buying a tortillon, or stump, which is simply a compressed roll of paper or leather which can be used to rub and blend pigment. There is also a burnishing stencil available which can be helpful.

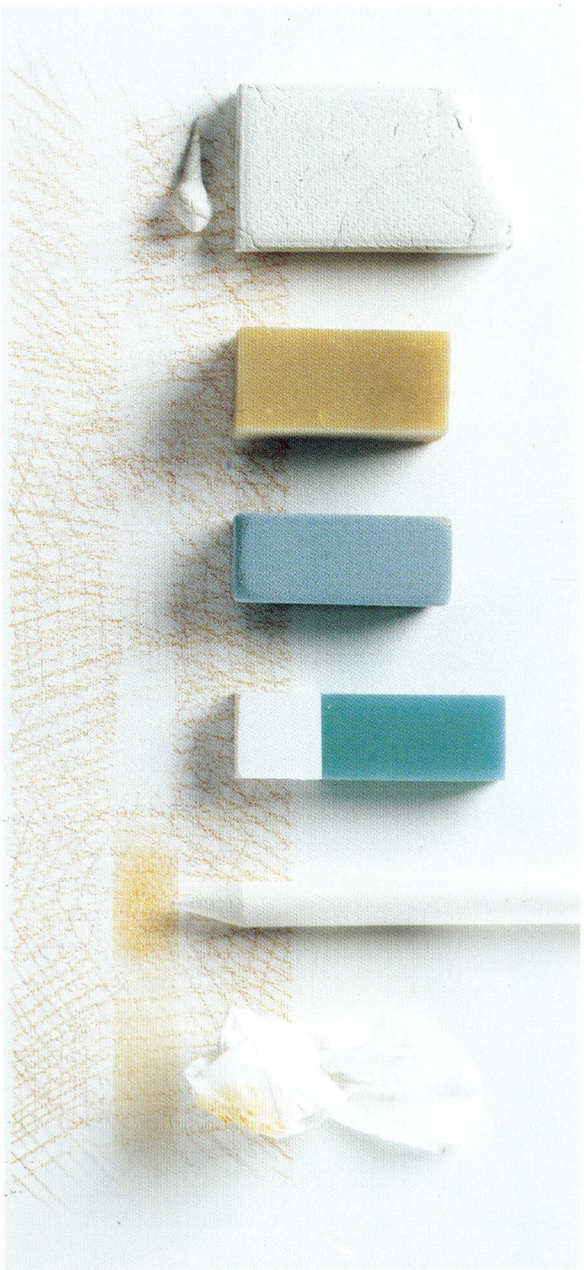

LEFT
Erasing and burnishing (from top): putty, gum, all-purpose vinyl, stump or stub burnisher, and simple tissue.

BELOW
A range of blades and sharpeners. The straight-edged blades are used for cutting, while the curved edges are valuable for scraping the surfaces of drawings.

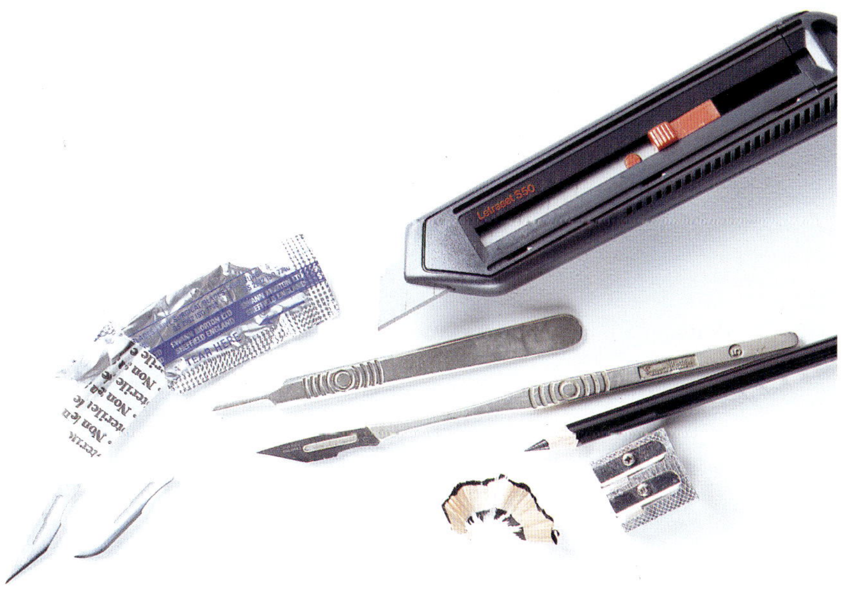

3. Using the Materials

This section is designed to try to do a number of things.

1. Experimenting with the materials
By testing the materials through a whole range of exercises, we can attempt to discover some of their limits and possibilities. These exercises can be a good model for testing most other artist's materials.

2. Experiencing the materials
While doing these exercises, largely free from what might normally be called 'drawing', it is possible to develop a number of useful skills. The experience and examples that you like may become part of the way you use these materials. This can be the beginning of a real understanding of the medium, laying the ground for the development of a personal 'visual' language.

3. Looking at some basic principles
While we are investigating how these materials perform, the examples can show the basic elements and principles used when we make art. It is a measure of these colored pencils that they can perform well in all these spheres.

Quality of Line

An obvious starting place for our inquiry into color pencils is in the range and qualities of the lines and marks they make.

Exercise 1 On your sheet of cartridge, longways, simply draw three lines. Use any of the three types of pencil.
Draw horizontally:

1 As fast as you can
2. As slowly as you can
3. A medium-paced stroke
4. A really heavy line
5. A really light line
6. A doodling meander
7. A hatched line
8. A cross-hatched line
9. A regular strip of dots
10. An irregular strip of dot marks, using different directions and energies
11. A dynamic scribble
12. A range of shaped leads

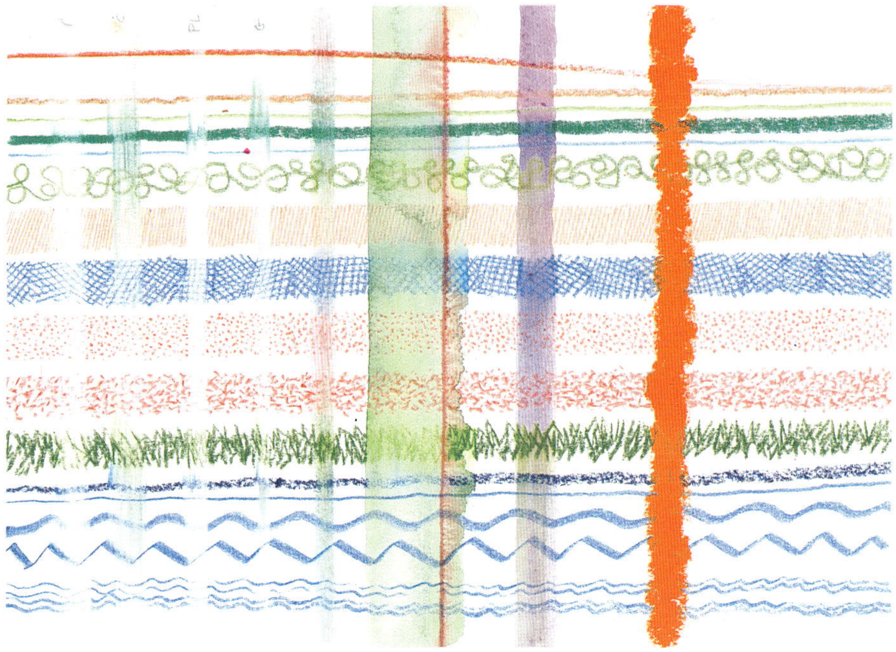

ABOVE
Quality of line: the horizontal lines illustrate Exercise 1, examples 1–12, the vertical lines illustrate Exercise 2, examples 1–7.

Exercise 2 Now draw vertically:

1. Using different erasers, make erased lines
2. A burnished line
3. Using clean water, make a wet brush strip
4. Using a soluble pencil, draw through the wet strip
5. Using the wet brush, collect pigment and paint a wet pigment strip
6. When dry, erase and burnish through these painted areas
7. With a hair drier, warm up the heat-sensitive pencil and draw a plastic line

Drawing is closely related to scratching and scoring marks on viable surfaces; these marks carry with them the same sort of feelings and associations. A mark might be a fast, forceful gouge, a slow, heavy, dragged score, or a delicate, thin cut. If we look hard at a drawn mark, we can see a sort of sign or signature of the way it was made. Even when there is no proper representational drawing, we might still sense the speed and swiftness or the slow cramped heaviness in a line. Hunters can read an animal's trail, so we can 'read' the marks.

RIGHT
John Raynes
Portrait Study
This drawing admirably illustrates a whole range of marks, from light, fast, open drawing to dense, thick, opaque passages, here used for light and shadow.

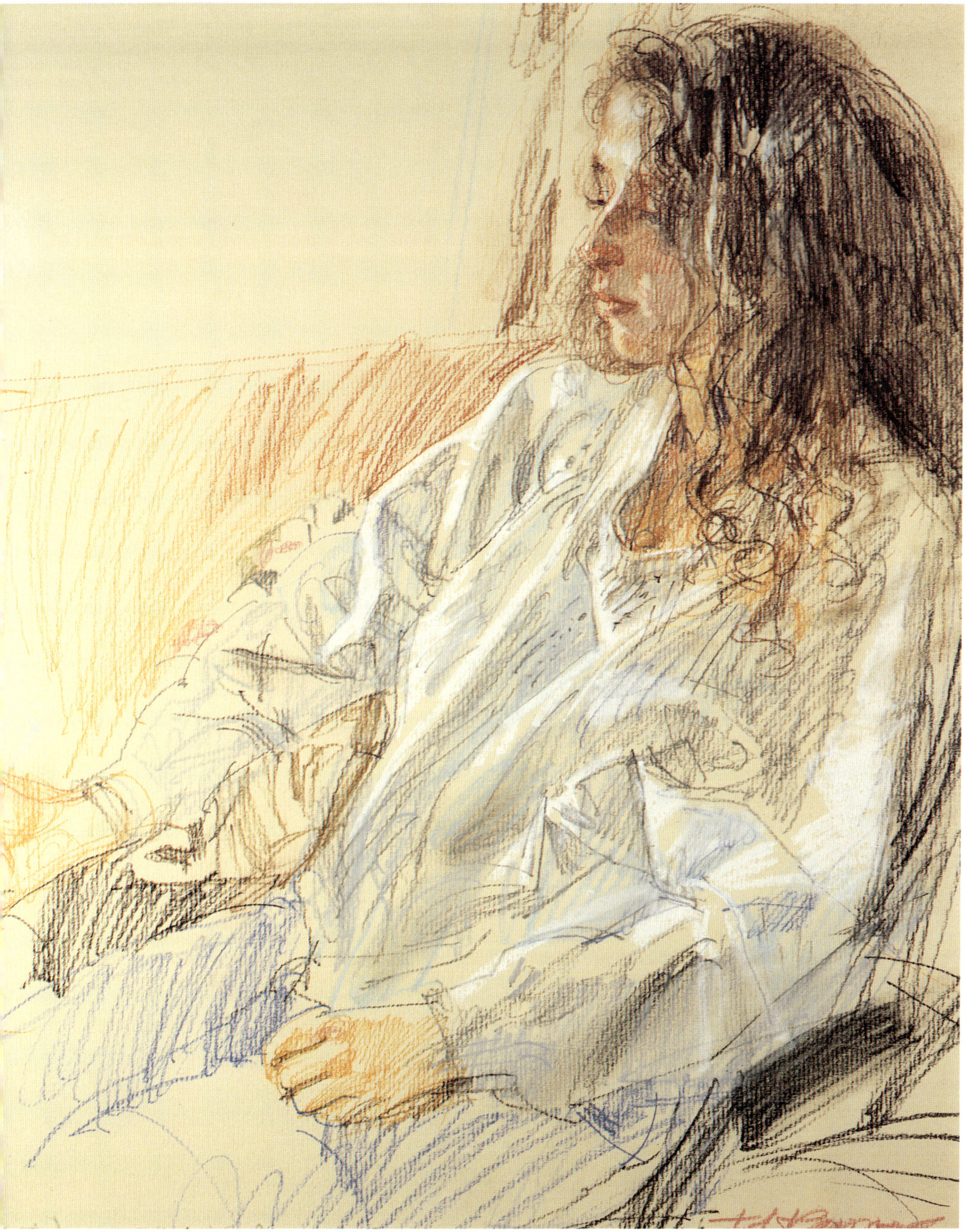

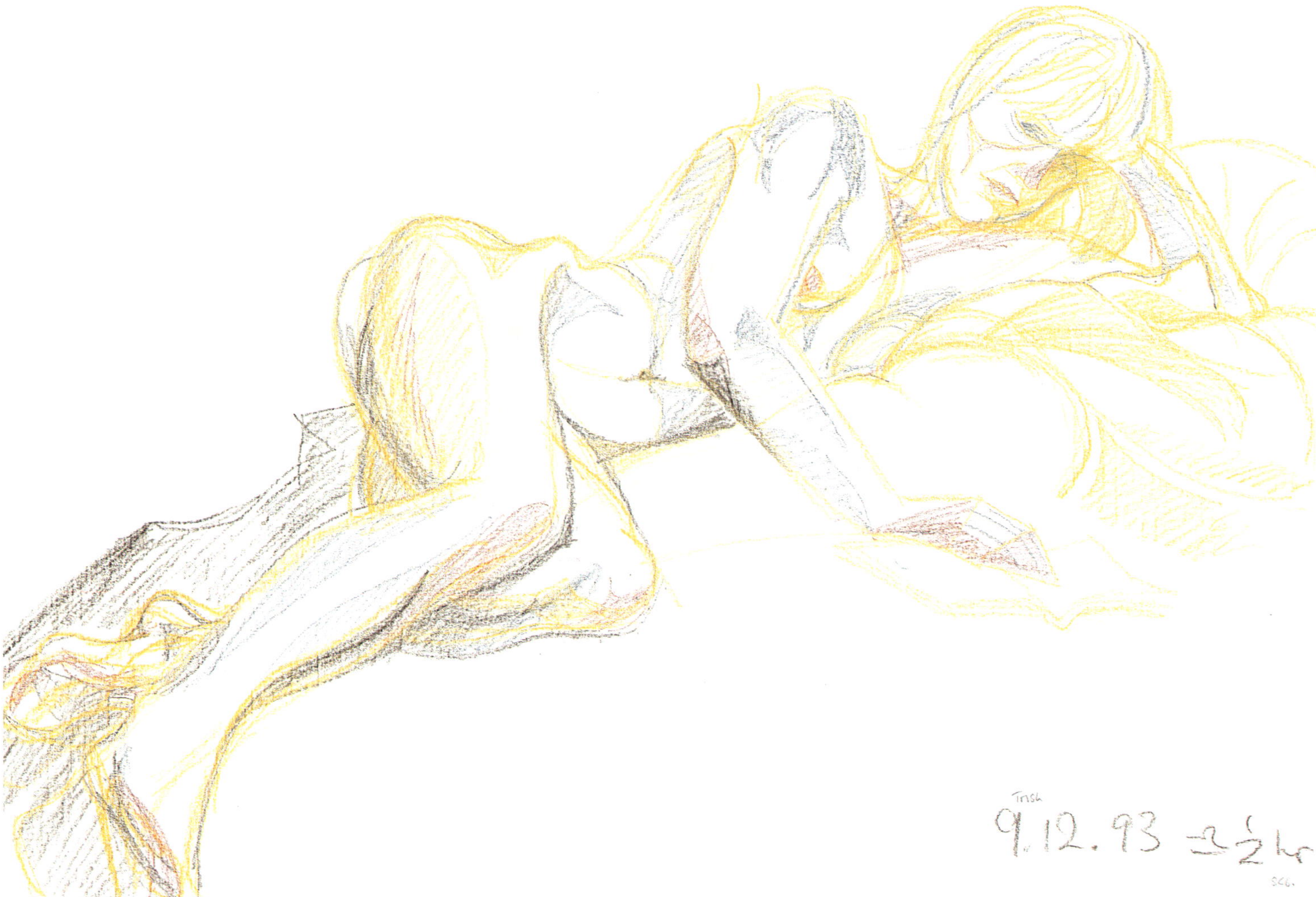

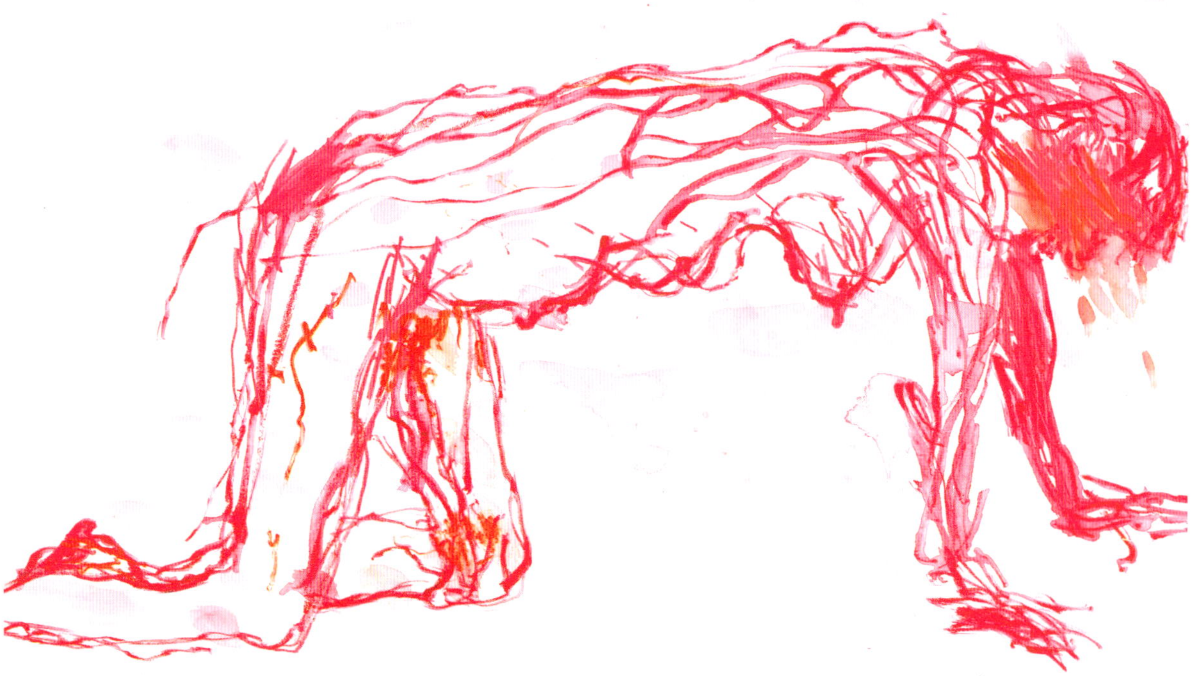

ABOVE
Sandy Brown
Figure Study
Here the artist is trying to build the form of the model with simple color contours made from earlier curving lines.

LEFT
Barbara Nicholls
Figure Drawing
This experimental drawing is made with heat-sensitive pencil. The dynamic marks suggest rather than explaining the form.

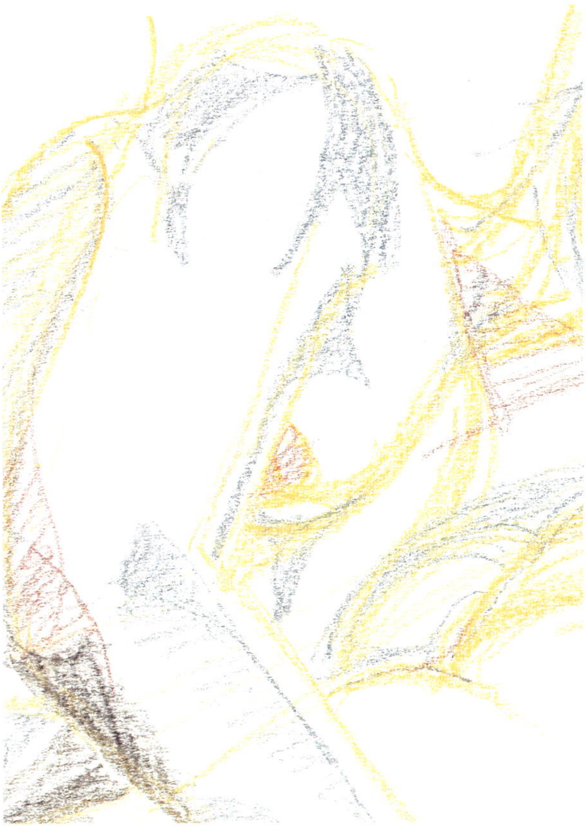

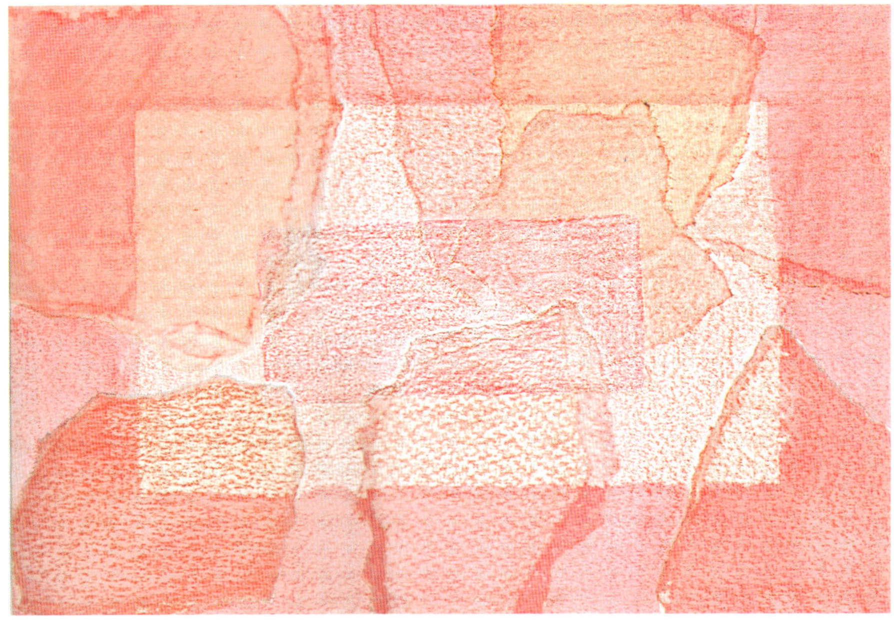

ABOVE LEFT
A close-up of Sandy's curving lines.

ABOVE
Quality of surface, Exercise 1.

If you look at some artists' drawings, just as abstract marks, I think you can see just how special and particular these marks are; they have the qualities of a signature. They are just as difficult to forge or imitate as written signatures. The way to get near these marks is by using the same materials and surfaces and the same energy in drawing them. Then we may produce a mark that is similar to the original.

Quality of Surface

Paper and Surface

Butting together lots of torn paper and gluing it on some A5 cartridge, we can look at the way that different surfaces obviously affect the marks. Use any paper you can lay your hands on; you only need small pieces for this exercise.

Exercise 1

1. Glue onto an A5 piece of cartridge paper a mosaic of different types of paper.
2. When dry, paint a shape across these varied paper surfaces somewhere in the middle.
3. Using a soft, soluble, colored pencil, you can show the change in texture by gently and evenly shading over the whole area.
4. With a wet brush and clean water, lift the pigment around the outer edge of the paper.

Impressed or Negative Line

Practically all papers can be scored with any suitable sharp instrument that will compress the paper texture. This will then be revealed as clear white paper, as the pencil shading misses the depressed lines.

BELOW LEFT
A close-up of Barbara's dynamic lines.

BELOW RIGHT
Impressed or negative line, Exercise 2.

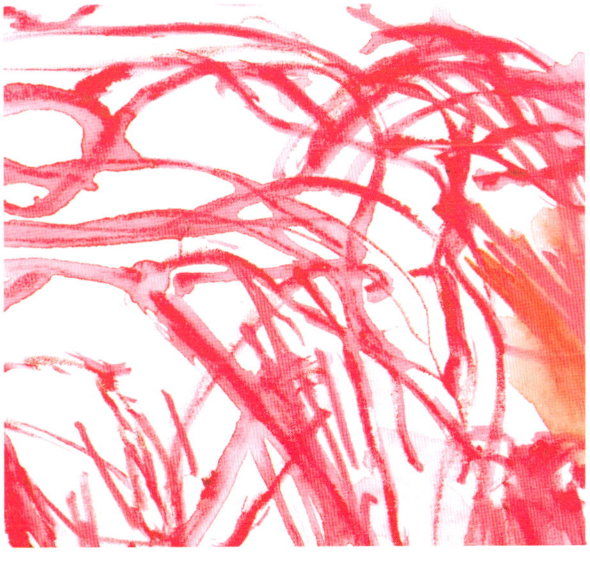

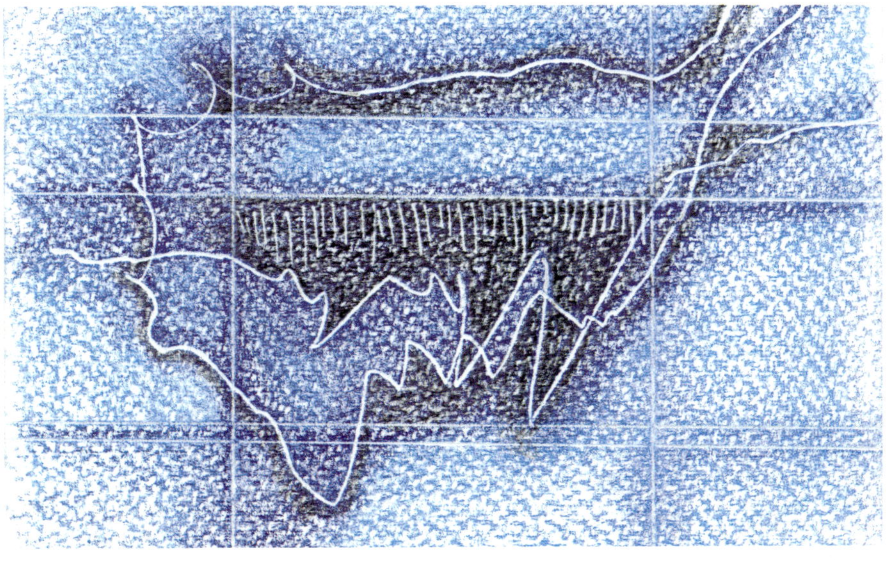

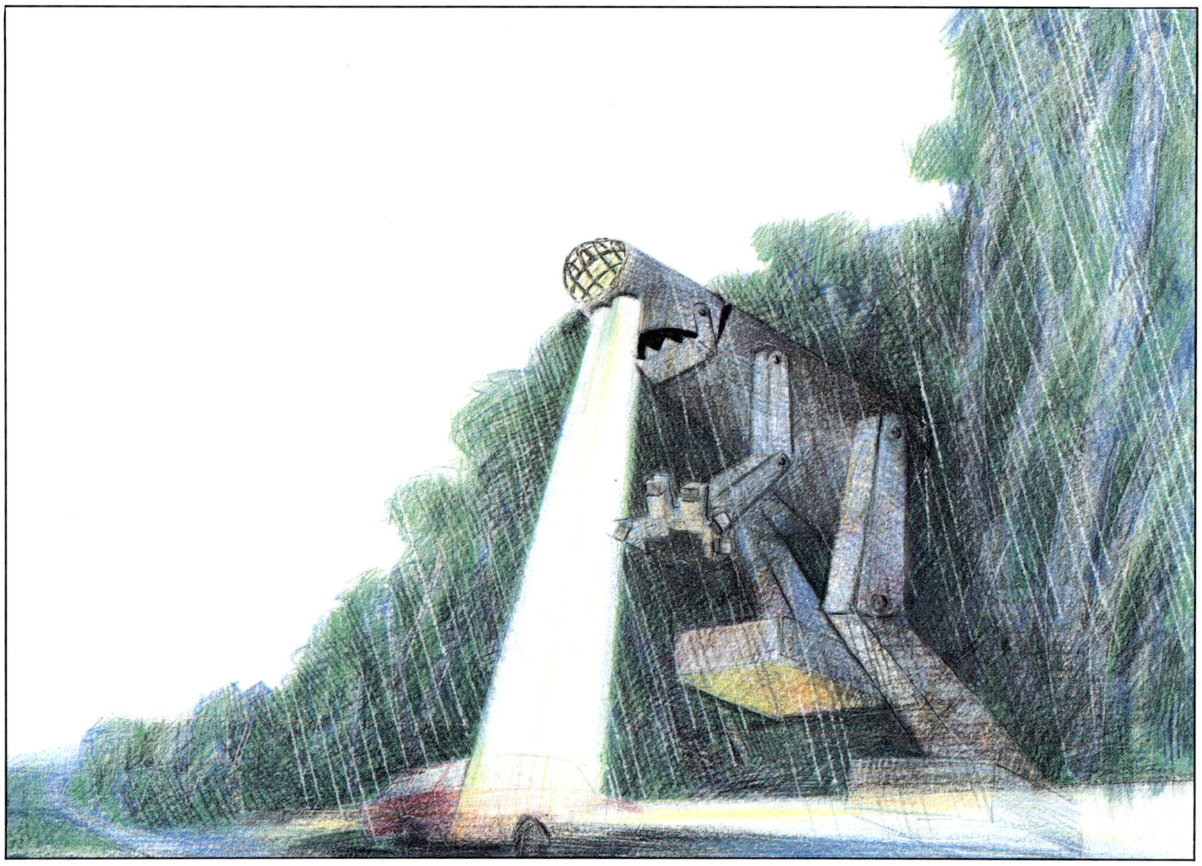

Exercise 2

1. Using a piece of A5 cartridge or, even better, some rough watercolor paper, score the surface. Use anything you think suitable; try a hard, sharp pencil through another piece of thin paper. Similarly, try a ballpoint, the end of the brush, the back of a knife, anything you can find that will do the job.
2. Use a soft, strong, colored pencil and reveal the marks by gently shading.

Frottage/Rubbing

This technique was used by Max Ernst. The idea is to capture texture from various surfaces, such as wood, stone, etc., by rubbing over the paper surface with soft pigment.

Exercise 3

1. Use thin paper, detail or typing paper will do. Find some interesting textured material, such as concrete or old wood, and place the thin paper over an area of it, taping it in place with low-tack tape.
2. Using a soft pencil, gently rub the surface. Try and keep the tone even until you have captured your texture.
3. By carefully moving the paper and taping it down, say a couple of millimeters away from its original position, you can repeat the process with another color. This can really bring out the representation of the texture.

Graffito/Scraping

This was originally a way of decorating plaster walls. A layer of pigment is covered with a contrasting color, and is then revealed by scraping and scratching the surface.

Exercise 4

1. Choose two contrasting colors, one from the harder pencils, and one from the soft pencils.
2. Using the harder first, cover the A5 cartridge with a dense, saturated layer of pigment.
3. Next use the softer color, gently at first,

LEFT
Madeleine Baker
The Iron Man
This humorous illustration for a children's story uses an impressed line for atmosphere and the lighter lines for rain.

BELOW
Exercise 3, frottage/rubbing.

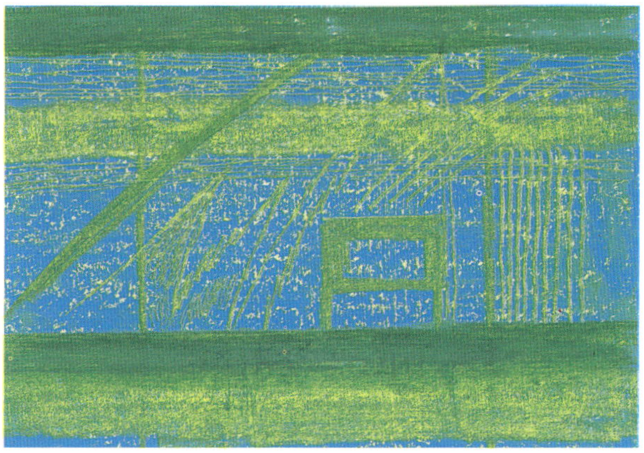

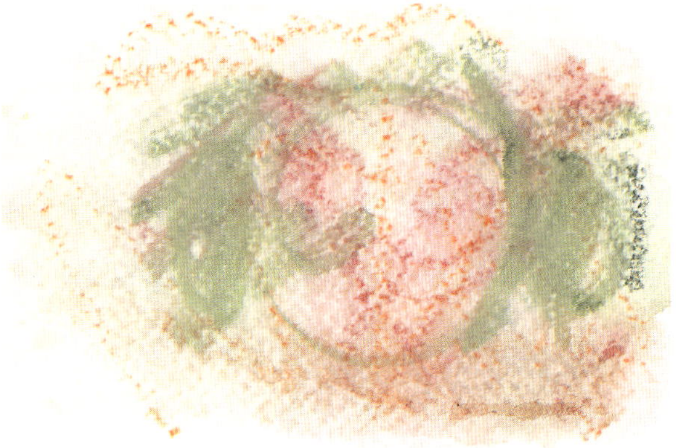

FAR LEFT ABOVE
Exercise 4, graffito/ scraping.

LEFT ABOVE
Exercise 5, surface printing.

FAR LEFT AND LEFT BELOW
Exercise 6, surface printing.

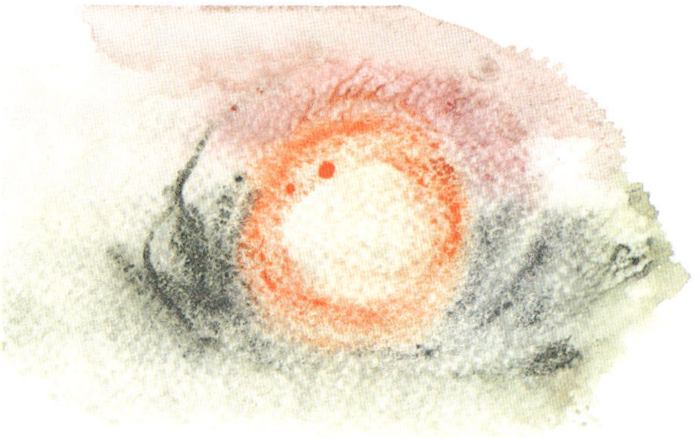

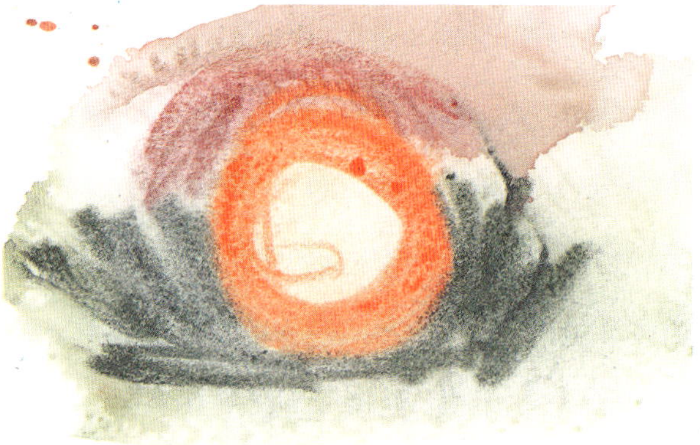

and overlay the pigment until you achieve a color change.

4. Taking a blade, scrape away pigment. Try different types of scratching; a curved blade will reveal the surface below differently to a straight blade. Try cutting back an area with sandpaper; try another area with a flat blade.

Surface Printing

Any pigment in its plastic or fluid form can be transferred by simply pressing the painted or marked paper onto another surface. All sorts of marks and effects can be attained in this way that would be extremely difficult to achieve through normal painting and drawing.

Exercise 5

1. Prepare a piece of A5 paper by covering it generally with any marks that you like.
2. With a contrasting color from the soluble range, mark and wet a separate piece of paper. Before it dries, press the two pieces of paper together firmly without allowing them to smear. Open up the two blots. Which is the more interesting?

Exercise 6

1. Repeat steps 1 and 2 above, but this time using the heat-sensitive pigment for one of the papers. Do not peel them apart.
2. If you apply gentle heat to this sandwich, perhaps a hair-drier or iron, you can release the pigments across the two surfaces. The heat required for this exercise is not very great, it is about the temperature of a hot bath.

A Ground: A Field of Tone and Color

Simple Line as Tone

Just using a free-hand line, try and make an evenly spread tone. Use straight lines first; they do not have to be horizontal, but should be roughly parallel.

Meandering Line as Tone

Lay a curving line right across the middle of the paper from left to right. Above and below this line, repeat the same shape as evenly and regularly as possible, building up a sequence.

Network as Tone

Repeat the simple line exercise and add a set of lines with similar spacing at roughly right-angles to the first. This will produce an even network.

Meandering Network as Tone

Repeat the network exercise but this time start with a slightly flatter set of curves. At a right-angle to the first set, draw a second set of meandering lines.

FAR LEFT
Simple line as tone.

LEFT
Meandering line as tone.

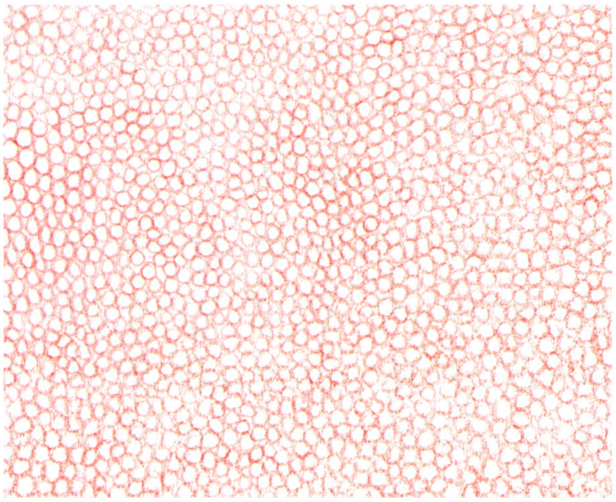

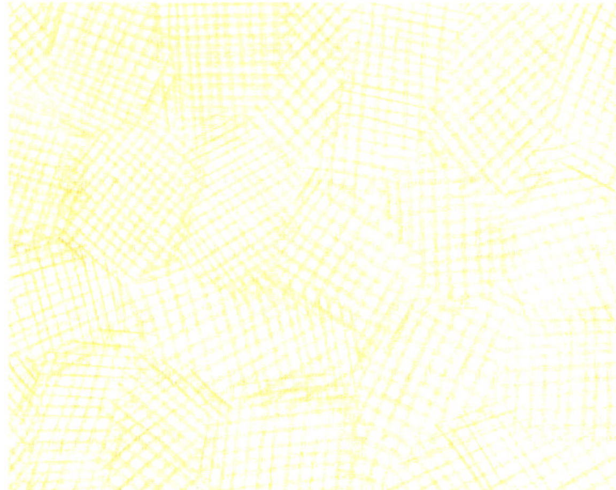

FAR LEFT
Modular tone.

LEFT
Cross-hatching

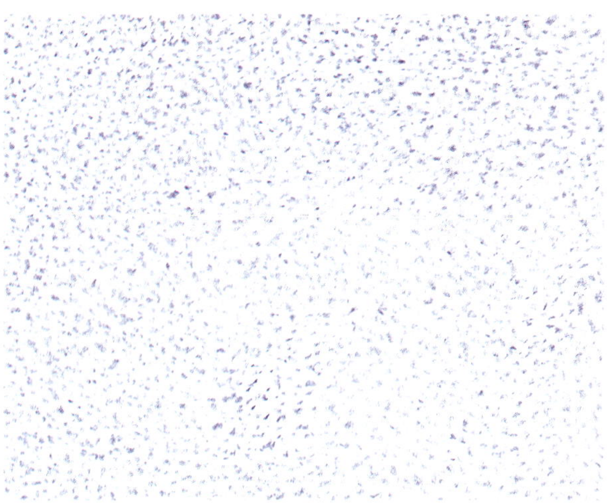

FAR LEFT
Dots/stipple/pointillism.

LEFT
Dry on dry, pigment particles.

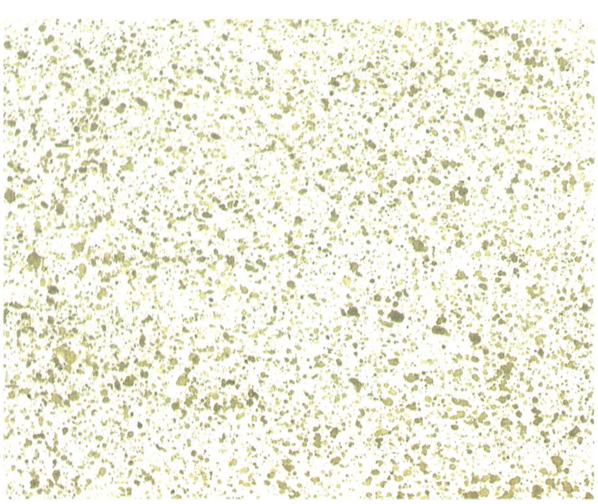

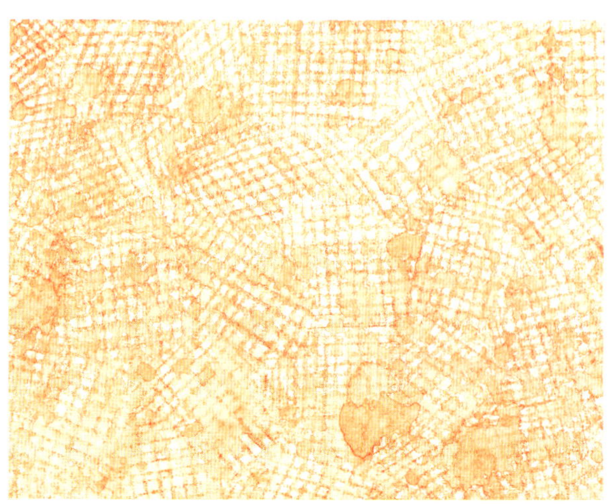

FAR LEFT
Splatter.

LEFT
Clear water spray.

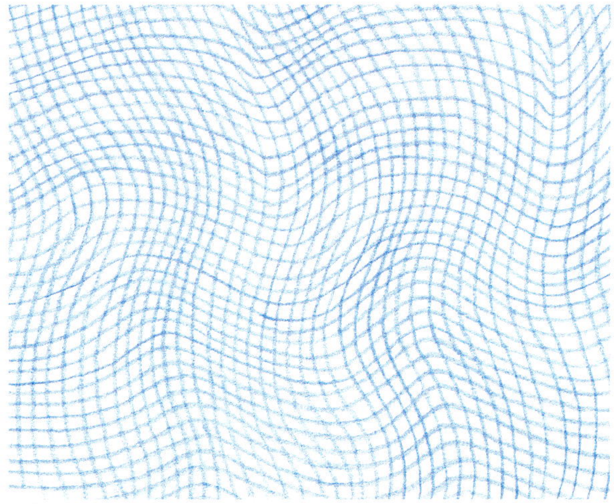

FAR LEFT
Network as tone.

LEFT
Meandering network as tone.

FAR LEFT
Free-form scribble.

LEFT
Paper texture.

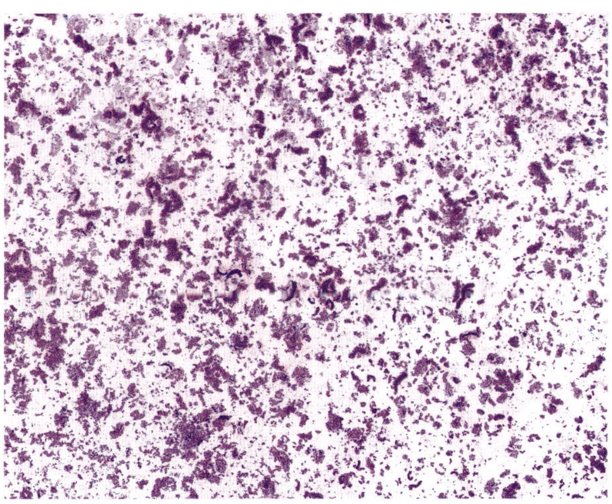
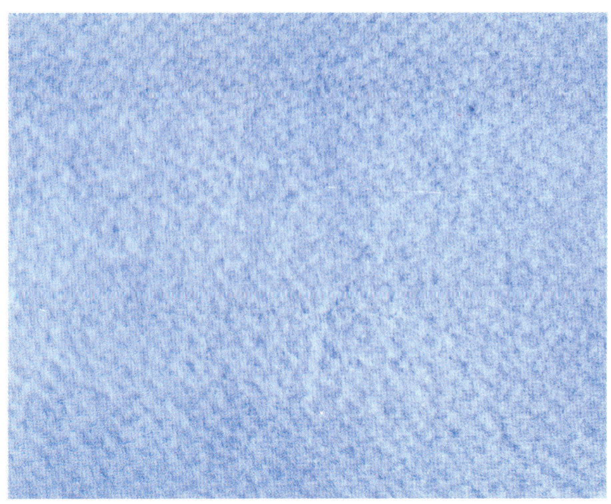

FAR LEFT
Dry on wet, particles on wash.

LEFT
Watercolor wash.

FAR LEFT
Thick opaque pigment.

LEFT
Transferred pigment.

Modular Tone

Use a repeated shape, which can be anything you find easy to mass-produce. Similarly sized squares, circles, beans or lozenges, anything like this as long as it is a closed shape. Space your shapes evenly to build a sort of wall or texture.

Cross-hatching

Cross-hatching is a commonly used method of making a tonal drawing. This is quite difficult to control at first. Draw a small network of spaced lines anywhere on the paper, next to that and slightly overlapping it draw another, and so on until there is an even tone, even though the effect is a little chaotic.

Free Form Scribble

By just scribbling over the surface in a regular manner, you can make an evenly toned area. Try and maintain an even distribution of clear paper.

Paper Texture

Gently using the side of the pencil, reveal more pigment with a blade. Rub enough pigment onto the texture to reveal the paper's surface. Try not to show any small lines.

Dots/Stipple/Pointillism

Using a slightly blunted pencil – a sharp point will need continual sharpening – make a series of evenly spaced dots.

Dry on Dry, Pigment Particles

Take a pencil that has been shaped with a long point and, holding it as if you were going to sharpen it, scrape a blade over the pigment, allowing a light rain of pigment particles to settle on the paper. Again the difficulty here is to get an even fall of pigment. Gently rub with a soft pad of cotton wool or tissue.

Dry on Wet, Pigment Particles on Wash

Wet the paper with a brush loaded with clean water. Using the same method as with the dry on dry exercise, drop powdered pigment as evenly as you can. A light rain of particles of pigment will settle on the damp paper. Again the difficulty here is to get an even fall of pigment. When the paper is dry, blow away any residue.

Watercolor Wash

Use the same scraping method of producing particles of pigment. This can also be done by rubbing a pencil on sandpaper, but beware of any loose grit. Collect the particles in a saucer. With a clean brush and water, mix the pigment into a clear pool of watercolor.

With your drawing board at an angle of about 45 degrees, wet the paper with clean water; a one-inch house-painting brush is excellent for this. Wait for the water to settle in, but before it is dry, load a sable brush with watercolor and lay down a wash of color using horizontal strokes. Reload the brush frequently and make sure there is no untouched paper. Try not to go over areas that have been painted. Leave it to dry; it should dry a perfectly even color.

Splatter

Take a wet sable brush and brush it across the exposed 'lead' of a soluble pencil, a few inches above the paper. The splatter will fall on to the paper like colored rain, and it is possible to direct the spray. Try and achieve an even distribution of splatter.

Clear Spray

Using any of the methods outlined above for laying an even ground and soluble pigment, spray fine droplets of water over the paper. This can be achieved with practice with a mouth-spray (see page 23) or a hand-held plant spray, if the delivery is fine enough.

Thick Opaque Pigment

Using soft heat-sensitive pencils, warm up your chosen color. A hairdrier is good for this task, or use a lighted candle to heat an old spoon; you can collect the warm pigment in the spoon as you work into it with the pencil. With the pencil sticky with pigment, mark the paper as thickly as you can. The pencil pigment will need to be softened repeatedly. The task here is twofold; we are trying to make an even distribution of color, and an interesting physical texture.

Transferred Pigment

Prepare a piece of paper and pigment in exactly the same manner as above, with the exception that this time you need not cover the paper so heavily. Using the method described in Exercise 5, transfer the pigment to a second paper as evenly as possible.

All of these surfaces can of course be played with using the methods described earlier (see page 29). They can be washed with a wet brush or cut back with a knife.

RIGHT
This composition uses as many techniques as I can muster.

BELOW
Devayani Khakhria
Underwater Garden
Devi's imaginary world, created with soft pigment and collage, contains wonderful creatures that seem to be partly organic and partly musical.

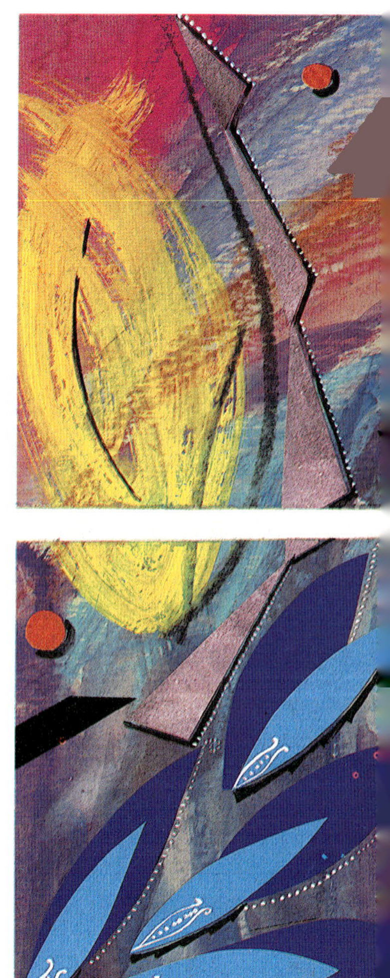

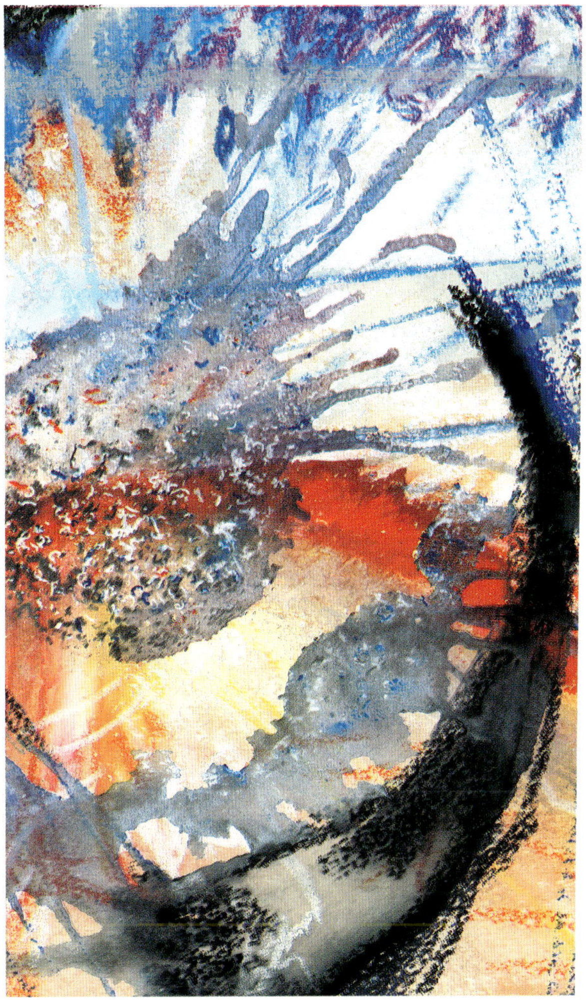

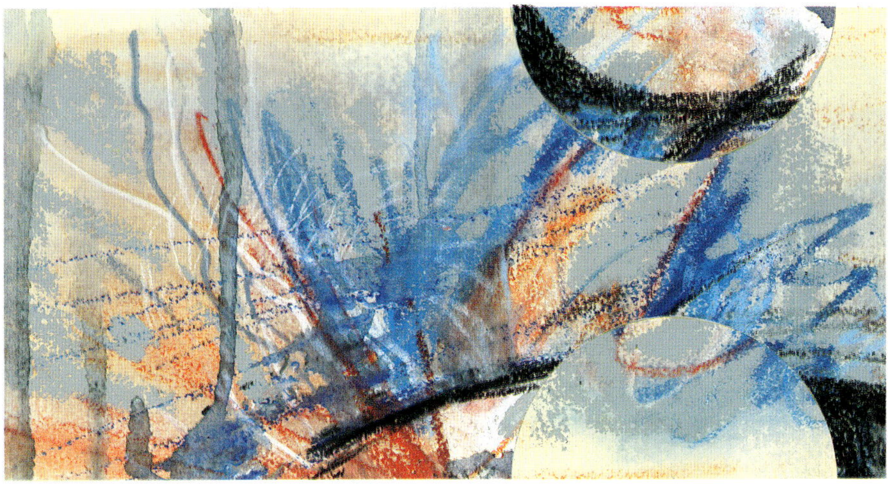

The marks we have made here show ways of rendering that can be useful in later drawing. They also have readable characteristics of their own. You might consider how you could classify them in terms of how they feel or what they remind you of.

We now have an understanding of the marks and surfaces available for color pencil drawing, and a repertoire of possible approaches, and we can now move on to some more basic elements and principles. If you have actually made these examples it would make sense to keep them as a resource.

ABOVE
A similar 'wild' composition to that shown left, this time with a pair of cut semi-circles which attempt to balance and control the piece.

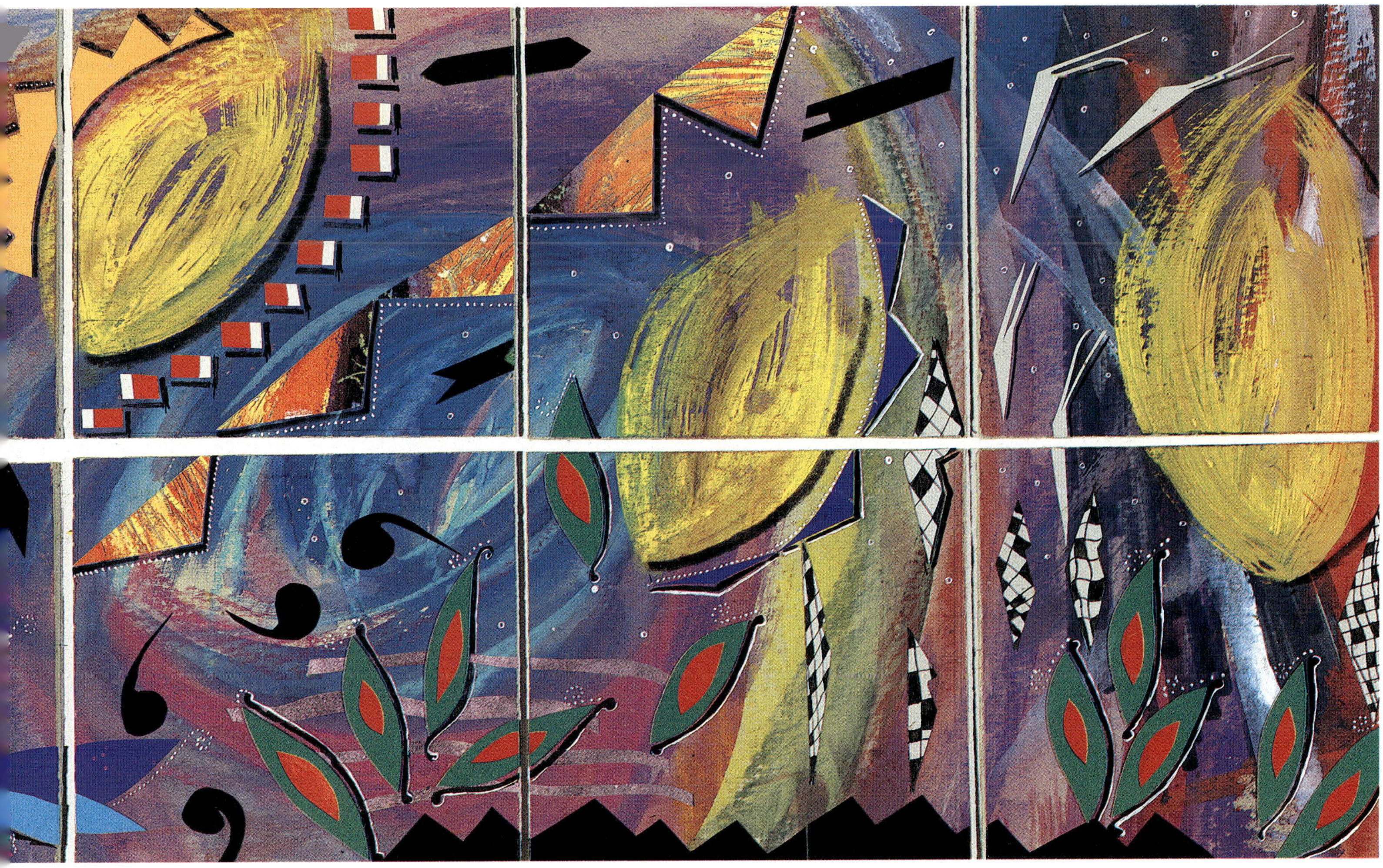

4. Color

Additive and Subtractive Color Theory

When we look at a picture, one of the first things we notice is the way an artist has used color. Historically color has been used in quite different ways, and for different purposes. The way it is used, of course, depends on the pigments available. It has been a long struggle to find a palette of color rich enough to satisfy our observations of nature, and this has perhaps only recently been achieved. Simply put, color can be used as a symbol; as a flat description (not necessarily naturalistic); as a description of nature (the way things look); and, more recently, as a personal quest for emotional meaning (the way things feel). Added to this, of course, is the delight in color for its own sake.

Additive Color Mixing

Science tells us that white light can be broken into the colors of the spectrum, the ones most of us can see in the rainbow. It is possible to reverse this process and remake the white light by re-mixing all the rainbow colors (in the form of colored light not pigment). It is equally possible to mix white light with just three colors, red, green, blue. These are known as primary colors for light. If just two of these primary light colors are projected and overlapped, each pair combines to form secondary colors.

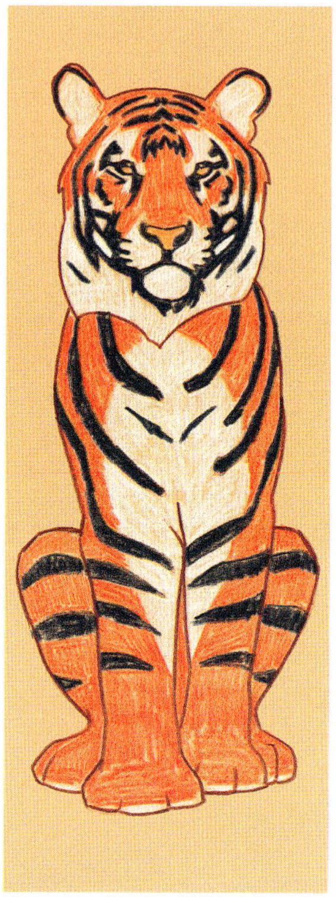

ABOVE
This tiger is harmless; the color and line is reduced to flat pattern.

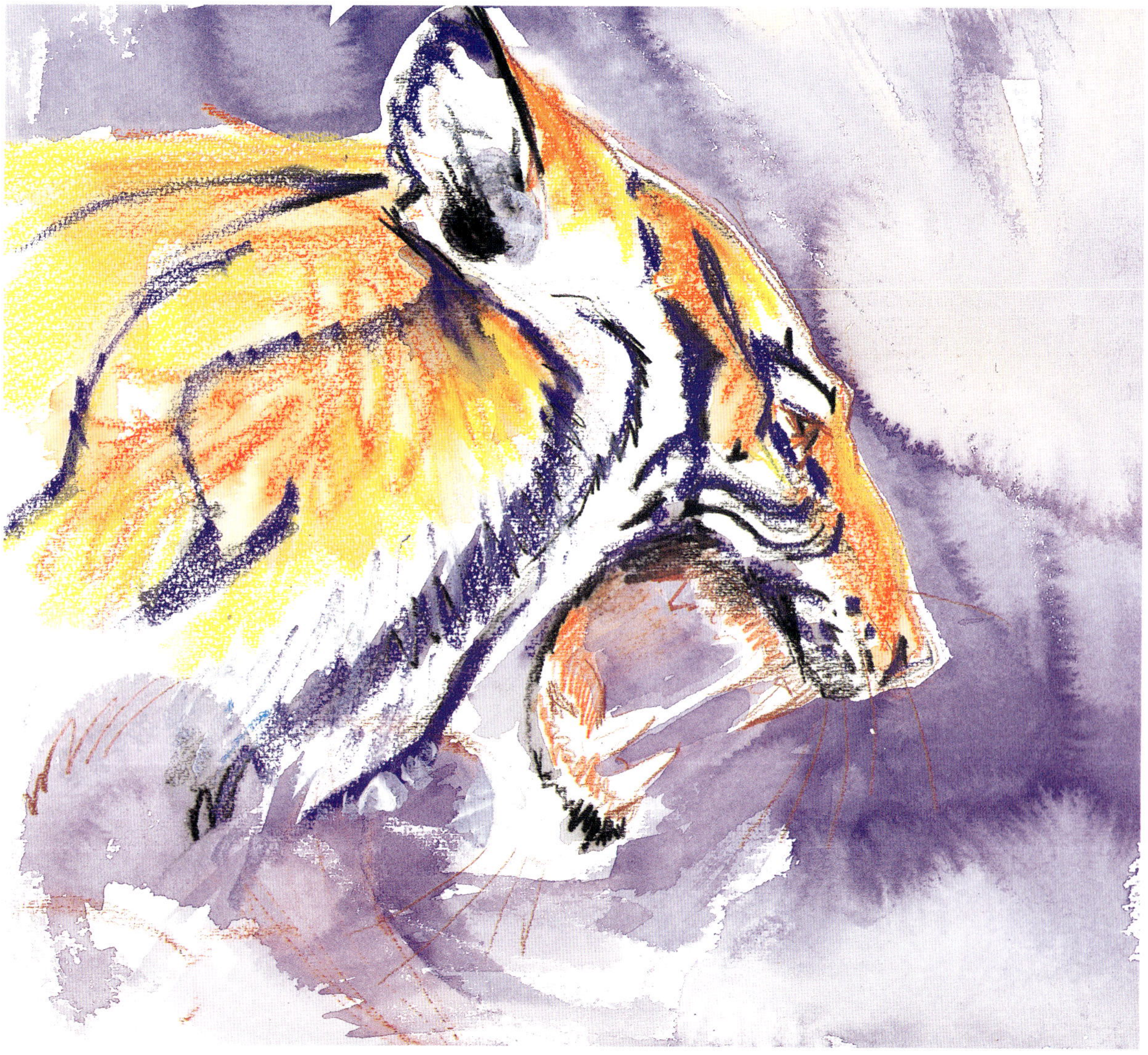

LEFT
Here the tiger is drawn more expressively, in terms both of line and color; the basic orange and black has been pushed toward yellow and purple.

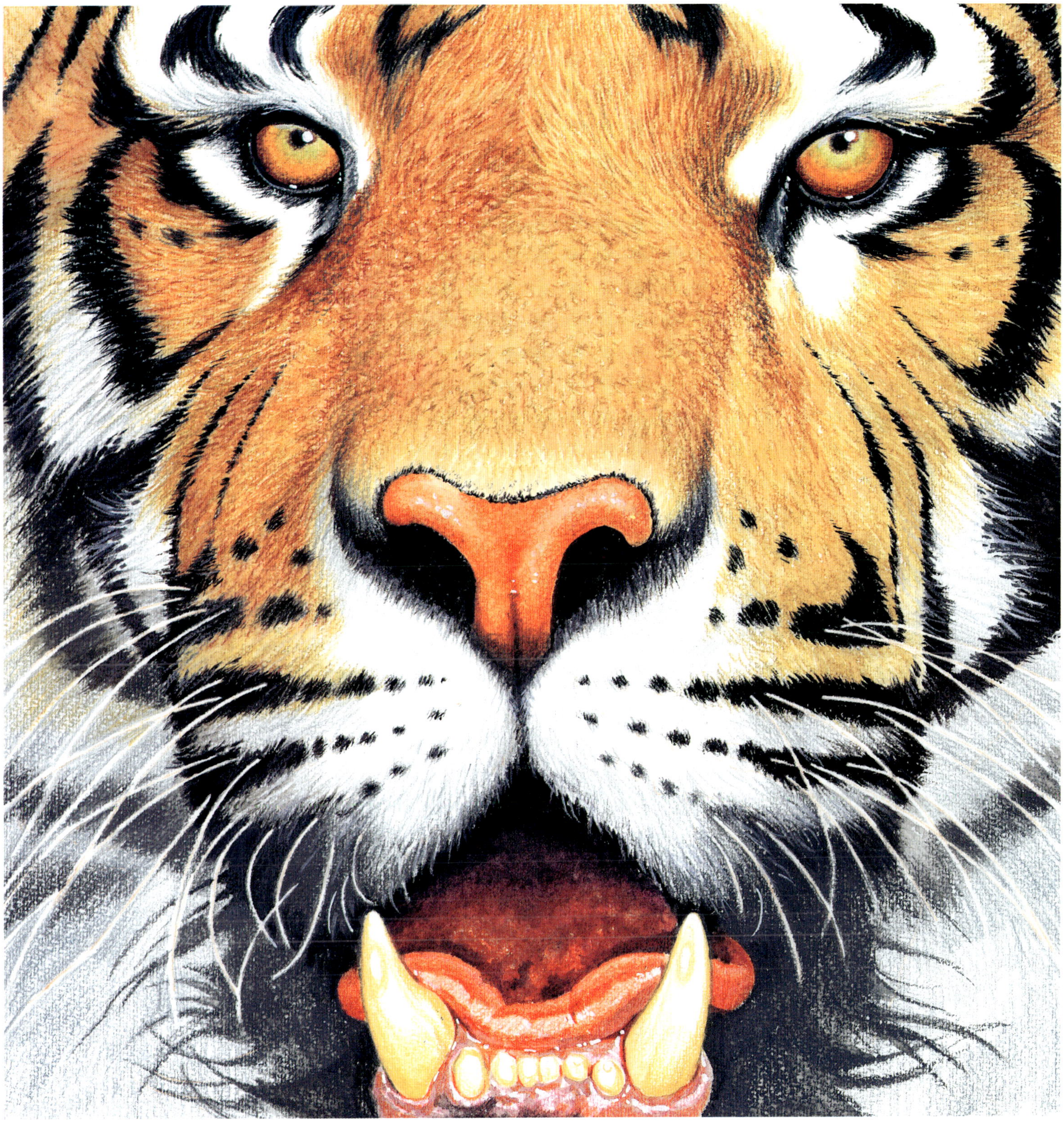

ABOVE
This close-up image is drawn realistically. The lines imitate the actual textures of the animal and the colors blend through natural harmonies.

Blue + green = cyan
Green + red = yellow
Red + blue = magenta
Red + blue + green = white

This phenomenon is known as additive color mixing, and the three colors that are produced are called secondary colors.

Subtractive Color Mixing

The color theory that is important for our purposes looks at what happens to the pigment. Colored pencil pigments, like all pigments, produce their color by absorbing some light and reflecting the rest. Something that appears red, for example, will have absorbed all the spectrum, except red, and reflects back at us the red we see. Colored pencils are semi-translucent, in that they literally allow light, in some measure, to pass through them.

The paper, if white, can give the reflected color great brilliance. If the paper is tinted, the underlying color can be seen to affect all the pigment and provides an overall harmony. If, on the other hand, the paper is dark or black, the pigment can lose its vitality and brilliance. The very soft pencils can produce more opaque color, however, which can block out the dark support and maintain its own brilliance. We can therefore see that color pencils and soluble color pencils are, as a general rule, more brilliant when used lightly, and the more opaque soft pencils are brighter as thick pigment.

The three primary colors for pigment are magenta, yellow and cyan. When we mix or blend pairs of primary colors, we can get green, red and blue. This is known as subtractive color mixing.

Magenta + yellow = red
Yellow + cyan = green
Cyan + magenta = blue
Magenta + yellow + cyan = black
(In practice black is usually dark gray/brown)

The next set of exercises will test the colored pencils and show some ways to blend and mix colors.

Exercise 1

Using only the three primary colors from the three types of pencil, make three rainbows. Your pencils will probably not be labeled; choose the nearest to the example illustrated. The sequence for our spectrum example is:

1. Magenta
2. Red (mix magenta and yellow)
3. Orange (mix magenta and yellow)
4. Yellow
5. Green (mix yellow and cyan)
6. Cyan
7. Blue (mix cyan and magenta)
8. Violet (mix cyan and magenta)

Using a simple shading technique, you should overlay one color over another to achieve a suitable color mix. If the mixed colors are a little dull, it is because your

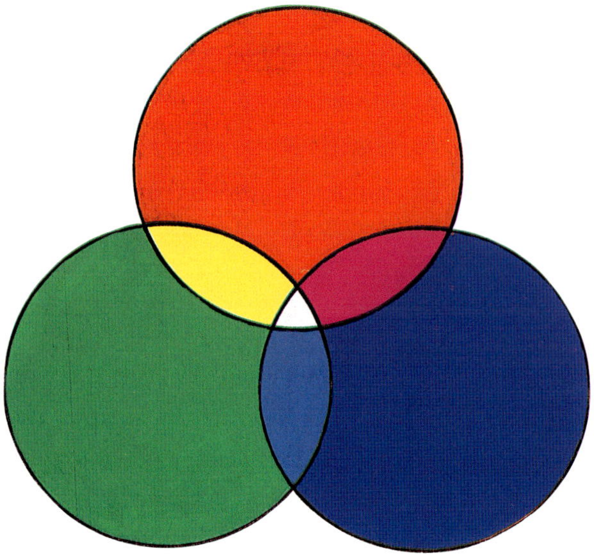

LEFT
Additive color mixing; three primary colors of light are mixed to produce secondary color.

FAR LEFT TOP
Magenta and yellow blended to red on paper.

FAR LEFT CENTER
Yellow and cyan blended optically to green by means of cross-hatching.

FAR LEFT BELOW
Cyan and magenta blended as dots to dark blue.

BELOW
Primary color blended as powder to black.

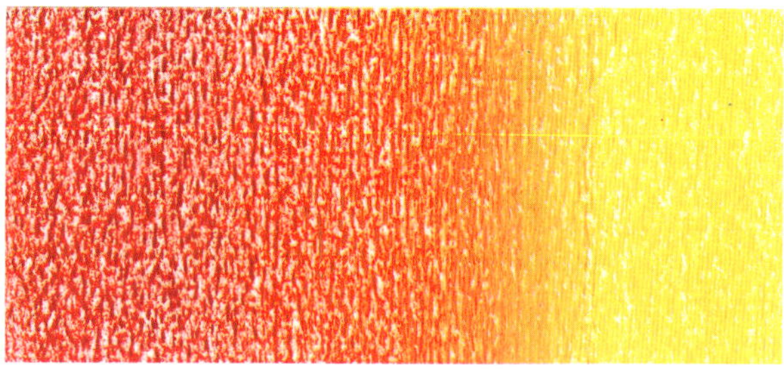

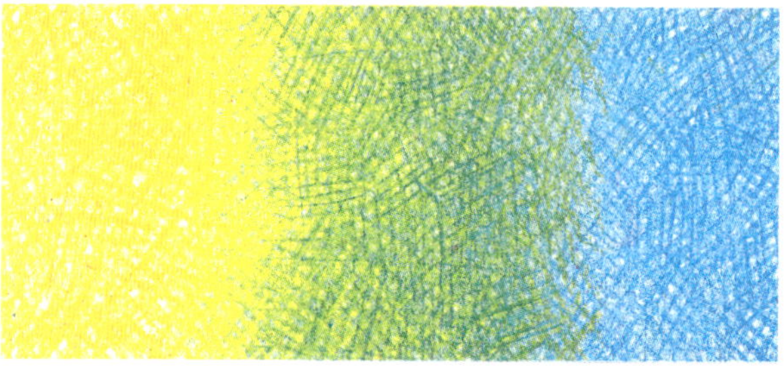

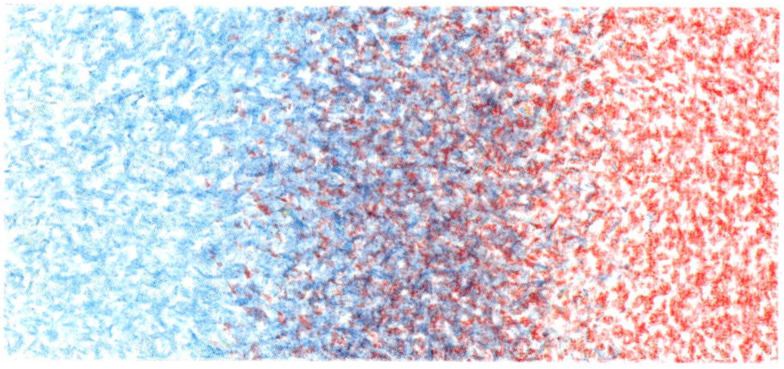

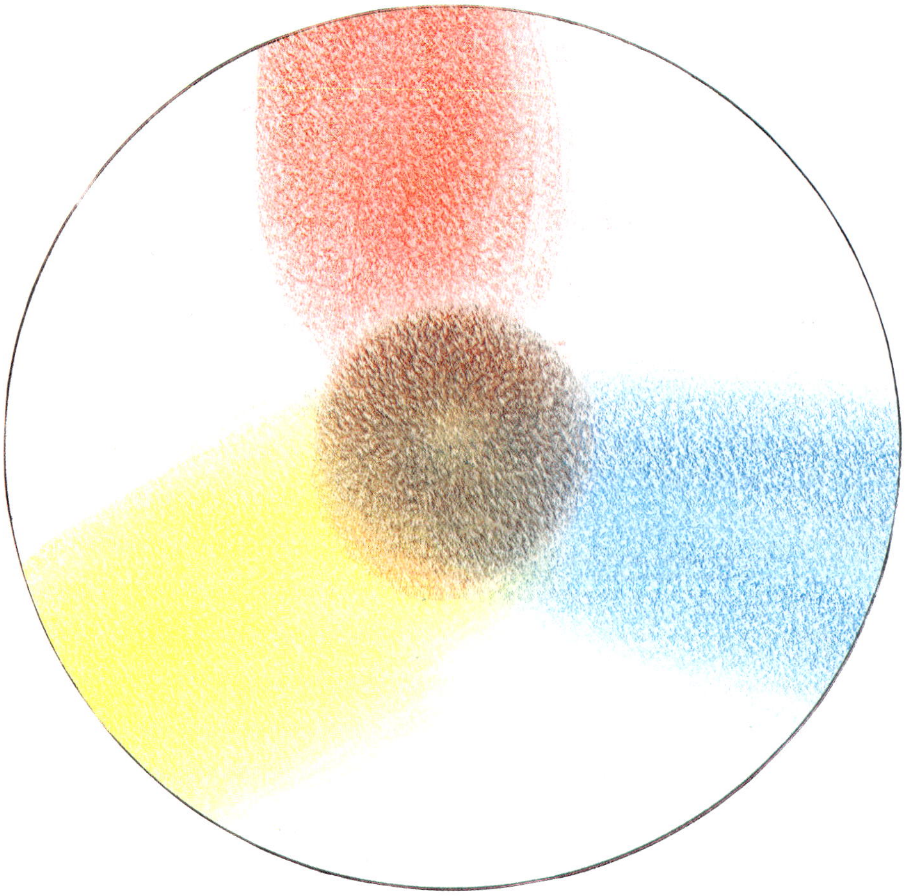

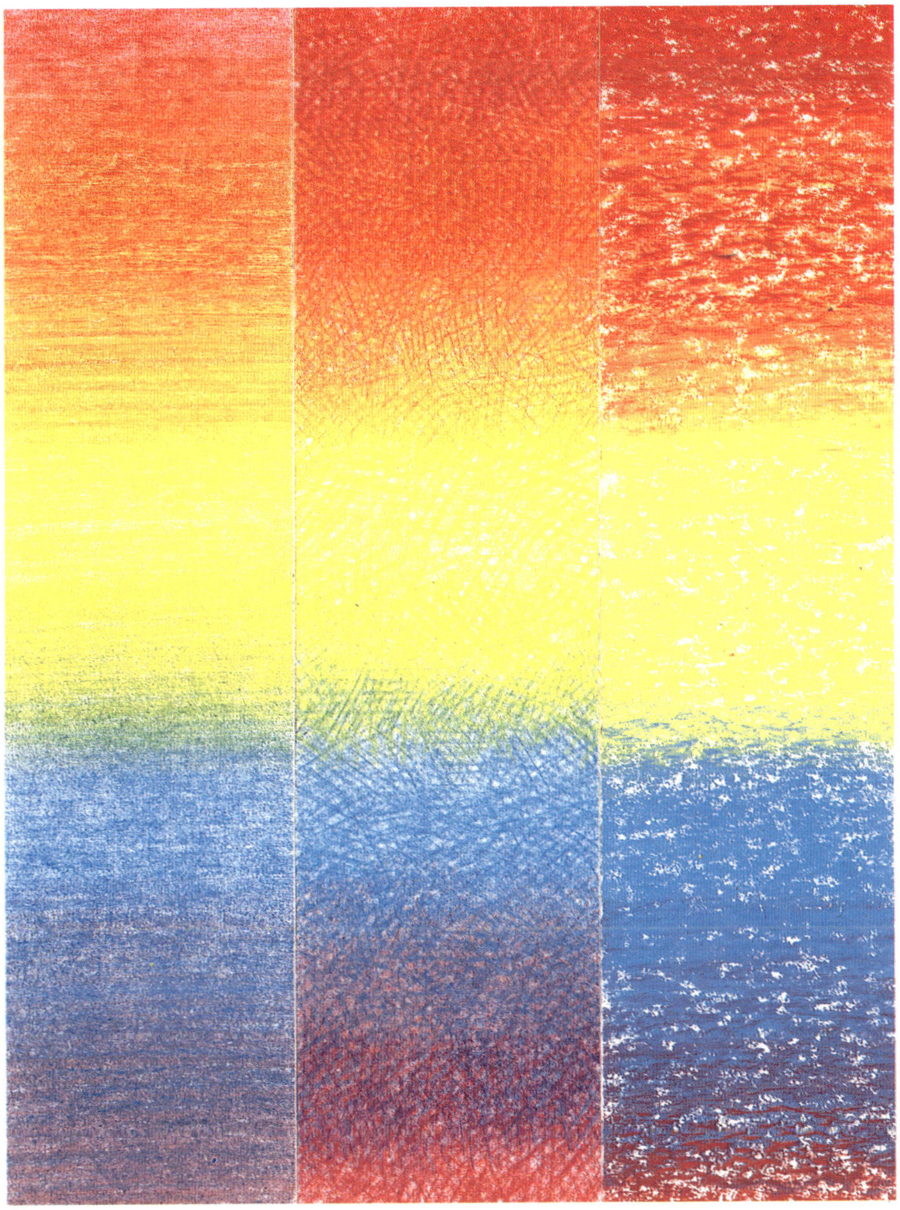

FAR LEFT
Three spectra based on primary colors from each pencil range (from far left): simple color pencil; soluble color pencil; soft soluble color pencil.

LEFT
A spectrum of color using the whole range of pencils: magenta, red, orange, yellow, green, cyan, blue, violet.

primary colors are a little less than perfect, and blending by overlaying shading often gives the last color laid down too much prominence. From your earlier experiments you should now have a range of blending techniques. Again with the three primaries and three types of pencil, try these techniques and see how they perform:

- Revealing the texture of the paper
- Cross-hatching
- Pointillism (optical blending)
- Dry on dry
- Dry on wet
- Wet on dry
- Wet on wet
- Brush blending
- Burnishing – stub
- Burnishing – gum eraser

Color Wheel

If you look at the most successful of your blended rainbows, you can see that the two end colors could equally well be blended together to form a circle. This chromatic circle, or color wheel, is an old favorite of art teachers, but it also shows us some strengths and weaknesses when we test different media. It also shows us some basic ideas about color relationships, and the way this one is made can also introduce the idea of optical mixing.

We can see that using just the three primaries (1), it is possible to make a complete spectrum. Looking at the wheel, we can demonstrate that equal amounts of primary color mixed as pairs produce the secondary colors (2). Similarly, by mixing a primary with the nearest secondary, we can achieve tertiary color (3). This can go on for ever, of course, depending on the number of divisions in our circle.

For our purposes the interesting thing to notice is that the two colors opposite one another on the wheel, known as complementary colors, display the greatest possible contrast. When placed side by side, these two colors each enhance the other's tone and color. This shows us something about how our eyes work. Look at the circle on page 42 for about 30 seconds and then look at a white area; you should see a ghost image or a rhomb. What is interesting is that this rhomb will be in the complementary color of the original, like a negative color photograph.

In a similar way the triangles on page 42 are the same color physically, but optically we experience the green with an induced hue that is the complementary color to the

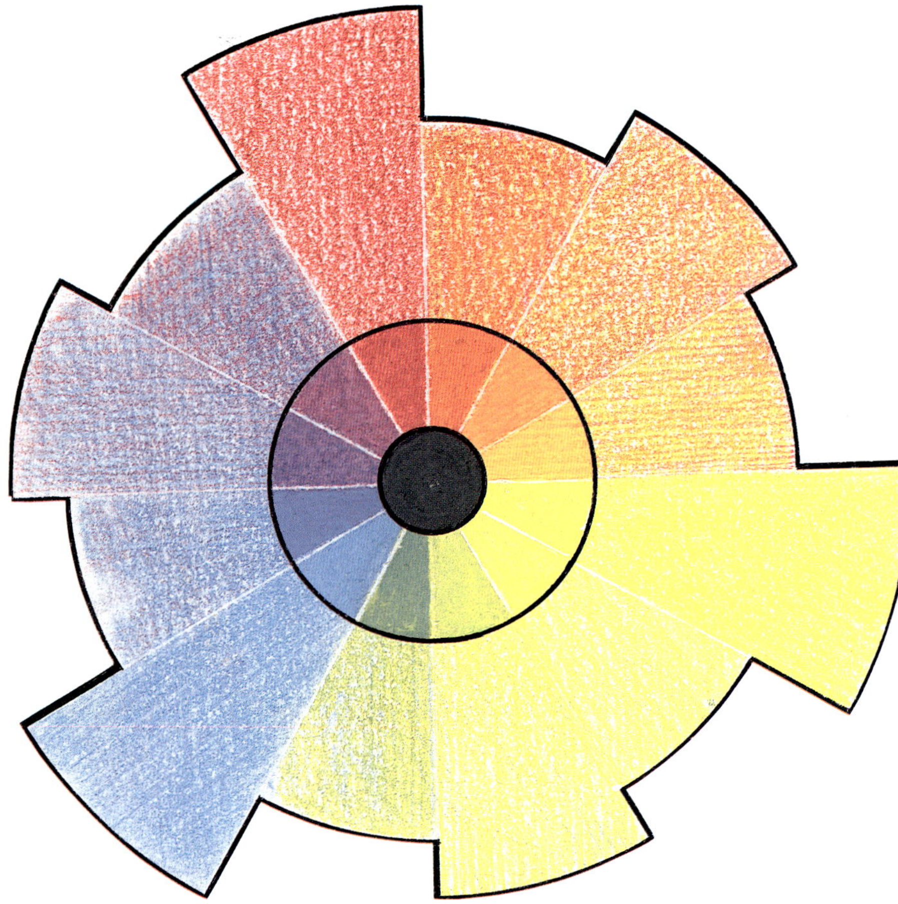

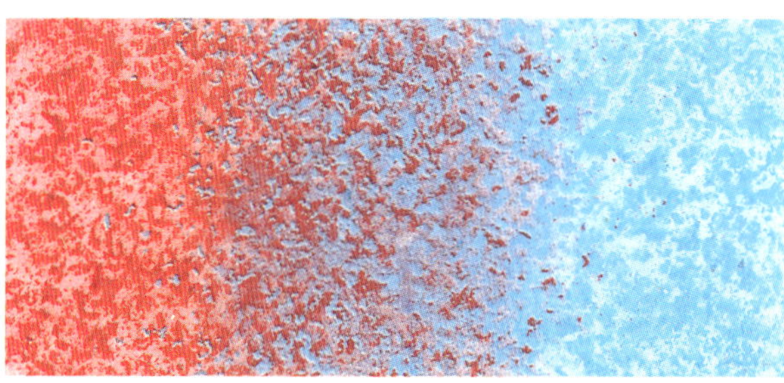

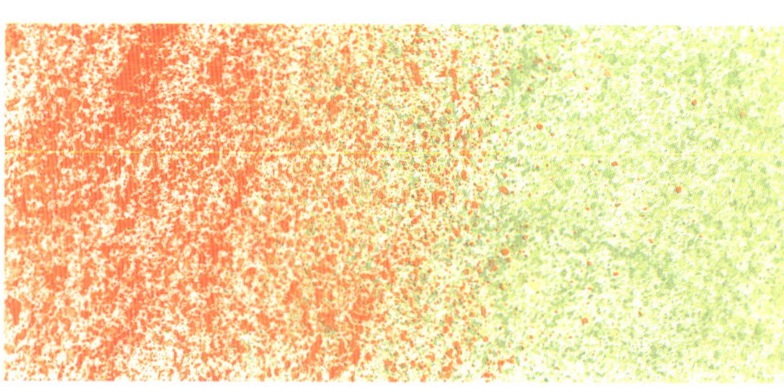

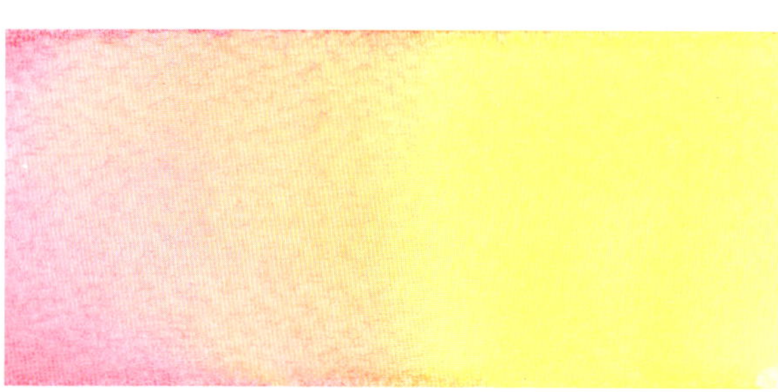

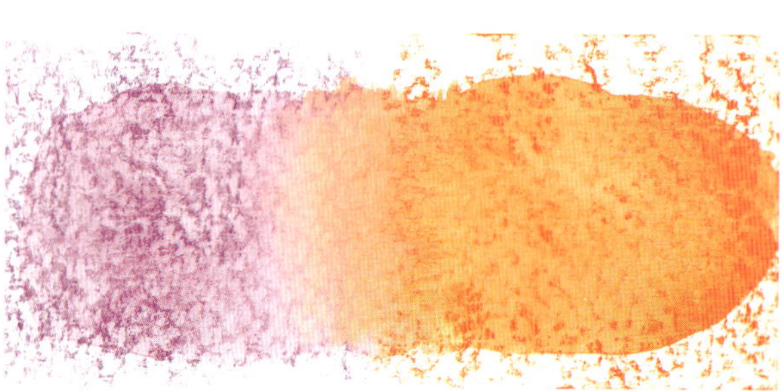

surrounding color. This gives us another view on the importance of positive and negative shapes (figures and backgrounds). We can affect the color of a figure by changing the surrounding color toward its complementary. When we make a color mark, it also affects the space around it.

If we look at the color wheel again, we can see a general division between colors that we would describe as warm and those we might call cool. This sort of description is common when artists choose a range of working colors. Harmonious color is any close group of colors existing side by side on the wheel.

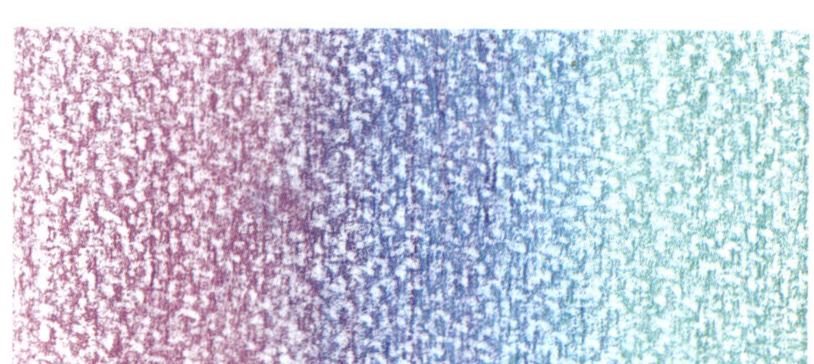

ABOVE
A simple color wheel made from three primary colors (from the outside ring): three primary colors; three secondary colors; three tertiary colors; intensified color (with water); color mix (black).

FAR LEFT FROM TOP
Orange and violet to red/brown, blended by dry powder on dry paper.
Magenta and cyan to blue, blended by scraped pigment on wet paper.
Orange and green to brown, blended by wet brush splatter on dry paper.
Magenta and yellow to red, blended by wet pigment wash on wet paper.
Violet and orange to red/brown, blended by wet brush over dry pigment.

LEFT ABOVE
Violet and cyan to blue, blended by stub.

LEFT BELOW
Cyan and magenta to blue, blended by gum eraser.

RIGHT
John Raynes
Portrait Study
Here the warm base color and the bright yellow ocher controls the harmony. The sparse open drawing is almost luminous and very effective, and the yellowish and pink flesh tones mix optically over the warm brown support.

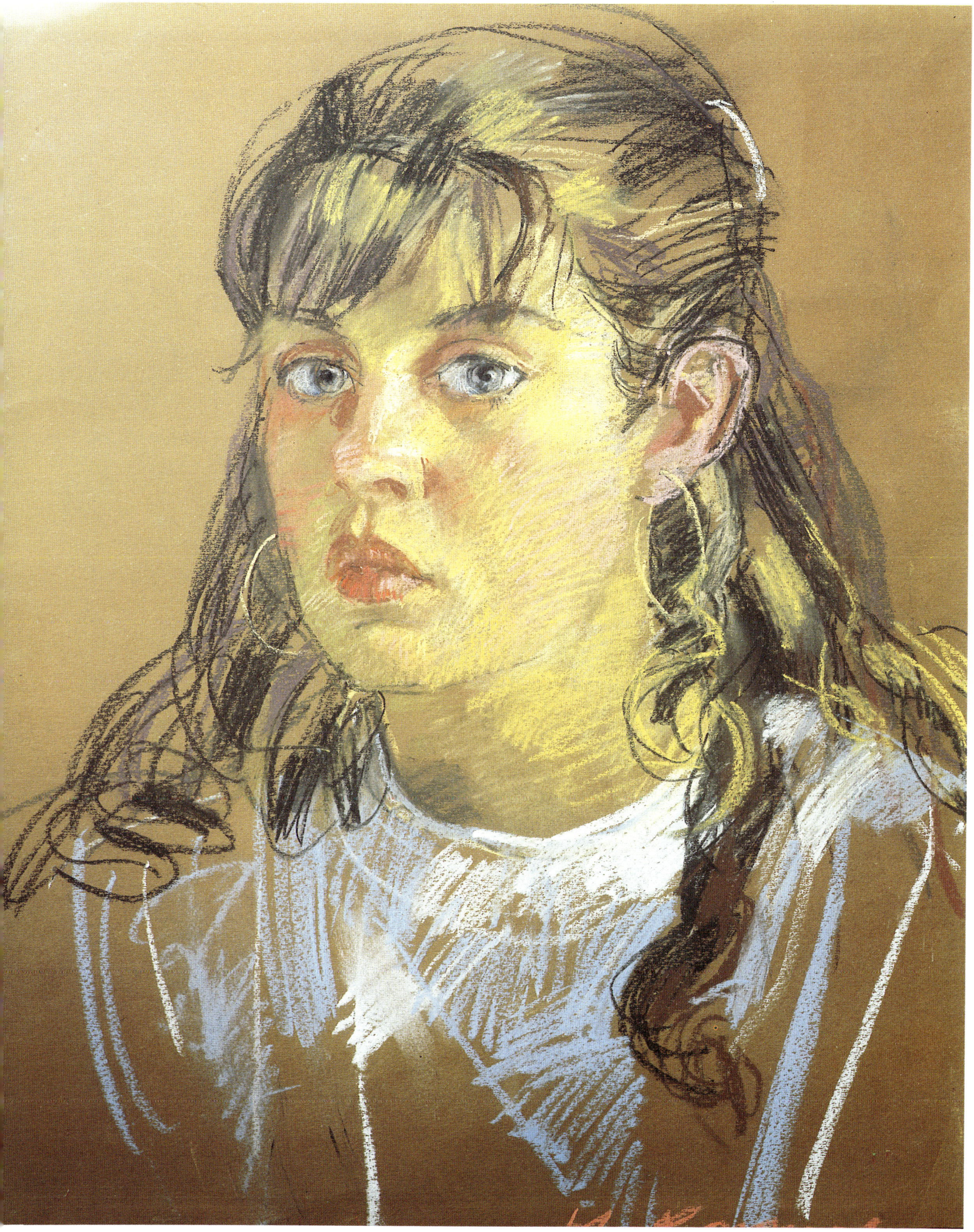

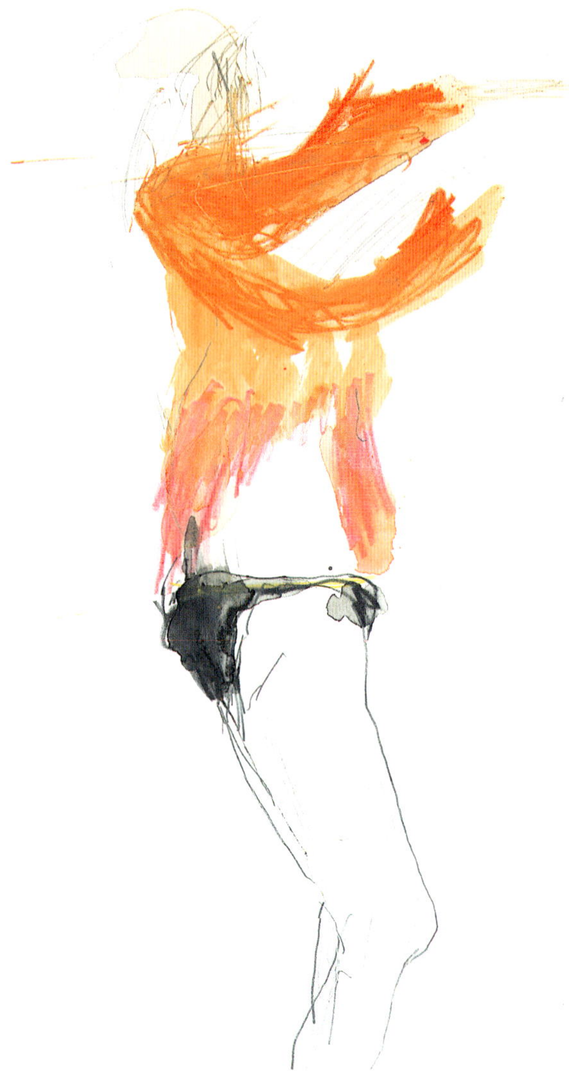

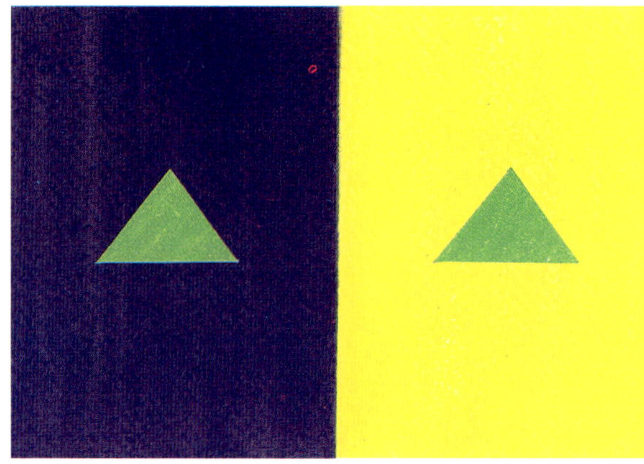

A different sort of harmony, with perhaps more energy, can be achieved by using colors across the wheel – a contrasting or complementary harmony. If we mix these pairs of complementary colors, we can achieve a whole range of brown and grays.

We have played with color by just using the three primary colors; to achieve some of the secondary and tertiary colors can involve a lot of heavy loading of pigment. Fortunately we have up to 100 colors available, although about 12 is sufficient. The other good news is that by the appropriate use of colored or pre-stained papers, we can achieve good color harmonies because the color pencil pigment is semi-transparent.

Color is what we all find attractive, it is the key to our emotional responses to art. Color gives us ideas of space and rich pattern, and it is fun.

FAR LEFT
Barbara Nicholls
Figure Drawing
A 'wild' drawing that focuses on the exciting contrasts in the marks and colors offered by the materials.

LEFT
Simultaneous contrast; complementary colors enhance each other's tone and color. The same green appears yellower on dark blue and bluish green on yellow.

RIGHT
Devayani Khakhria
Celestial Flame
This gorgeous pattern uses the harmonious colors of the soft pencils and punctuates the shapes with complementary orange and yellow-gold.

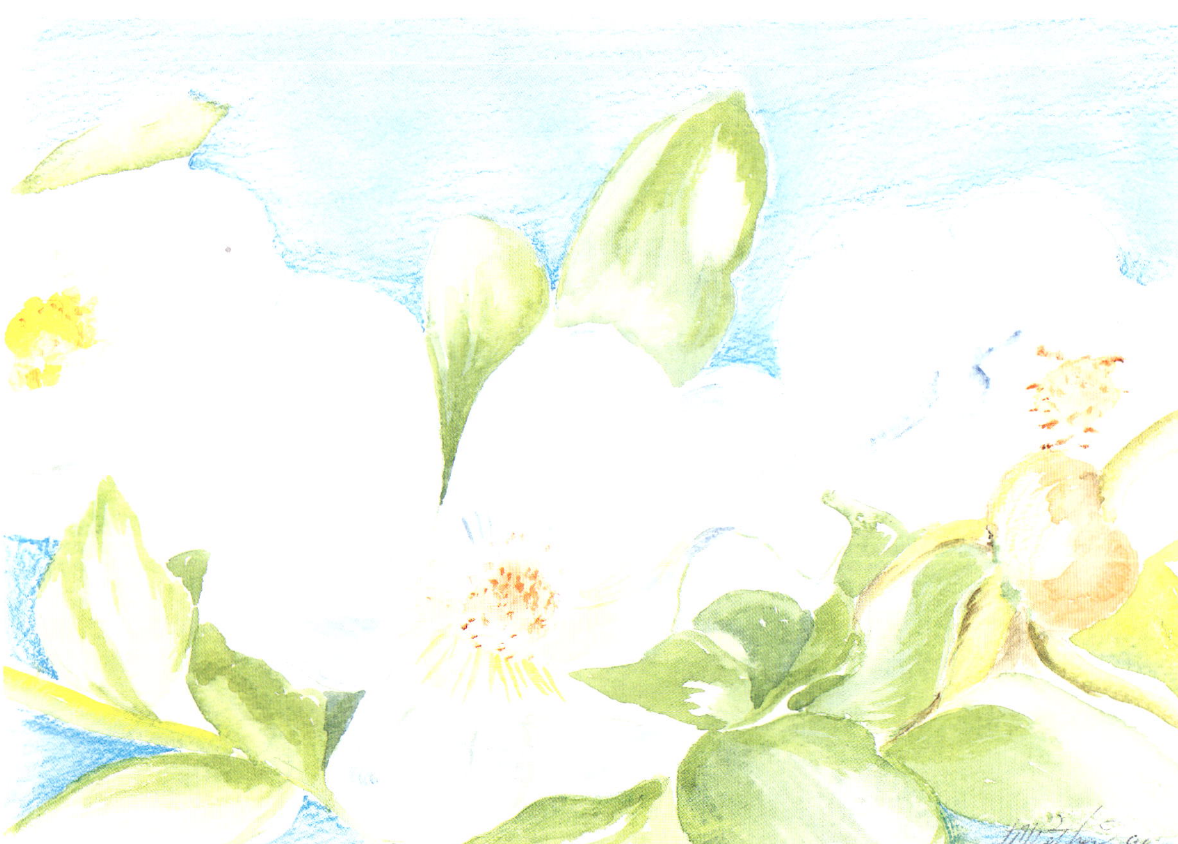

BELOW LEFT
Ivy Pether
A delightfully simple flower sketch using harmonious color.

BELOW
Complementary 'ghost' image. Look at the pale magenta patch for about 30 seconds, then look at the white space. You should see a ghost image or a 'rhomb' in the negative or complementary color.

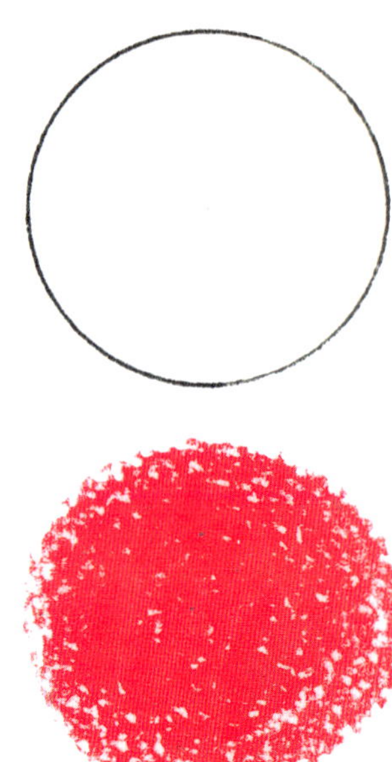

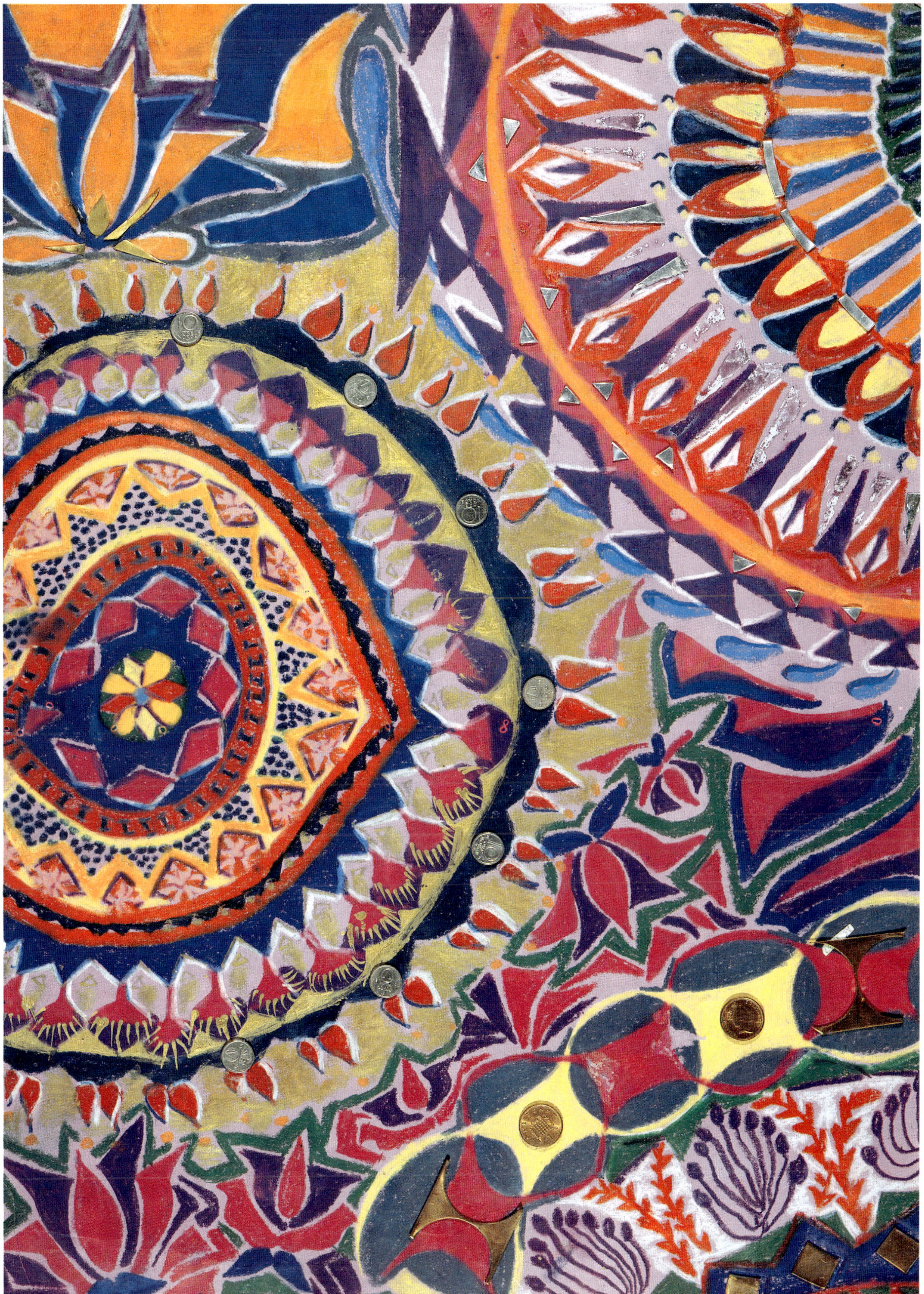

5. Composition

The term 'composition' means how an artist arranges and organizes all the different elements into one harmonious whole. When we make pictures they obviously come in all shapes and sizes. This is not accidental; how we place the drawing on the page is the fundamental problem of composition.

It is useful to look at three basic elements that make up a picture. These are positive shapes (the subject of the picture, objects or figures), negative shapes (the space around the figure), and the containing format (the length and breadth of the surface). People new to art are often so attentive to the thing they are drawing, that they disregard the boundaries made by positive and negative spaces and the edge of the format. Experienced artists understand the importance of these three elements. They know that if care is taken over these issues the picture feels right.

Format

Composition is the organization of all the parts that go to create the picture, including

BELOW LEFT
A chair treated as a positive shape.

BELOW
The chair revealed in profile as a negative shape.

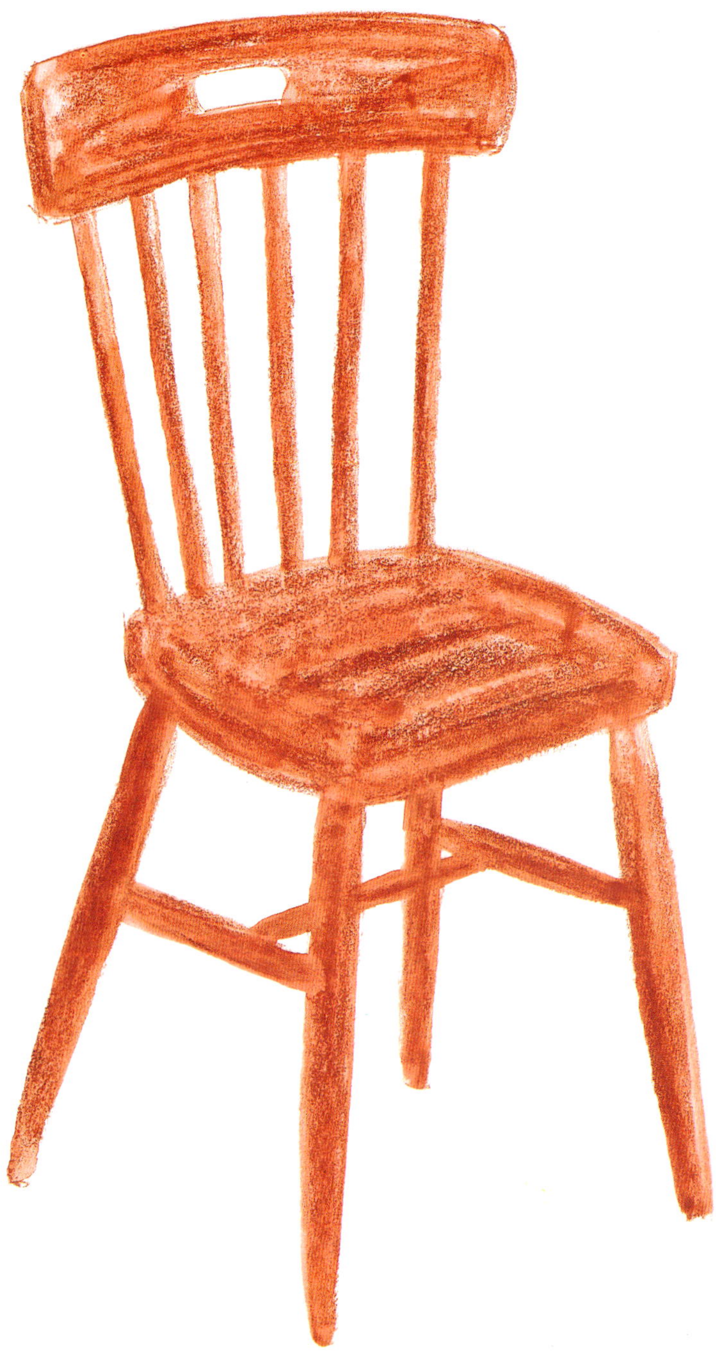

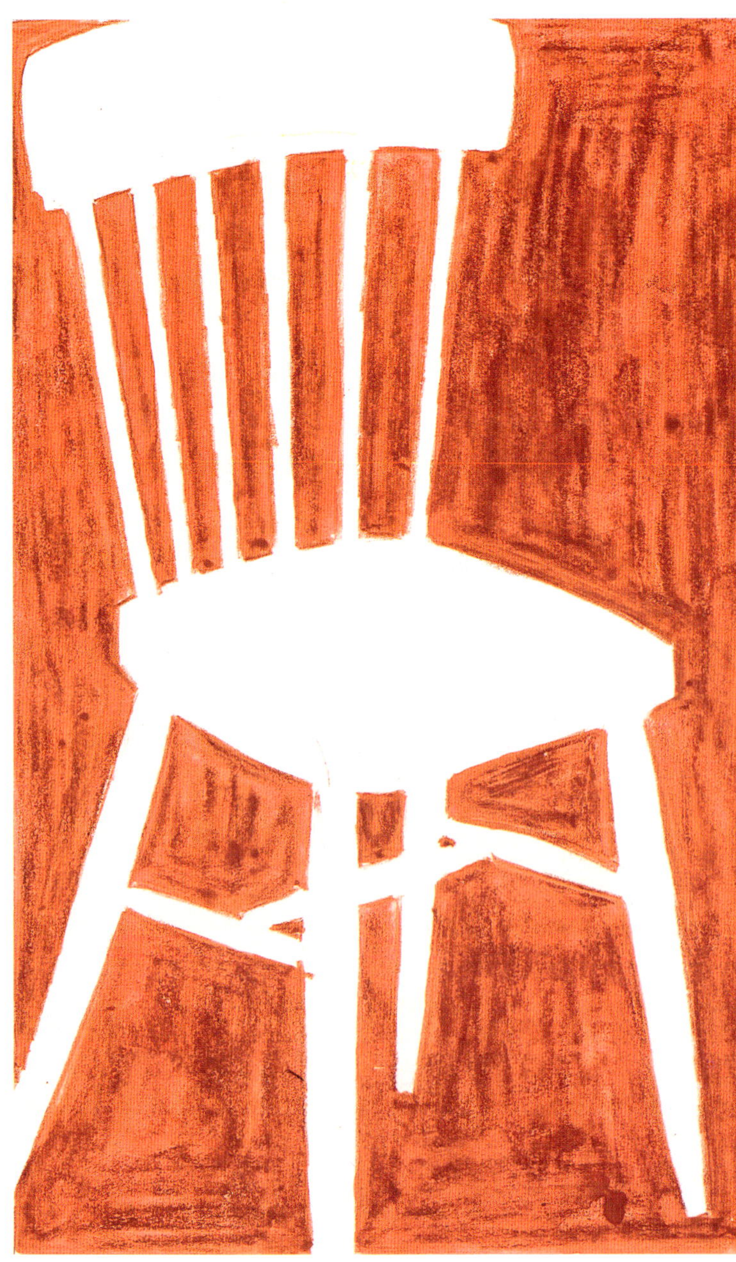

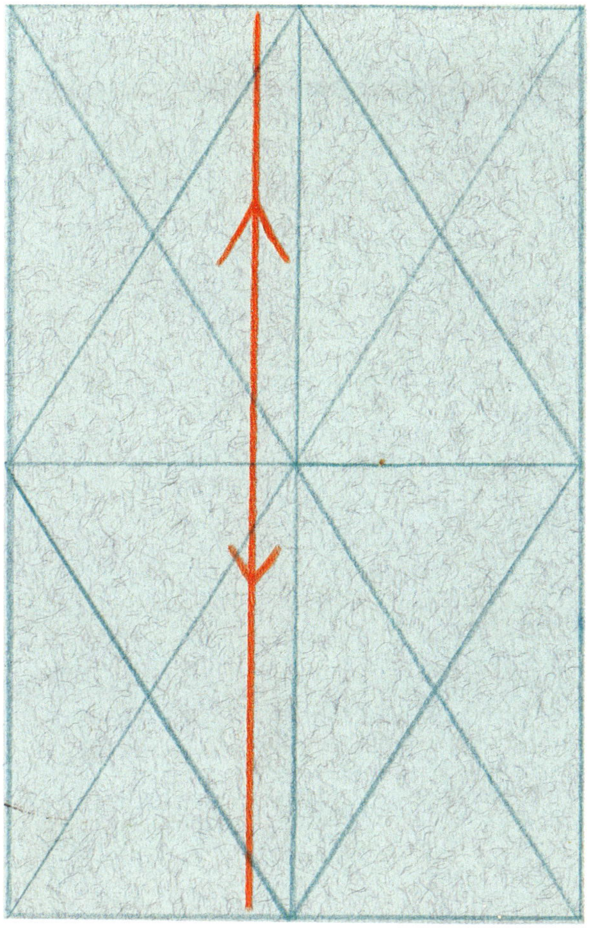

the containing format. Historically a range of formats have been used for their special qualities, in much the same way as architectural shapes were used. In fact the picture formats owe their shape to the architecture that originally housed them. These framing shapes can often influence the way that our attention moves over their surfaces, even as empty spaces.

Horizontal Rectangle

The horizontal rectangle produces a very stable impression, since its base is much longer than its vertical sides. Within this format the eye tends to roam over the surface expansively, from side to side. It seems only too ready to perceive imaginary depth (this is called 'recession'). This is a favorite shape of landscape painters, and is referred to as a 'landscape' format.

Vertical Rectangle

By turning the landscape format up on its short side, we can create a different response. Here the shape feels a little less stable. If it is higher than we are, it can even feel intimidating. While the eye is restricted sideways, it is encouraged to climb and fall to the limits of the shape. This is the format of some great religious paintings, with subjects that are larger than life. It was seen as

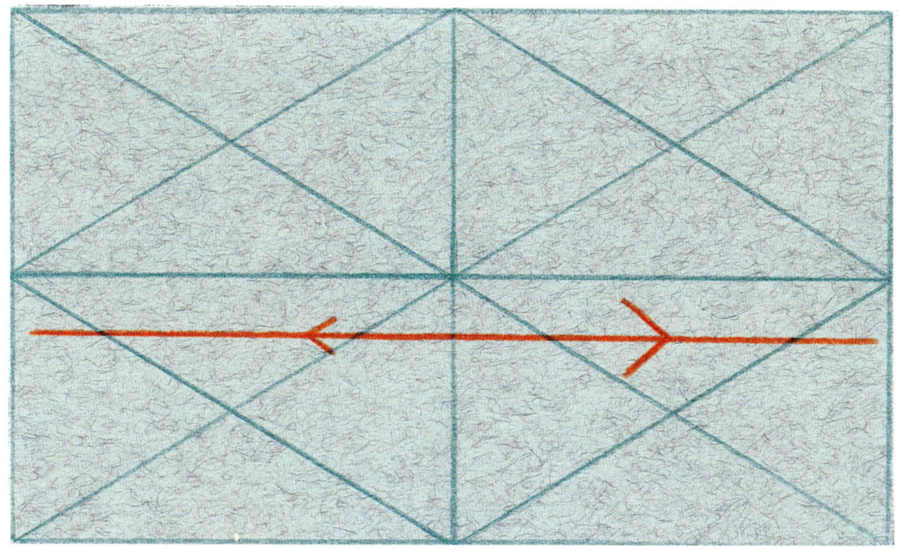

FAR LEFT
A vertical rectangle used to frame the picture space, known as 'portrait' format.

ABOVE
A horizontal rectangle, 'landscape.'

LEFT
An arched rectangle.

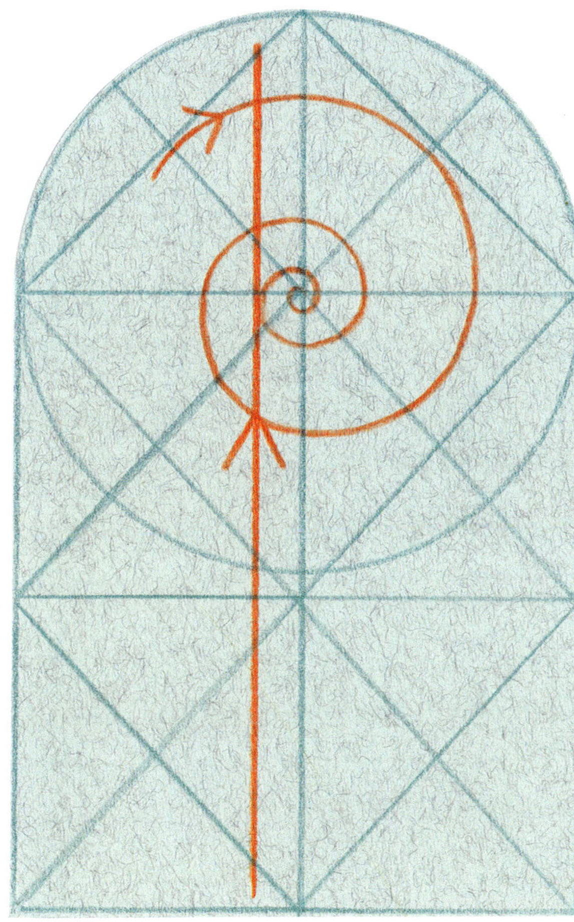

encouraging a feeling of awe and elevation. On a smaller scale the format is perfect for work on portraits and figures, and we know it as the 'portrait' format.

The Arched Rectangle

The arched rectangle shares the qualities of the portrait format, with a bonus effect from the semicircle, which can hold and focus our attention at the center of the implied circle.

Circles, Squares, Diamonds

Symmetry has a powerful focusing effect, conveying all sorts of ideas of wholeness or completeness. The eye can become trapped within the shape spiralling in to the center. With diamonds and circles, their stability is delicately poised, and it is quite challenging for artists to maintain the equilibrium of these shapes.

Irregular Shapes

Irregular shapes are a relatively new phenomenon in art, and can have a delightful effect by making the image seem more 'real.' However, we still tend to perceive these shapes as if they were contained within imaginary geometric shapes, and so sharing similar properties to those we have already looked at.

Proving Mounts Within the Format

With most pictures, there are some elements that will tend to divide the surface, and others that may dominate by virtue of their color or shape. How best to deal with these effects is our next consideration.

It is a good idea to cut suitably sized 'L' shapes from card. When held together these can make a whole range of rectangles. They give us a way to play with possible formats both at sketch and at finished stage. They can also provide ways of composing a scene in reality, by holding the proving mounts as a window and considering the best view and format.

Central and equal divisions, unless handled with great skill, hold little interest in your composition. Similarly, equal weights of tone or color can be boring, but it is difficult to make rules – you must consider all these aspects yourself. We need to take all these considerations into account to make a picture that works as a whole. These issues can almost become second nature with practice.

Example 1 This is a drawing using just the three elements, positive space, negative space and format.

1. Choose an object to draw. Chairs and stools have long been a favorite for this exercise as they work well as an isolated form.
2. Look at your subject through a proving mount; this is going to be the basis of your composition. Choose a view that you find interesting, look at how the positive and negative shapes interact with the format/proving mount, change the proportion in the proving mount, and move back and forward until you have found a really interesting view.
3. Tape the proving mount in the same proportion as you have chosen, and place it at the top left on your paper. Mark the corresponding bottom right corner, then lay a straight edge from the top left corner through the mark and draw a light diagonal. Any horizontal and vertical line making a corner on this diagonal will make a rectangle exactly proportional to the viewer. Draw the rectangle for your drawing.
4. Remember that you are only interested in the containing overall shapes. Hold the viewer as a window to your subject. Using a pale neutral color pencil, lightly sketch in the negative shapes, then the positive shapes. Judge one against the

ABOVE
Chairs
A finished composition made simply with positive and negative shapes and the enclosing format. The complementary colors have been transferred to wet paper, giving the added interest of saturated colors, and a degree of mixing where the colors meet.

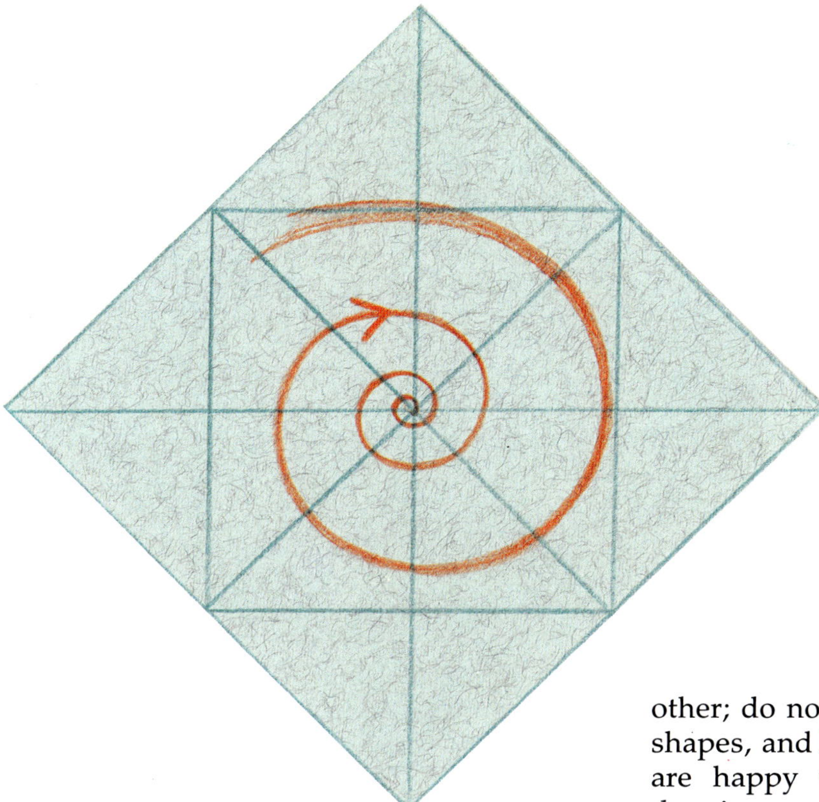

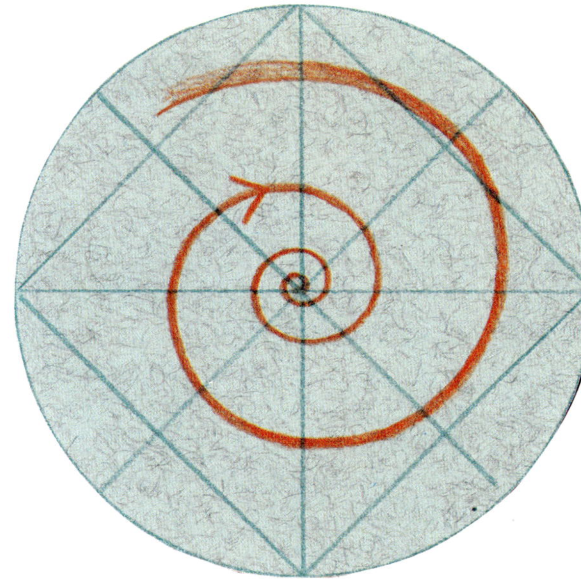

other; do not be afraid of correcting the shapes, and keep working at it until you are happy with the balance of your drawing.

5. Now you can move into a different gear, and assign one color for the negative space and one for the positive space. You might use contrasting colors. It becomes a more interesting piece if you give the same amount of attention to the space as you do to the thing itself.

ABOVE LEFT
Symmetrical formats; a diamond.

ABOVE
A circle.

LEFT
A square.

FAR LEFT BELOW
Irregular shapes.

LEFT BELOW
Proving mounts.

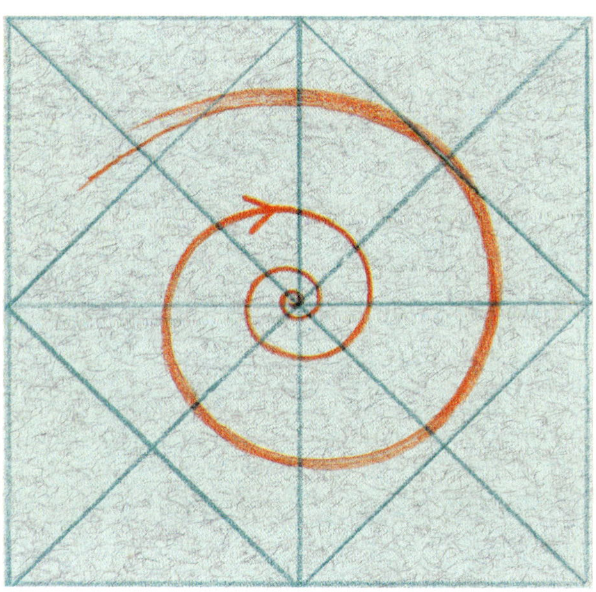

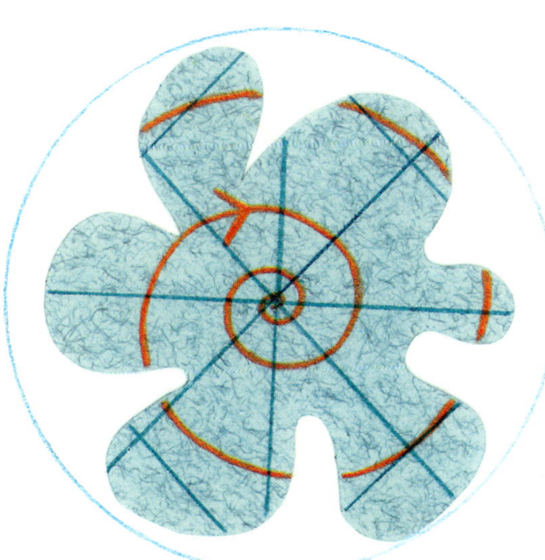

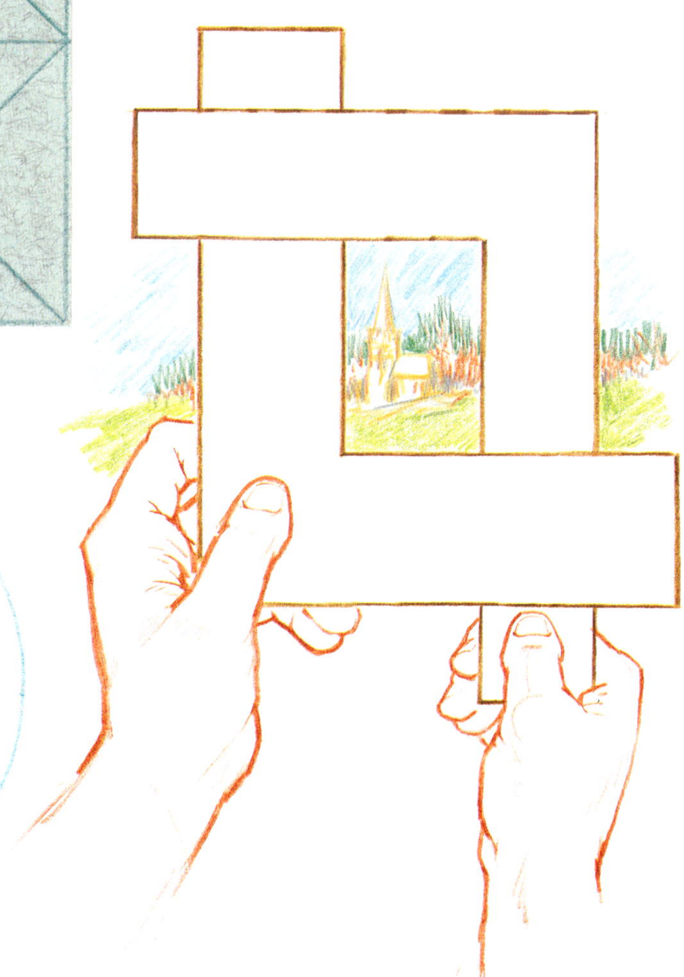

6. Drawing

A drawing can be part of a process toward some finished project, as well as a beautiful object in its own right. Charcoal, chalk, pieces of colored earth, each known to us as pigment, have all been used in drawing since man first started to make pictures. From burnt wood on a cave wall, to a designer's mechanical pencil on a finely surfaced line board, all of us are involved in what is basically the same physical process. What we do, for different reasons, is to leave a pleasing track of pigment on a surface.

So far we have been dealing with the way that the material itself looks and feels. In the next section I want to look at drawing as a stage toward picture-making, and drawing as a finished product. Whenever we try and draw from the real world, one of the earliest issues that we come up against it that of 'recognition' – does it look right? Does my drawing look like the thing that I am drawing?

As young children, we seem perfectly happy with our delightful and very personal descriptive drawings, but sooner or later we find ourselves struggling against these problems of accuracy and recognition. This struggle can become such a barrier to the development of our visual skills that we tend to define ourselves thereafter as 'drawers' and 'non-drawers,' depending on how successful we are in overcoming these issues of recognition. Leaving aside for the moment the idea that drawing is more than just accu-

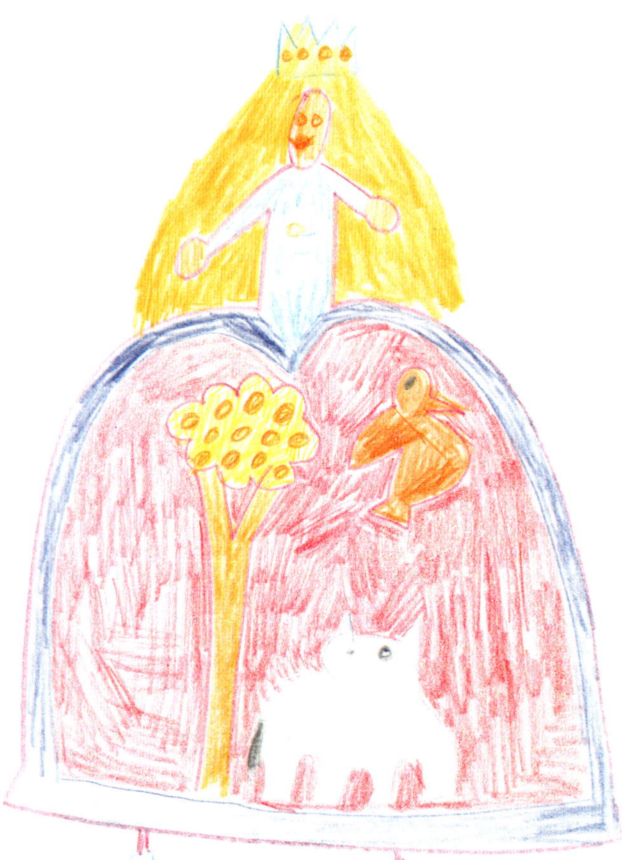

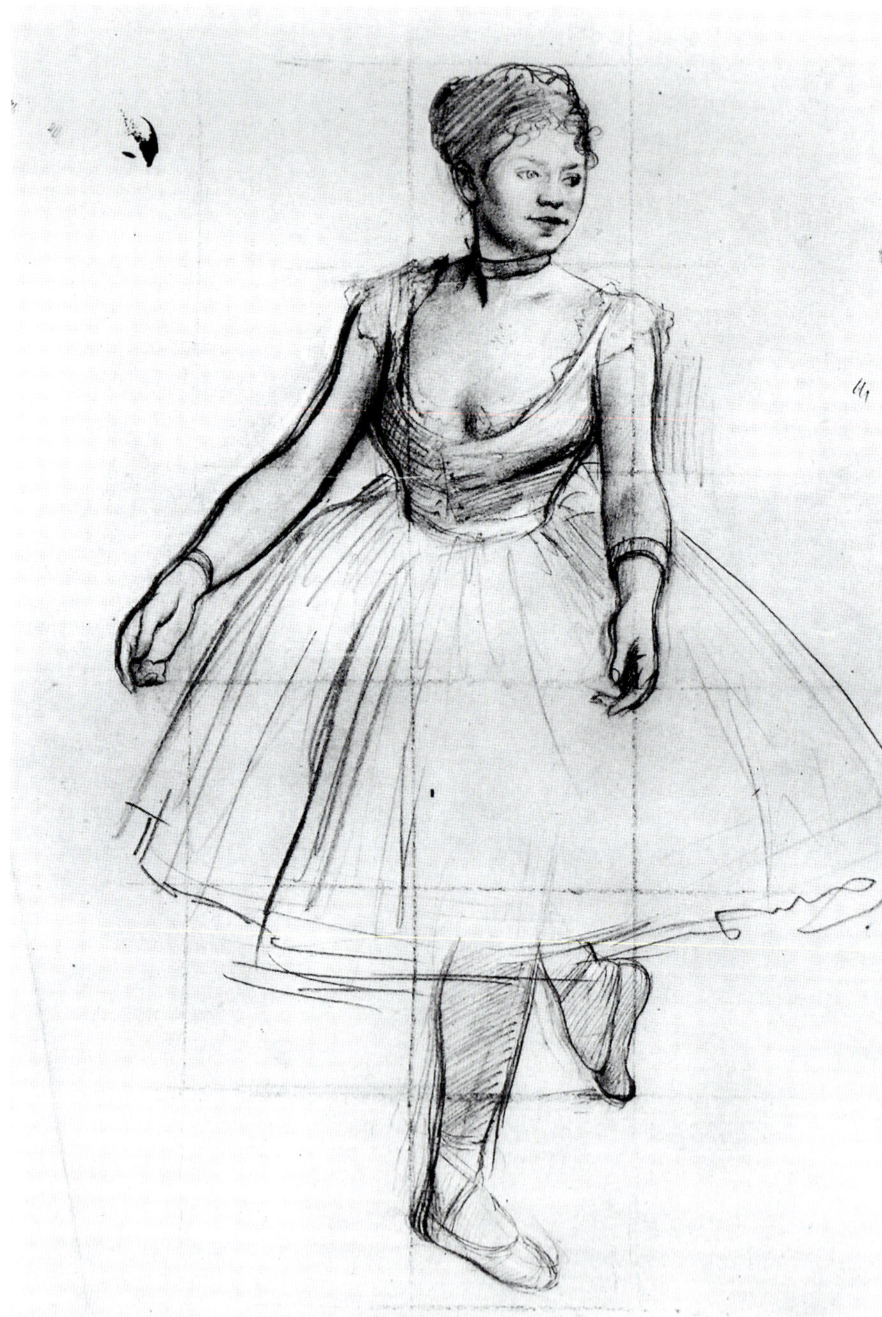

LEFT
A child's drawing; my daughter Sophie drew this when she was five or six years old.

ABOVE
Edgar Degas
Ballet Dancer in Position,
1872
Many artists base their observation on a simple grid structure.

rately describing the world, there are skills and strategies for this descriptive drawing that can be taught and confidently used by all of us.

These skills and strategies can be looked at separately, for our purposes, both as examples and as exercises. However, most drawing will freely combine all or some of these elements.

Drawing from Memory

Young children's drawing usually comes from their memory. Recalled and reinvented people, stories and events live in their pictures. These reconstructions basically reflect their visual memory. The drawing from memory is, of course, not the actual memory, nor is it the thing observed; it is a simplified view that often gives prominence to features that are personally important, with all sorts of happy accidents that the child is content to leave, or even embellish.

The mind has skills that involve the visual memory, so that it can monitor very complex visual information and simplify the scene to what it finds relevant. When, for example we walk through a room, we can usually avoid the furniture without being really conscious of its details. When we recall or invent scenes, this same sort of selection takes place, and the drawing has a similar simplicity.

There is a tendency for this imagery to have its own peculiar perspective, to flatten views and invent strong pattern. Children's pictures are often amazingly well balanced, with symmetry as a strong component. This sort of drawing is fine when an artist intends to show those qualities, but when we attempt to draw not from memory, but from observation, these tendencies get in the way. Most of our 'mistakes' in observed drawing come from using this visual memory.

Exercise 1

Draw from memory someone or something you are very familiar with. You might choose a pet, a close friend, your bedroom,

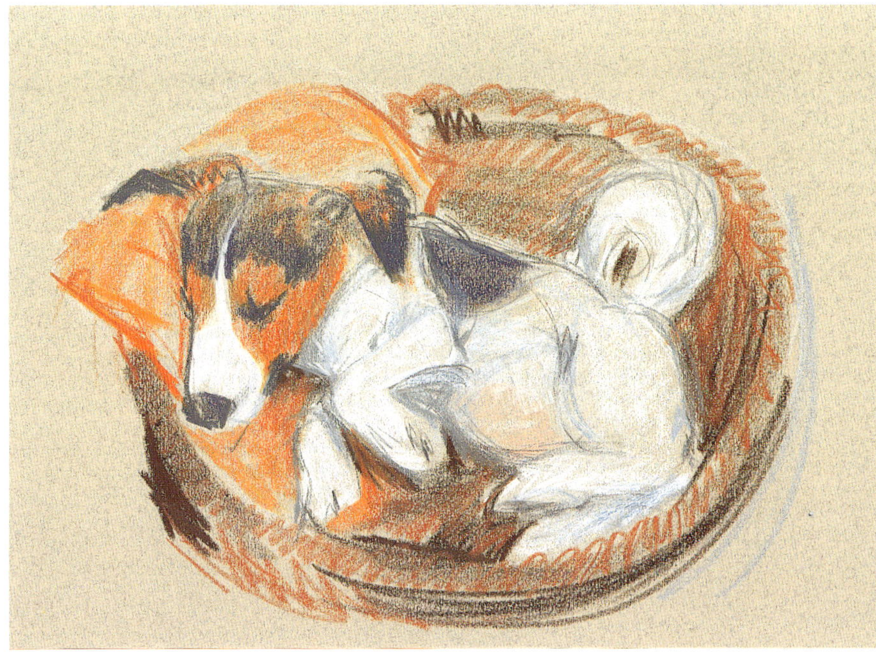

ABOVE
Drawing from memory, Exercise 1.

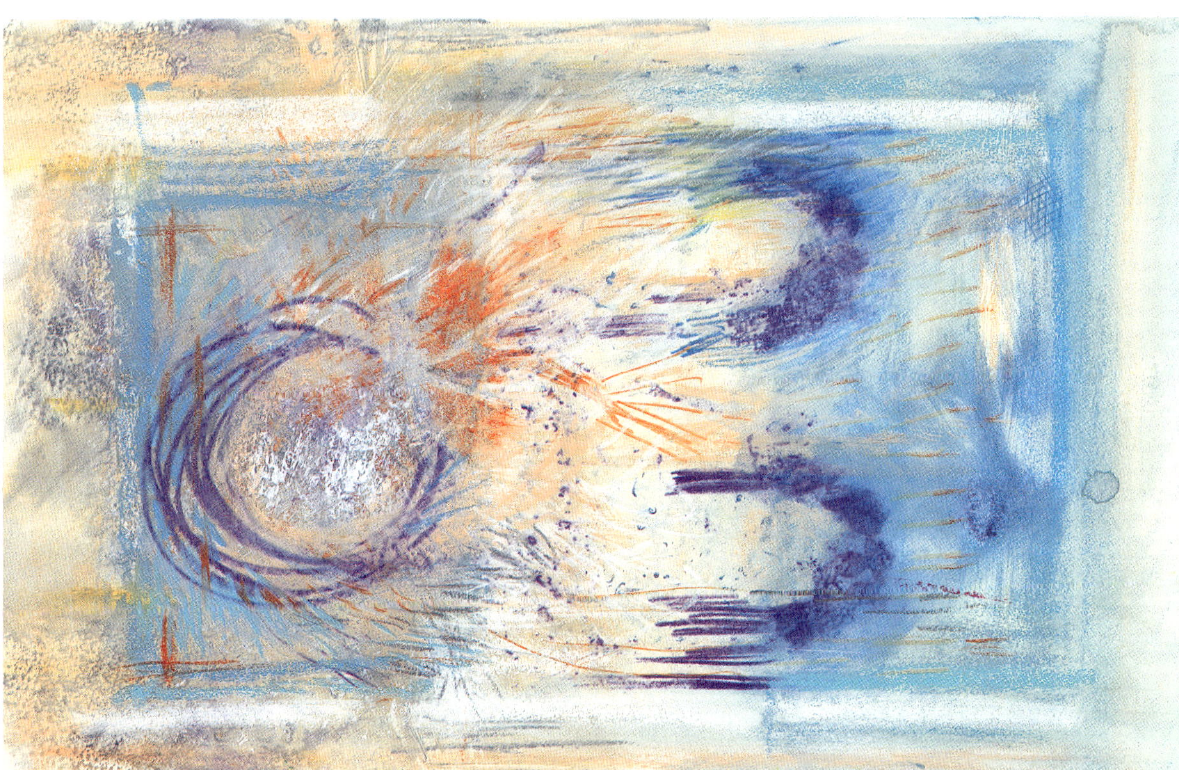

LEFT
'Automatic' drawing from memory. This composition tries to capture visually the feelings evoked by the word 'energy.'

anything at all that is really familiar. Using a simple line description first, and then moving freely and/or decoratively into a full range of materials, make your picture. Try and reduce your critical judgment, at least at the early line stage. Go for simple recognition. Nobody but you need see this. Imagine, if you can, yourself as a child, and doodle a drawing for fun.

On the other hand, drawing from memory is a very important and powerful resource in art. It can evoke feelings that are perhaps best described as 'poetic' or 'magical.' It can also expose deeper psychological layers of meaning which are more often concealed in observational drawing. The more we draw, the more this personal visual memory is strengthened. Most children have developed a rich visual memory just by being alive, looking at and responding to their surroundings, and through simple drawing. This is where we all start, and some of us stop. Very young children draw from observed life.

If we try and push this visual memory, however, it is possible to go to a deeper level. This initially needs the sort of distracted attention most of us use when we doodle. Remember the covers of your school books. If they were anything like mine, it was almost impossible to read the title for the layers of patterns and scribble. If I use the telephone, my attention is directed to the conversation, and yet when I replace the handset, some other 'me' has drawn a whole world of spirals, mazes and patterns.

This sort of 'automatic' drawing can be a rich source for artists interested in the way that the mind makes pictures from some deeper visual memory. This skill, which we all possess, can be focused with practice.

Exercise 2

This exercise is about drawing from feeling. Choose a word that describes some sort of emotional experience that you can recall. A range of experiences might include: peace, chaos, love, hate, joy, sadness, energy, depression. You might choose feelings of attraction toward: masculinity, femininity, family, isolation.

Next choose a color that might represent or enhance this chosen feeling. Using just line, and this is the hard part, do not draw anything pictorially, no hearts or flowers, no symbols of any kind. Just using an appropriate range of marks and patterns, try and represent your feeling. Remember from the section on mark-making the whole range of marks available: slow to fast, soft to hard, light to dark, smooth to rough. Using the three types of pencil, and perhaps a wet finger, make your doodle.

When you have built a satisfactory linear version, move into the full range of color that the pencils offer. The only requirement now is that what you do should help to maintain that feeling and not destroy it. It is worth noticing that, just as our range of words have opposites, so do the colors and marks, and with care these opposing values can be used to increase the feeling. Be honest: if you lose the feeling, start again. The bulk of the early drawing is usually done quite speedily.

What you have made has been the basis for a lot of modern art; it is a sort of personal symbol or analog representing your remem-

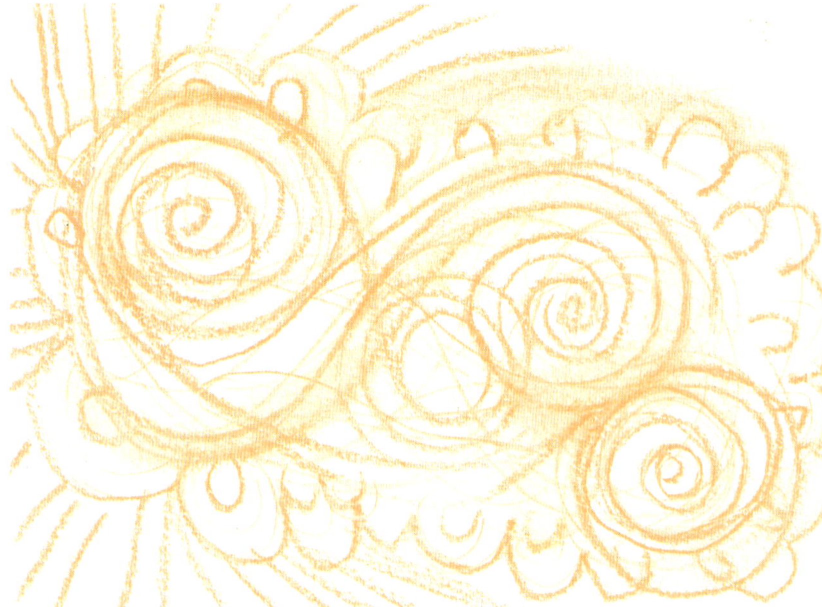

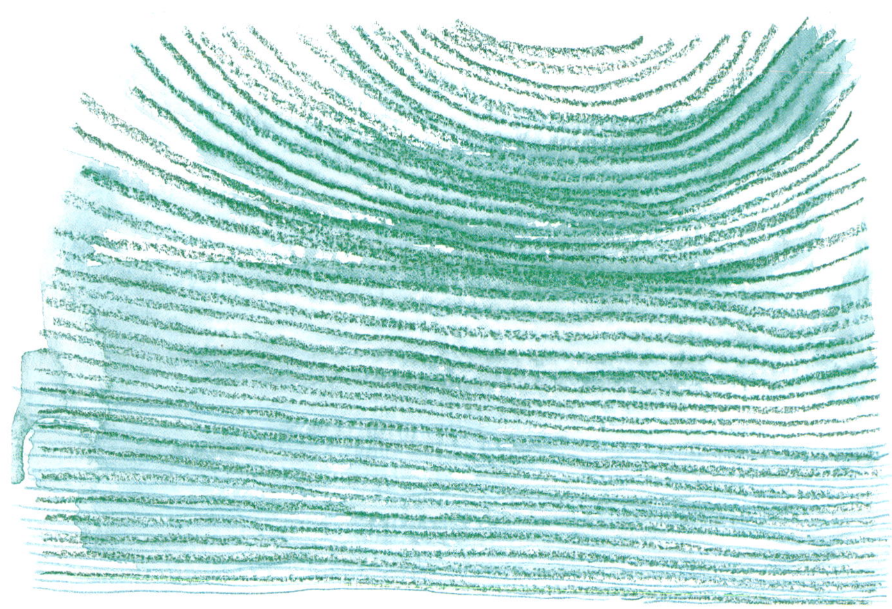

TOP
Exercise 2; student sketch inspired by the word 'feminity.'

ABOVE
Student exercise evoked by the term 'tranquillity.'

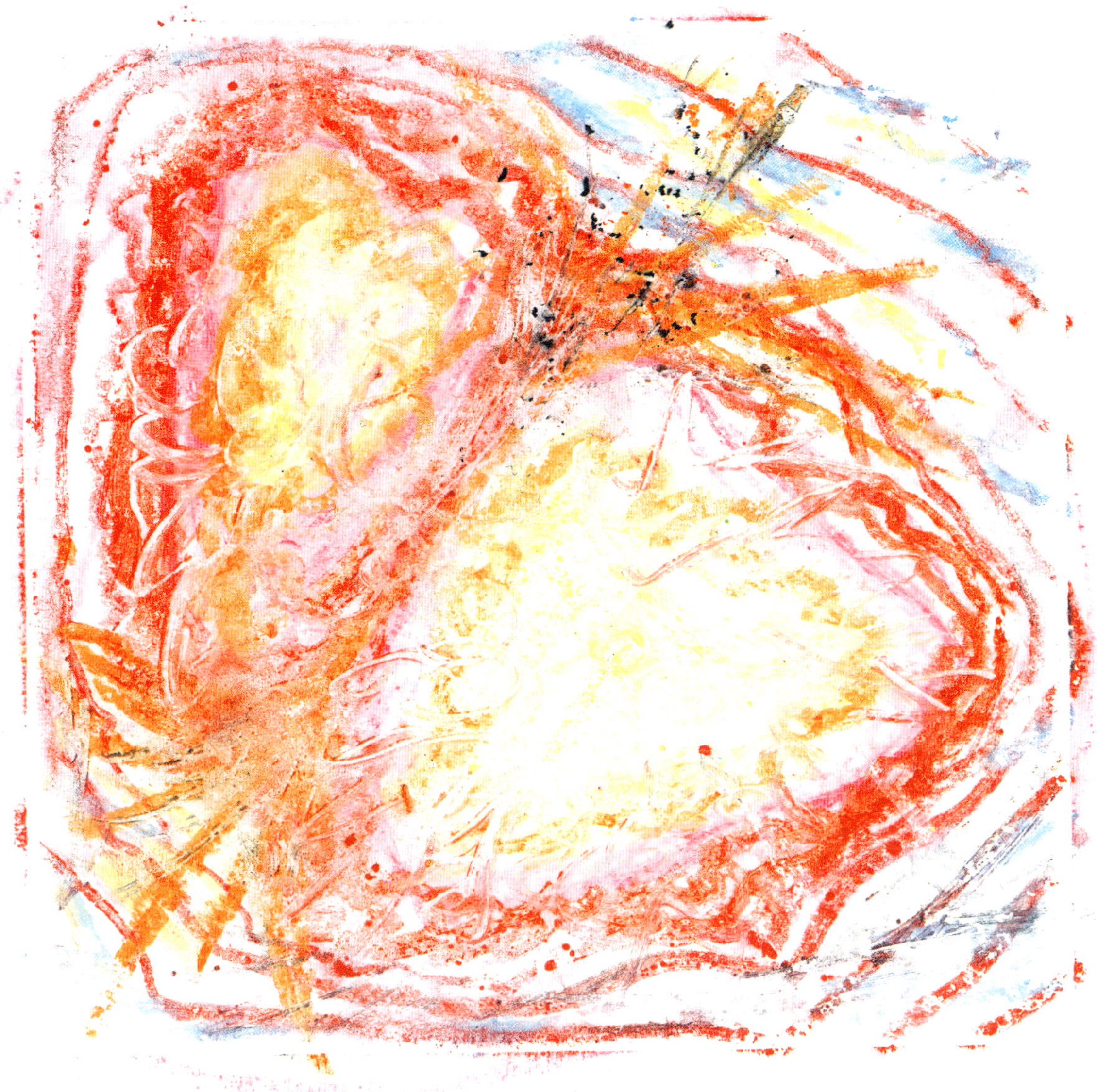

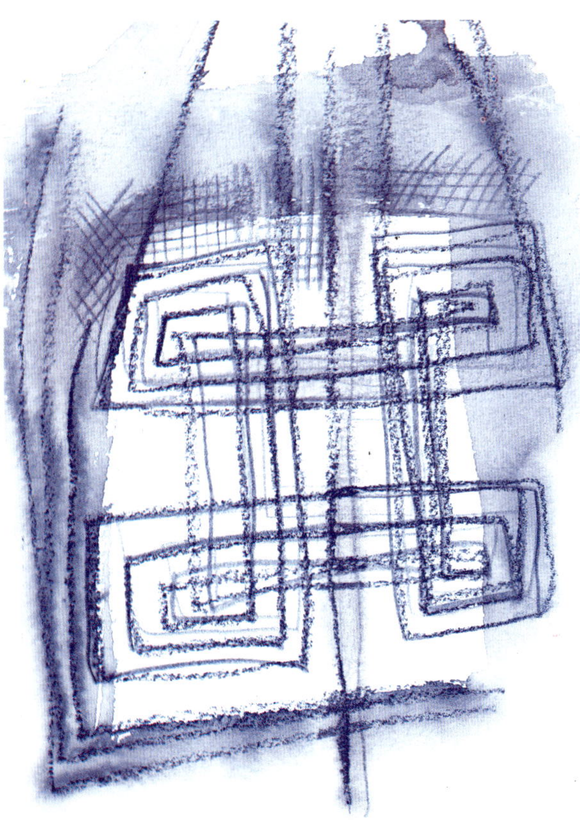

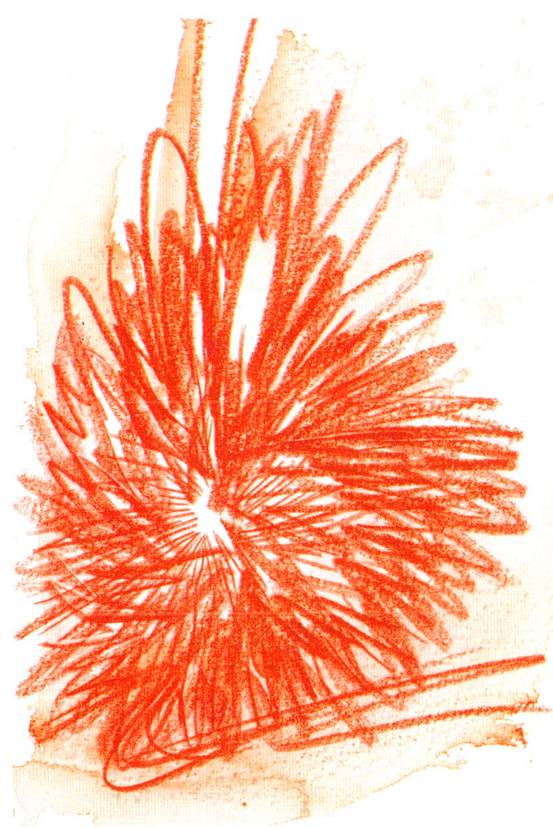

ABOVE LEFT
A developed drawing of 'energy.'

FAR LEFT
Student sketch of 'masculinity.'

LEFT
Student sketch of 'energy.'

LEFT
Water and Stones 2
This piece is developed from an earlier experimental composition, shown on page 24; here the aim is to evoke water lapping the stones in the cold winter light.

BELOW
Devayani Khakhria
Communications Satellites
Painting with celestial imagery; the great swirls of soft pigment make a space in which organic and structured forms dance and trail in the form of a collage.

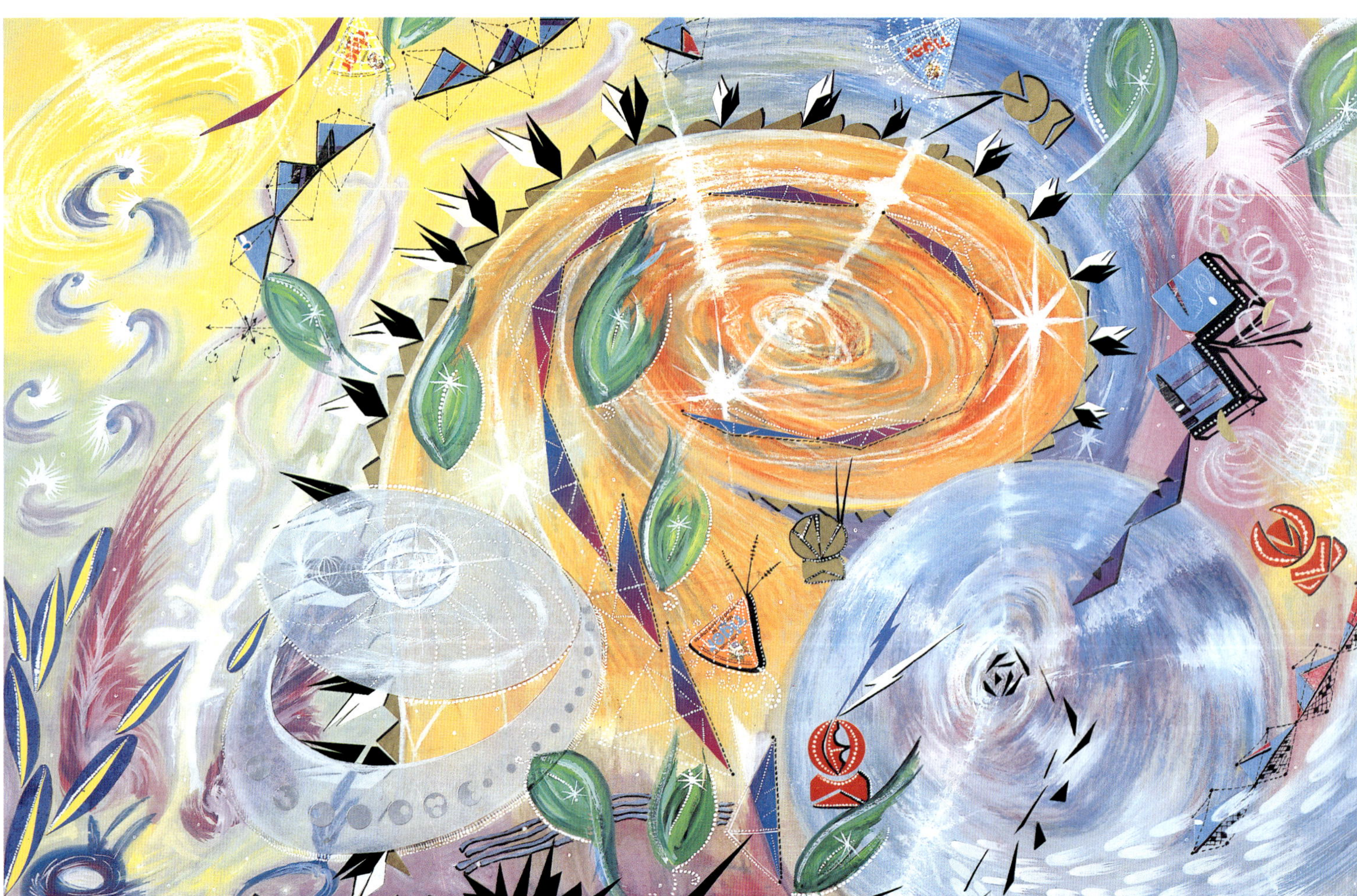

bered experience. If this was a rich experience for you, you might wish to experiment with these images, perhaps include figures and objects that increase the experience. Look at the composition as a whole and see if there are other shapes or formats that enhance the image. You might choose and prepare the paper, stick other surfaces on the image, draw over and paint out passages. This is an intensely personal activity, and you are the main critic as to whether it evokes what you intend.

Instead of using a remembered emotion as your subject, you might try drawing directly to music. What emotions/marks does a favorite piece of music evoke? Express it first as line and simple color as you experience it, secondly with added color and texture as you remember it.

You might make an abstract portrait of someone, by recalling the feelings they evoke and generating the equivalent marks, colors and textures. Because of their immediacy and breadth of response, color pencils are a great way to rehearse and produce these ideas.

Observation

This is a section about seeing things in their true relationships in space – as they really appear. To do this effectively we must put aside our old habits and preconceptions and take a clear look at what we see out there.

Perspective

Various cultures have favored different ways of representing the real world of three-dimensions on a two-dimensional surface. The word 'perspective' comes from the Latin word *prospectus*, which means 'looked forward.' Linear perspective was developed by

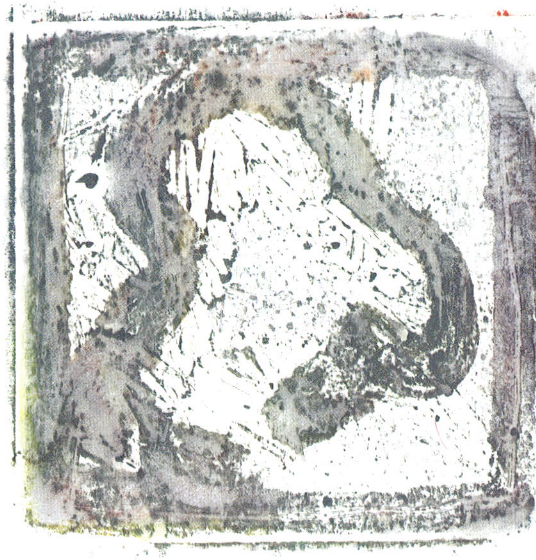

LEFT
An expressive surface print.

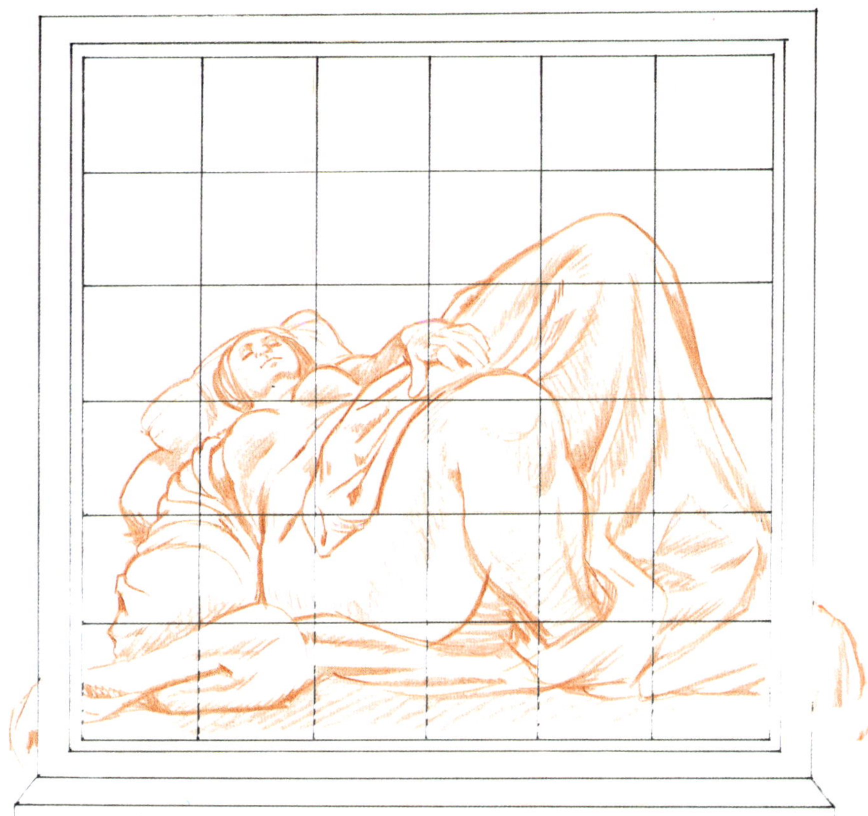

BELOW
An approximate view through the artist's grid shown in the Dürer print (bottom).

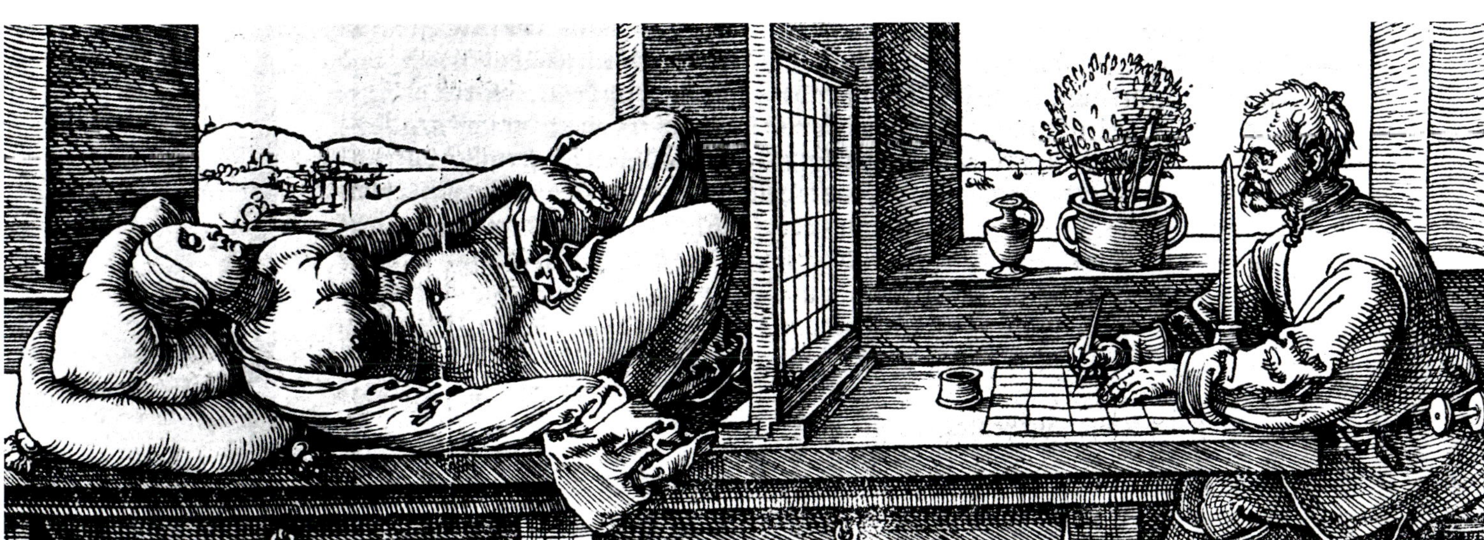

BOTTOM
Albrecht Dürer
Draftsman Doing Perspective Drawings of a Woman, 1532
An early example of the implementation of linear perspective; see page 54.

European artists in that incredibly inventive period we now call the Renaissance. Renaissance linear perspective is the closest system of drawing to the way that we in Western culture perceive objects in space. Forms appear to become smaller as their distance from us increases. Railroad tracks seem to converge and vanish at the horizon. This is the stuff of realistic drawing which is actually based on seeing and measuring.

The great artist and draftsman Albrecht Dürer (1471-1528) made an etching of the early implementation of linear perspective. Here (page 53) we can see how it works. The artist holds his head still, helped by a vertical rule. He looks through a vertical wire grid, a familiar device previously used on paper for drawing to a measured proportion. The artist sees a foreshortened view of the figure against the wire grid. On a similar grid marked on paper, he can mark off the points and lines observed. Drawing only what he sees in relation to the grid, he produces a foreshortened view on paper which shows sizes and shapes that are contrary to what we know to be true about the figure.

The system works extremely well, and was eventually codified into a sort of geometry that we know today as linear perspective. Artists had solved the problem of how to create an illusion of deep space on a flat surface. The shock of seeing this illusion beautifully executed must have been tremendous in its day.

Today, when we are used to this sort of imagery, there can be problems with linear

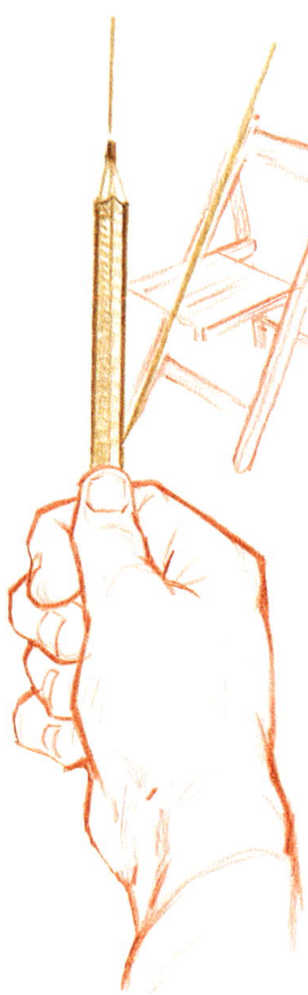

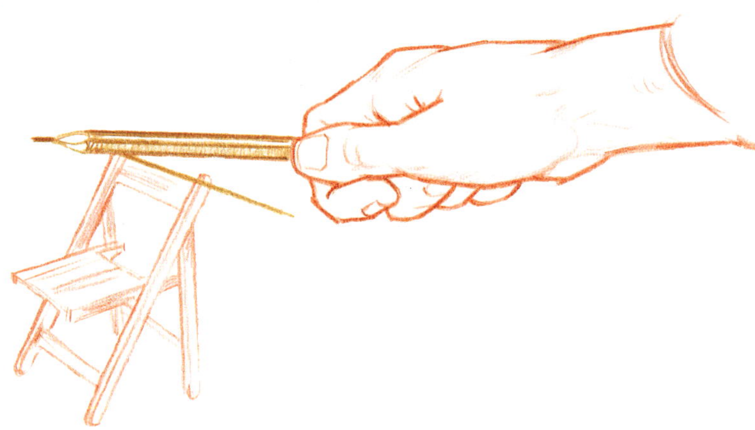

FAR LEFT AND LEFT
Taking preliminary measurements by horizontal and vertical sighting.

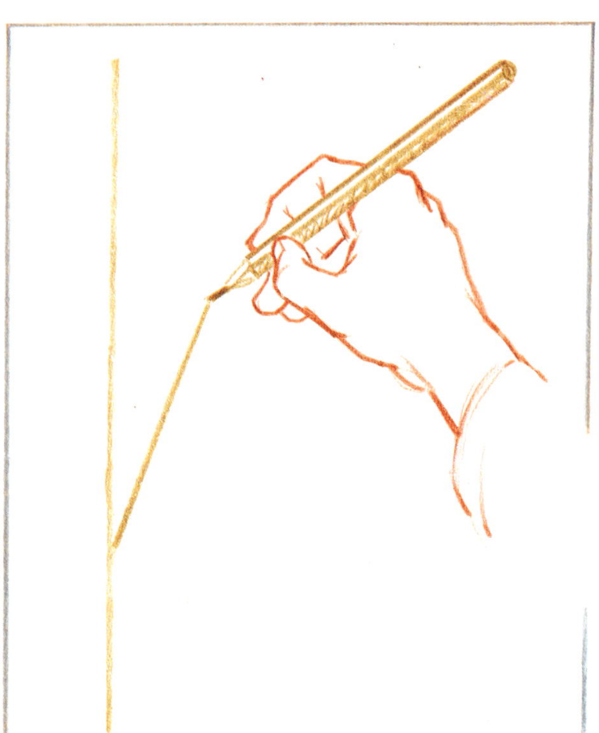

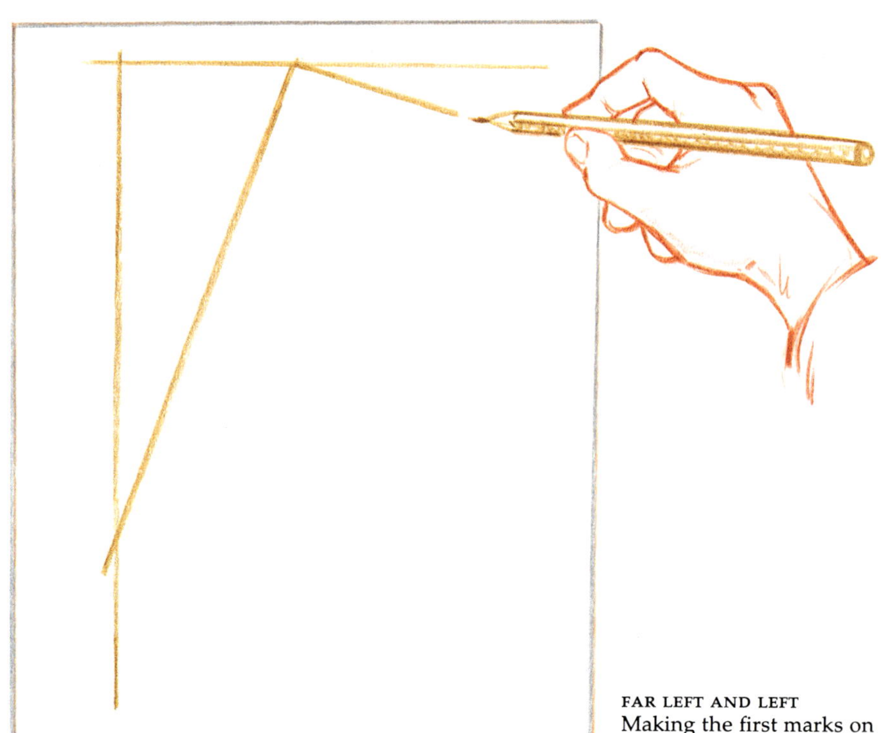

FAR LEFT AND LEFT
Making the first marks on your measured drawing.

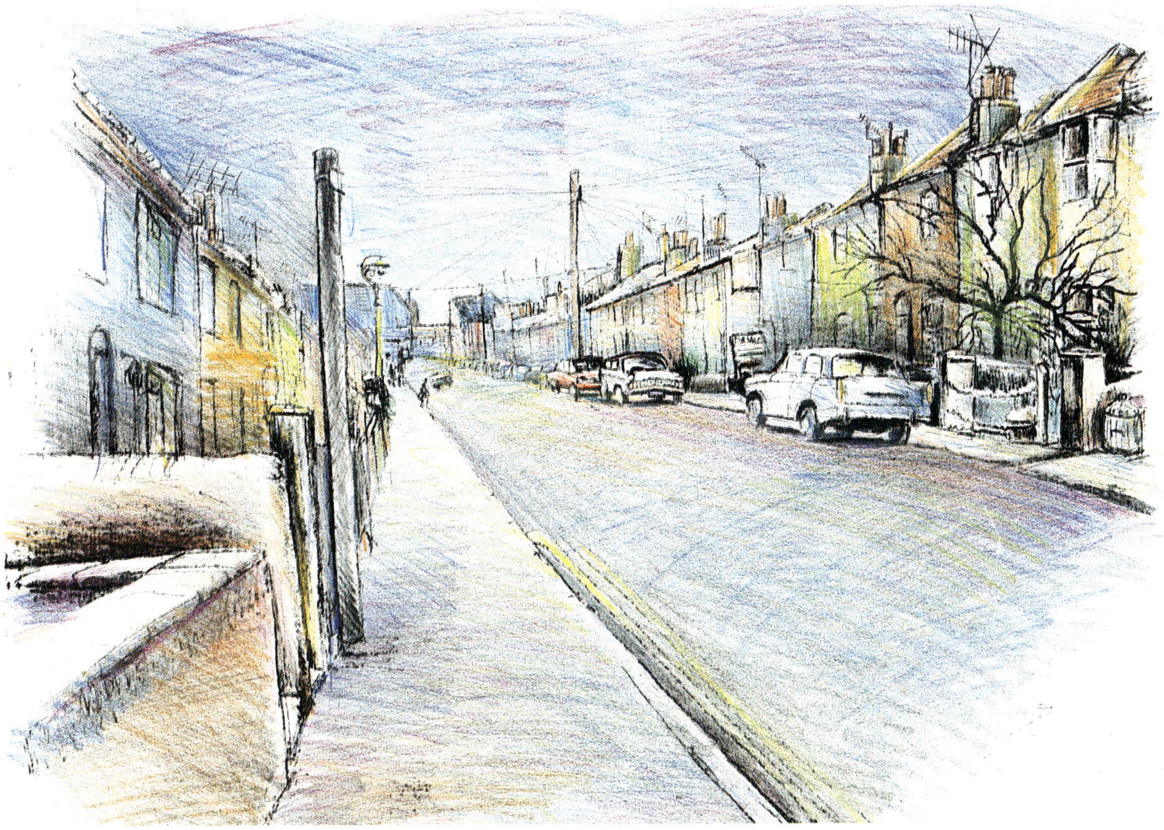

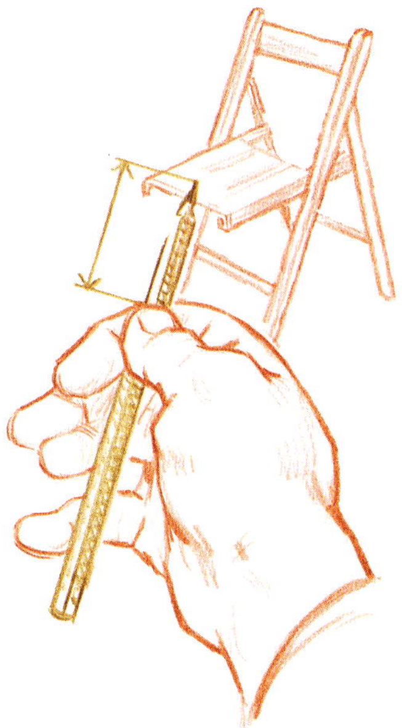

ABOVE AND BELOW
Completing the drawing by measured sighting.

ABOVE LEFT
Madeleine Baker
Street Drawing
This London street shows both linear and atmospheric perspective, with color turning bluish as objects recede.

perspective, especially when it is too rigidly practiced. Pictures can become over-analytical, reducing the range of ideas and perceptions that artists like to play with.

Fortunately, once we have a grip on the basic ideas, linear perspective can be held in reserve, as a resource for when we are in trouble. The best way of dealing with these issues of observation relies on seeing clearly, and this can be aided by a technique derived from linear perspective, that of measured sighting.

Measured Sighting

This is a way of comparing and measuring the placing and proportion of what you observe and draw. It does not need elaborate equipment, just pencil, paper and a simple technique.

Hold up a pencil vertically at arm's length, close to one eye, and observe directly some object, perhaps a chair leg, that makes an angle with the vertical of the pencil. Then draw that angle using the side of the paper

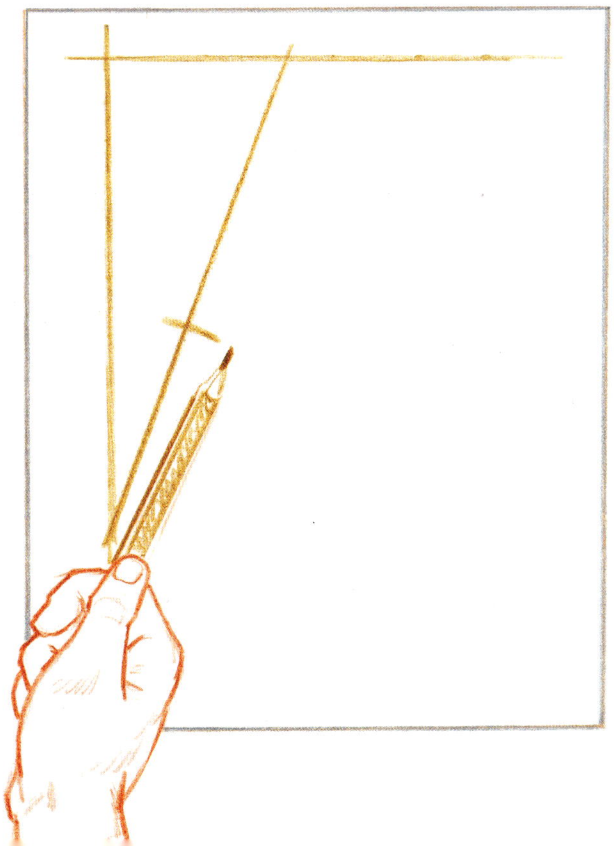

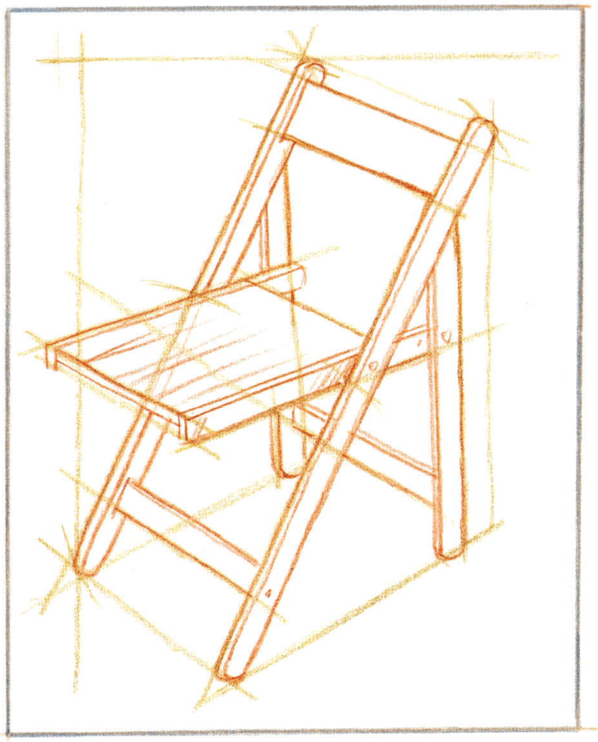

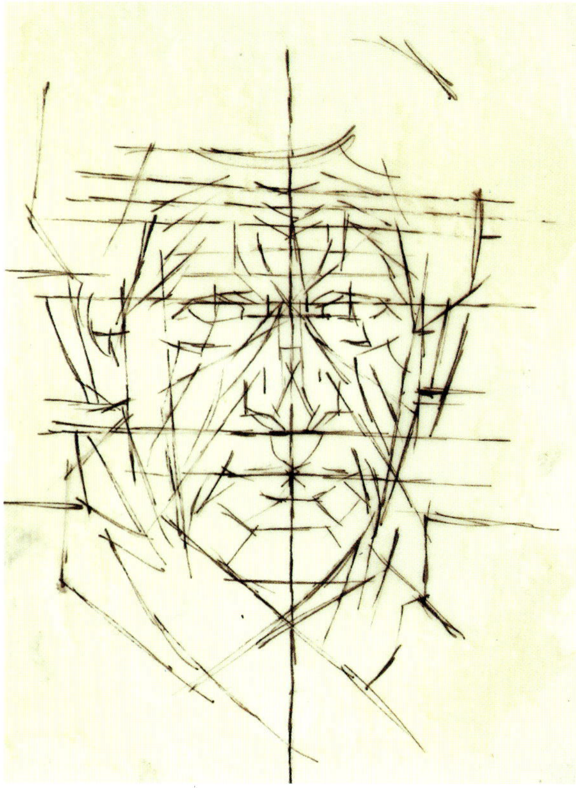

LEFT
A measured sighting construction of Giacometti's head, using photographs as a proportional reference.

It is also possible to make appropriate measurements in a similar manner. Using the top of your pencil as a pointer and the top of your thumb as a mark, measure the leg you first drew. It is important with measuring to keep your arm outstretched, with the same distance between your eye and hand, or the measure will be wrong. Keeping your hand and pencil measure, look at the second feature you drew. How does it relate?

Using the pencil as a rule, draw that relationship on your paper. It does not necessarily have to be the same size measurement as long as the proportion is the same.

By moving over the subject, by checking the angle against the vertical and horizontal, by measuring features and their proportional relationship with each other, a sighted drawing can be built up very accurately.

The technique uses your visual skill to see and observe key angles and lines in the subject of your drawing against the horizontal and the vertical. Then you draw the same angles and lines on the paper in relation to the vertical and the horizontal as given by the edges of the paper. Many artists' sketchbooks show underlying traces of gridwork and measured sighting applied to all sorts of subjects.

as your vertical reference. Repeat the procedure, but with the pencil perfectly horizontal, and find a related feature that is near horizontal or makes an angle with the level pencil. Draw this line using the edge of the paper as your horizontal reference.

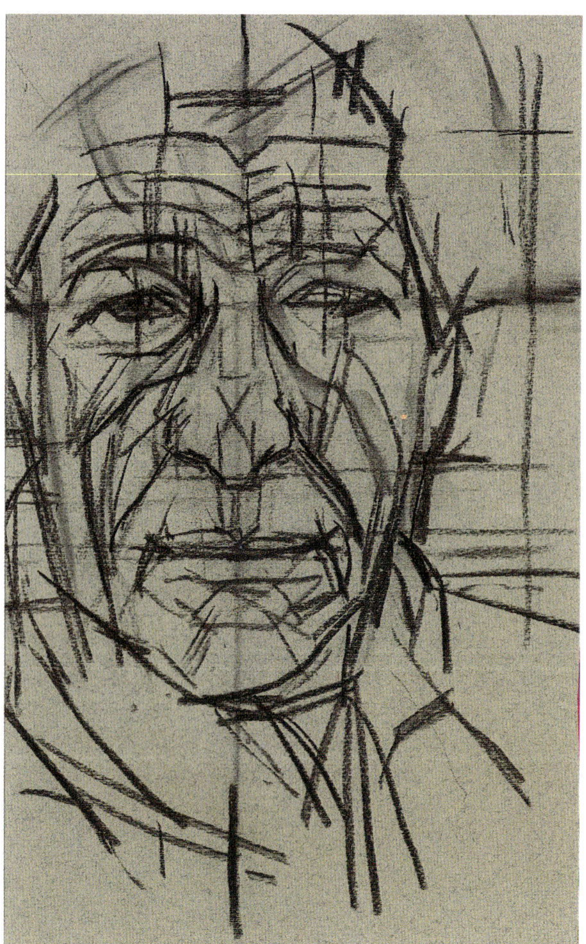

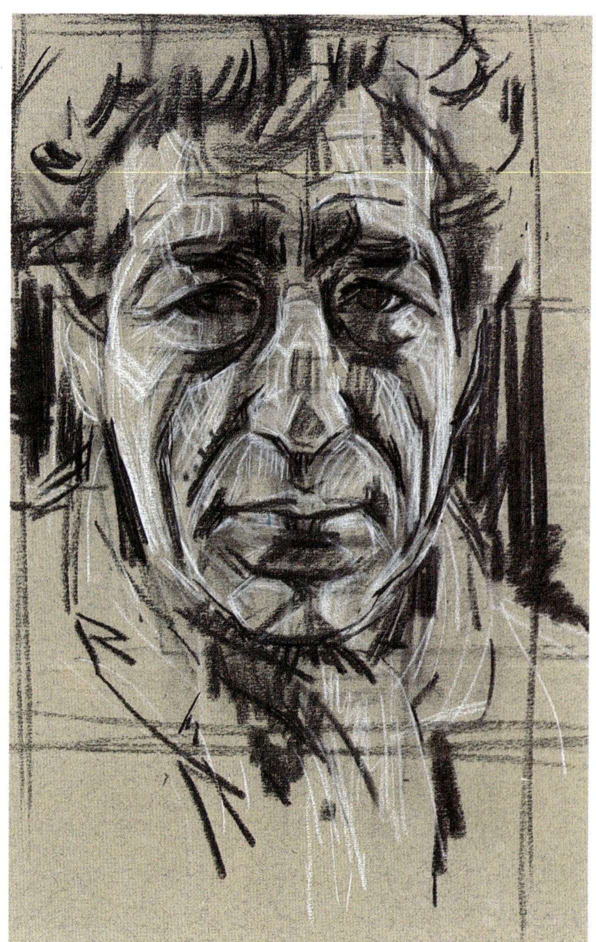

FAR LEFT
A reworking of the measured construction, beginning to build the head and the containing space.

LEFT
Adding shape and form, light and dark, and trying to understand the way in which the head works.

RIGHT
A new, finished drawing, using the information gained from the earlier sketches and selecting and limiting the description marks.

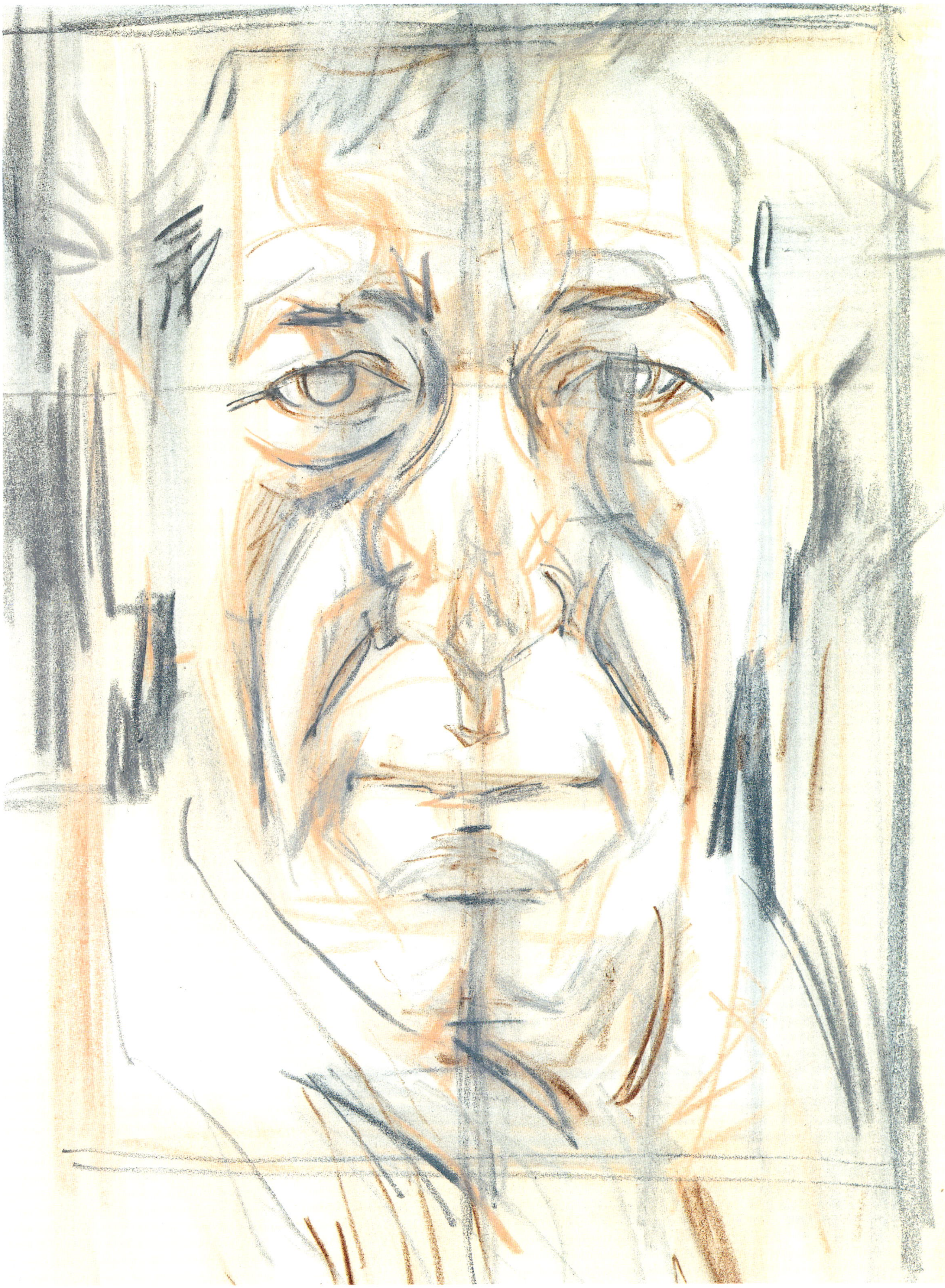

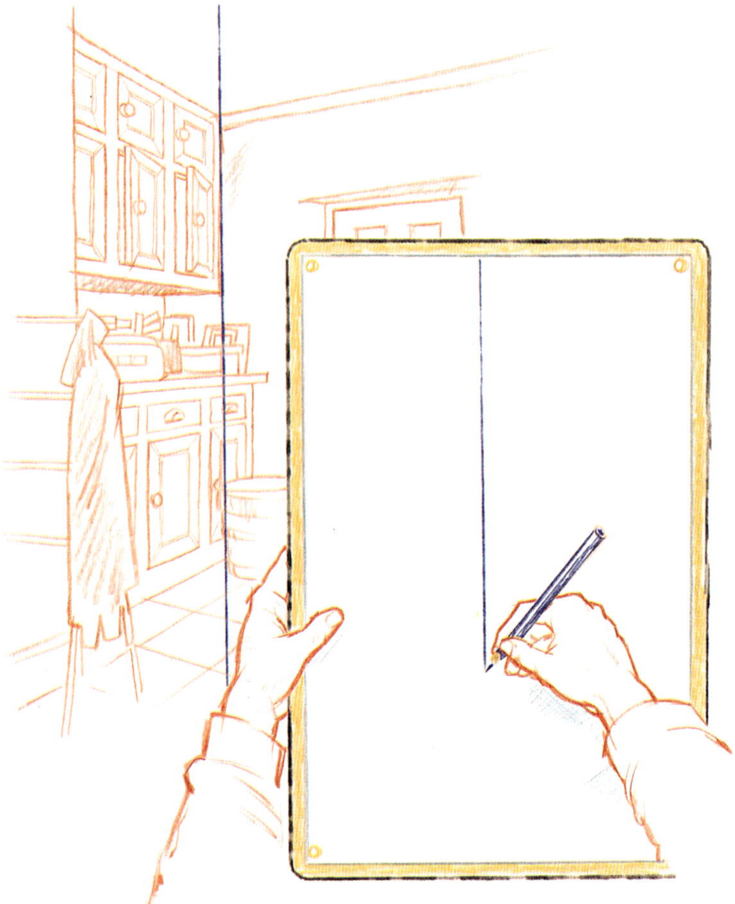

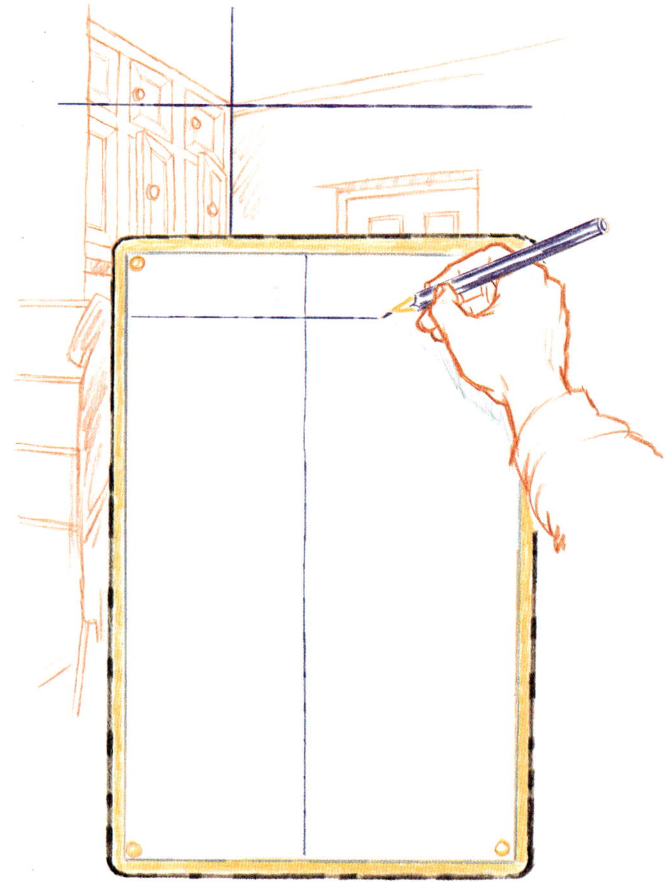

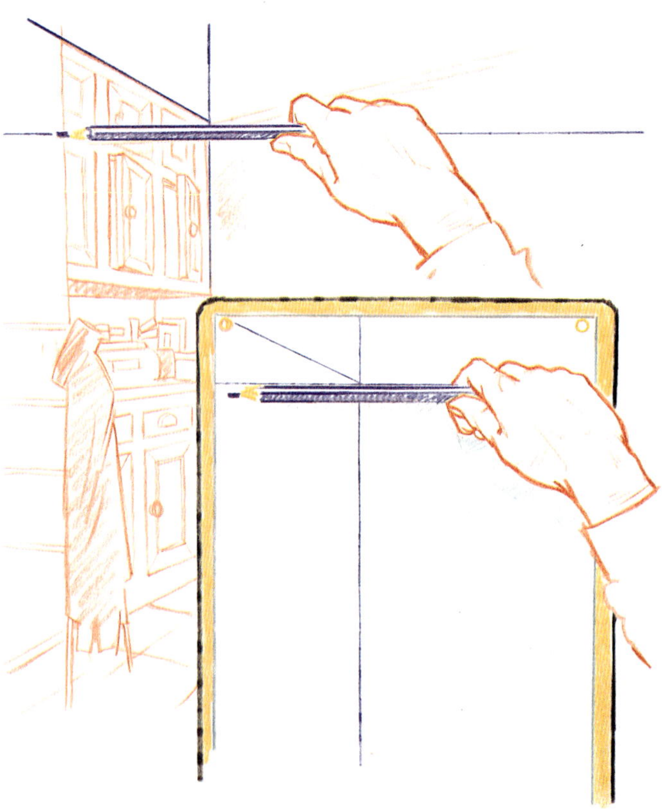

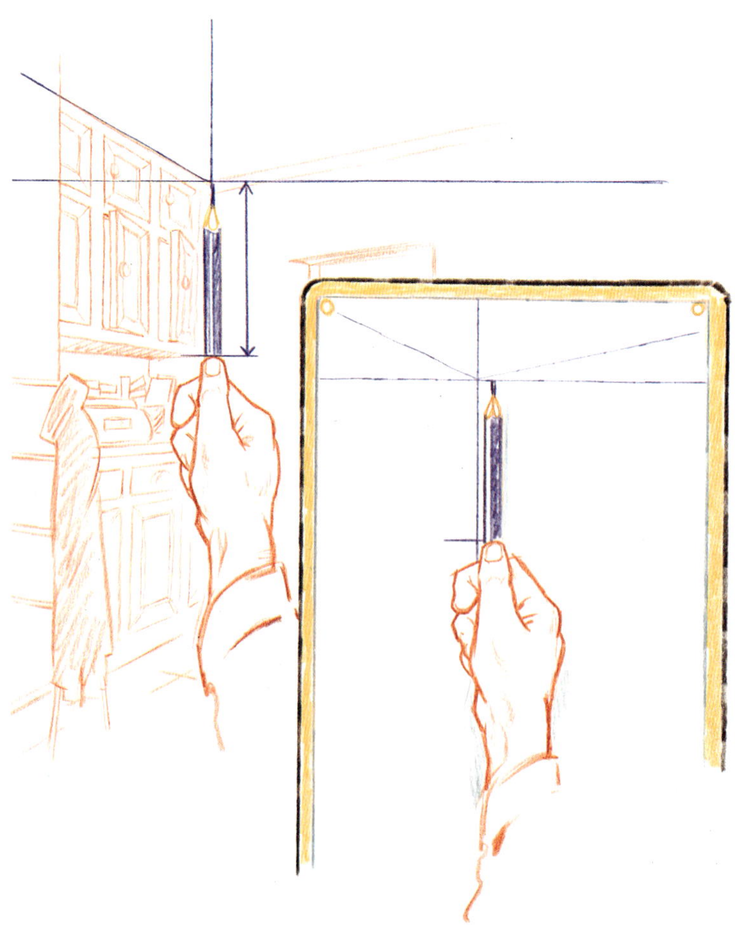

Exercise 3
1. Face a corner of your room.
2. Use a suitable piece of paper. This is now the boundary of your drawing and your reference to the horizontal and vertical. If you are using colored paper, choose a pencil that is near to the tone and color of the paper. If you are using white paper, use a pale color. We are not at this point drawing a colored representation of your corner, but a structural version on which we can build a more realized drawing.
3. Draw a light vertical line down the whole of your paper parallel to the sides of the paper; this will represent the position of the corner of your room.
4. Mark on this line your choice for the top corner, where the walls meet the ceiling, and draw a light horizontal line parallel to the top of your paper.
5. Holding your pencil at arm's length horizontally, place the pencil at the corner you have just marked. Close one eye, and look at the angles the pencil is making with the interaction of walls and ceiling. Lightly mark these angles on your drawing. Check them again with the pencil held vertically.
6. Using measured sighting, carry on building up a linear structure of the corner.
7. Using this linear version as a guide, complete the picture with a full range of color and tone. I have chosen a decorative approach to balance the rather analytical realism so far achieved. But you could also use this line version to study the whole range of realism, as represented by color, tone and surface detail.

Expression

So far we have looked at ways of expressing our visual memory and of building up our observational skills. Here, the two aspects come together. All drawing is expressive, by its nature. Remember that all the elements involved in picture-making – the paper, the marks, the way we use tone and color, the textures and structures of the composition – have a part to play in evoking what the artist intends. It really is a question of focus. In the exercise that follows there are two drawings of the same object. The first is an investigation of the thing by measured sighting. This is part of the process of understanding how the thing looks. The second is a fully expressive drawing. This drawing may contain elements of how it was made, how it looks, and how it feels.

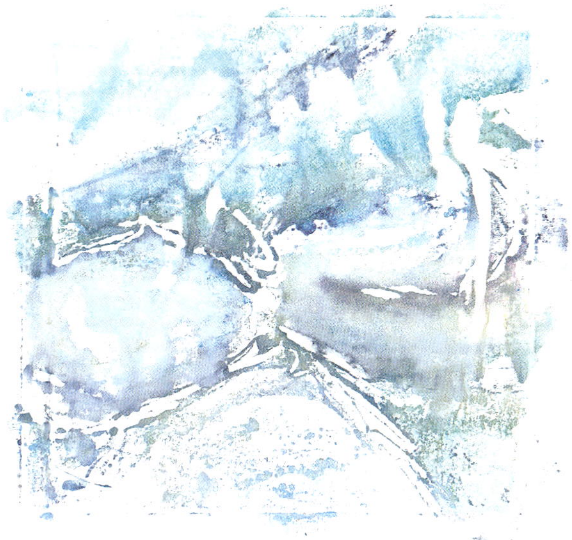

FAR LEFT
Four stages in building up the picture following Exercise 3.

BELOW
The finished drawing.

LEFT
An expressive abstract.

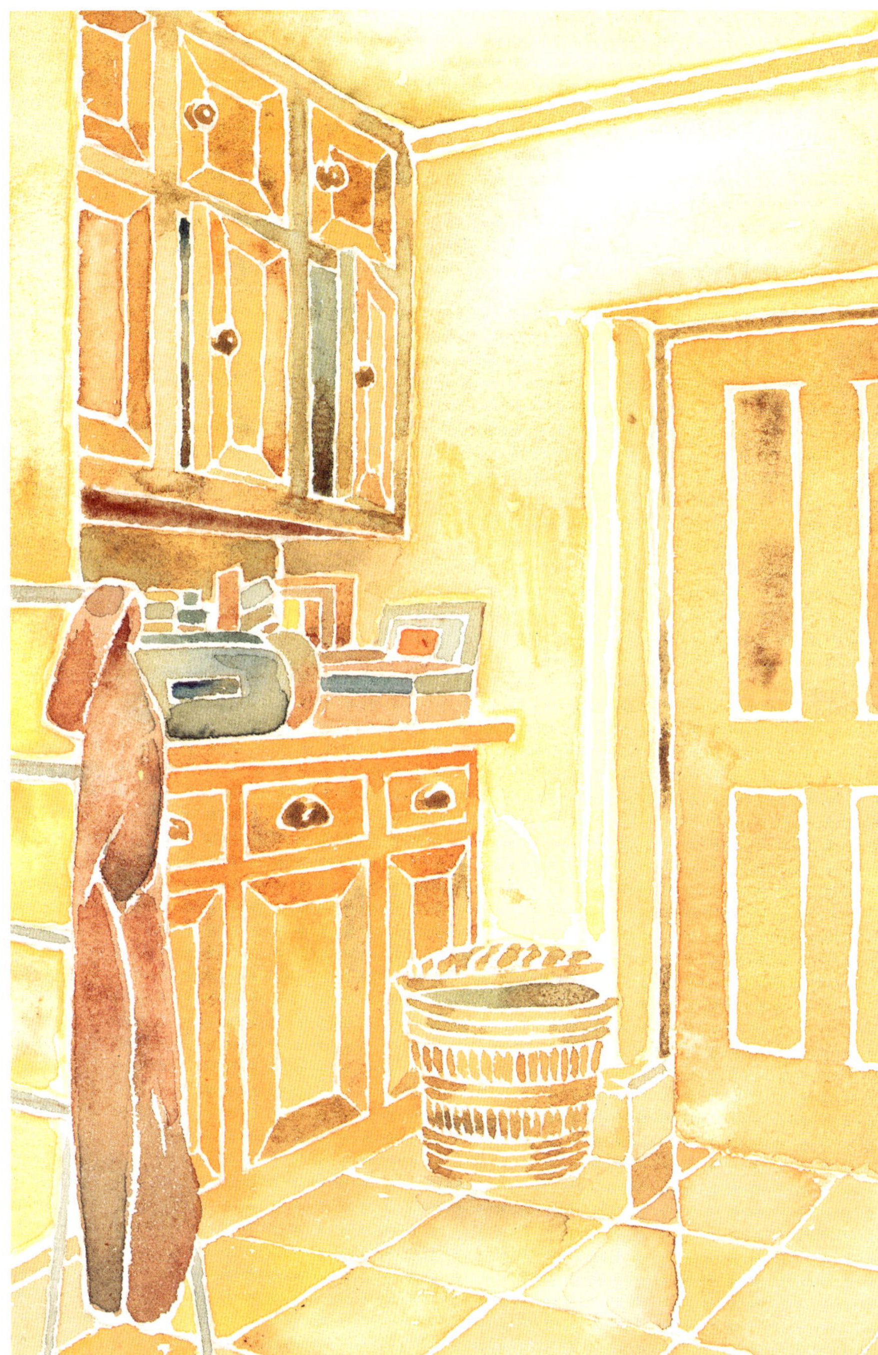

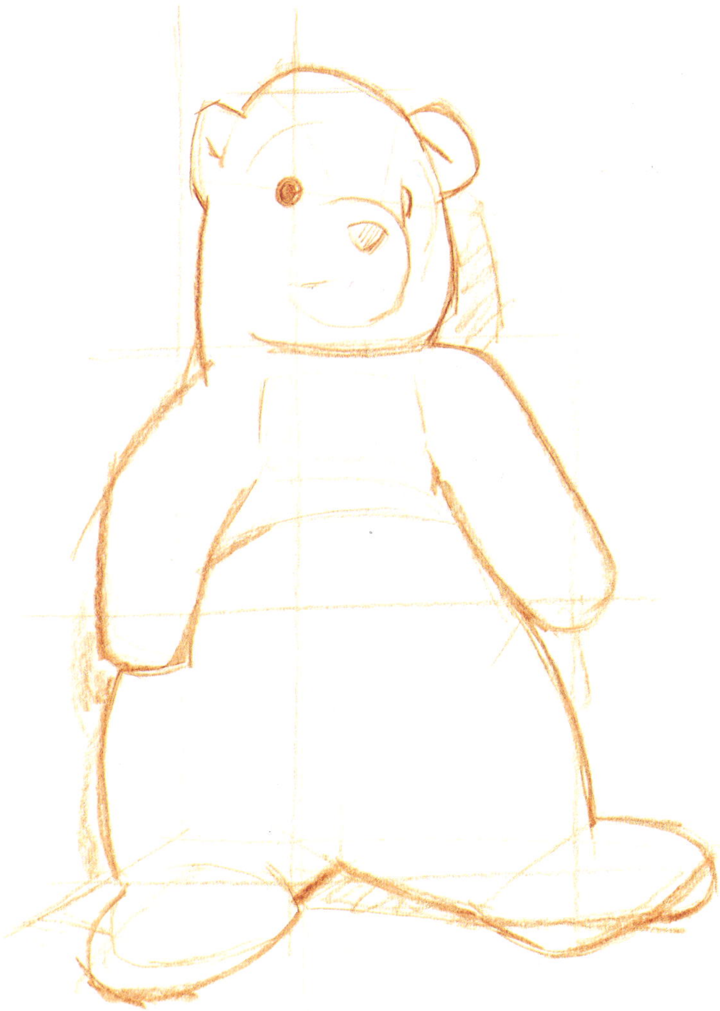

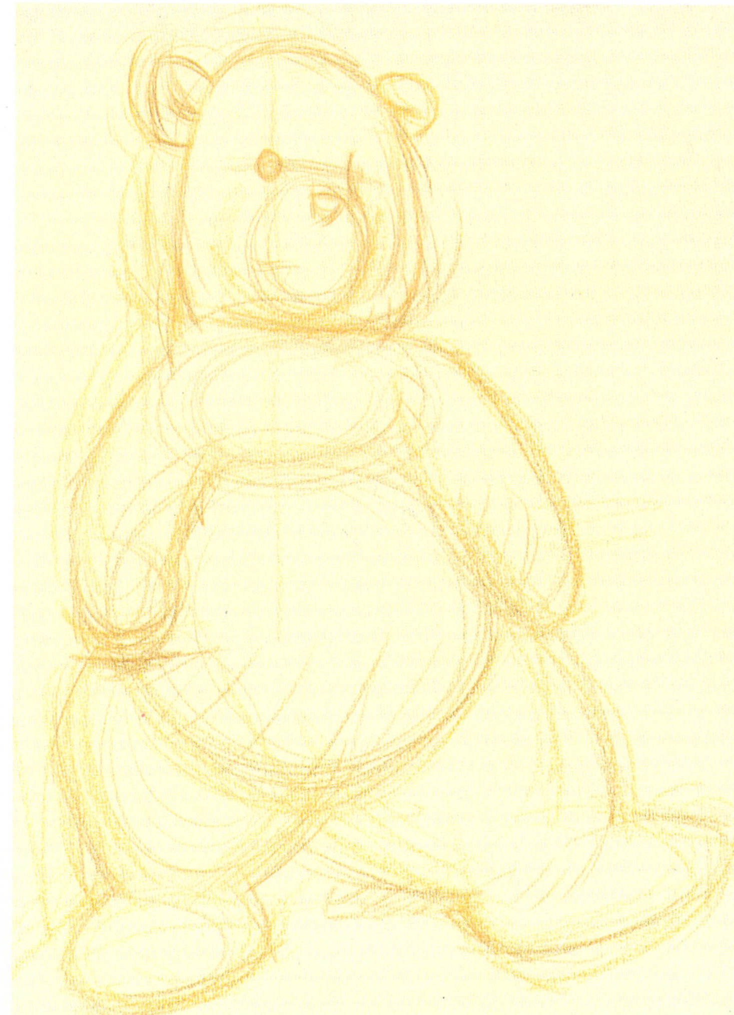

ABOVE LEFT AND RIGHT
Beginning your drawing, as described in Exercise 4.

Exercise 4

1. Choose an object that you know very well, and perhaps means a lot to you. It might be a toy from your childhood, or some collected figure. Set the thing up so that it looks right to you.
2. Draw a simple line version by measured sighting; this is your working drawing and a way of understanding the subject.
3. Consider this drawing. Although it is a good line version, it lacks lots of qualities that you like in the object itself. We cannot tell what color it is, or what textures and surfaces make up the object. Similarly we cannot really tell what the artist feels about this thing. The thin line does not tell us much.
4. Draw the object again, this time more freely. Choose your colored paper and first colored pencils carefully; the marks should be quite light. You now have some basic understanding of the subject. Make some light approximate marks that suggest the whole thing, no matter how crudely. Then accentuate those that look right and disregard the 'wrong' marks. All the marks will be visible as part of the process.
5. Although this drawing may be losing some of its observed 'correctness,' hopefully it now has new qualities that say something about your feeling for the object. Using the full range of color pencils, wet and dry, hard and soft, try and evoke some of the qualities you like about

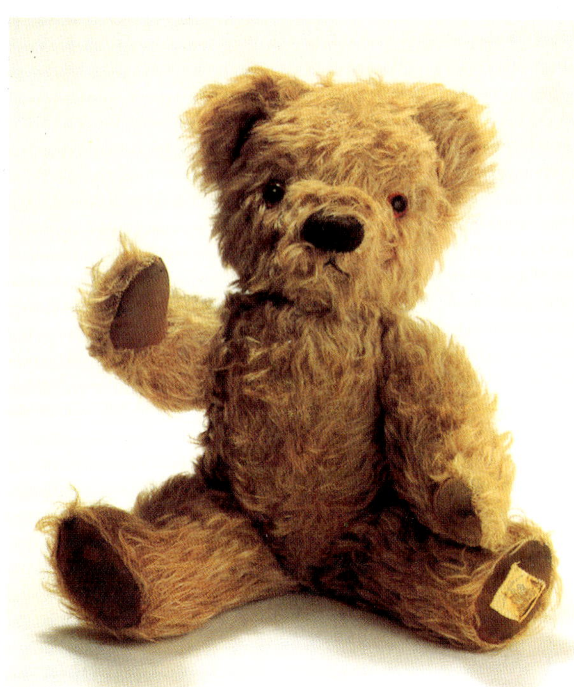

LEFT
A real teddy bear from the 1930s.

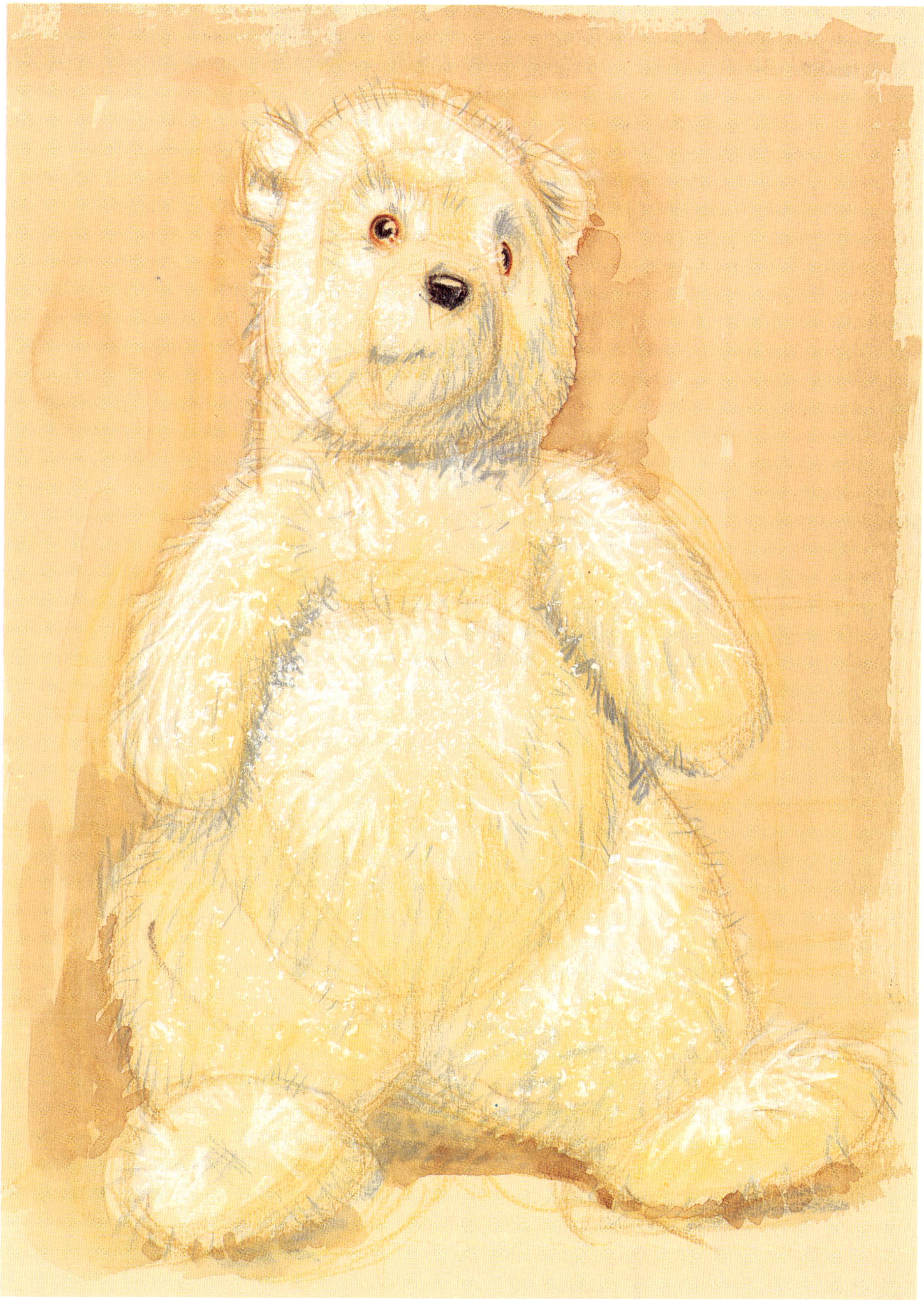

LEFT
The final stages in your teddy bear drawing.

the object. Be as free about this as you were in the visual memory exercise, except that now you have the object itself in front of you to remind you.

6. The finished piece should have a life of its own. It reminds us of the subject and the qualities we like, and embedded in the way it was made is something about our feelings toward the subject.

With practice, you should find that the first stage using measured sighting will not be necessary, unless you are making very realistic pictures. Different artists adopt very different approaches. Some artists choose to lose any reference to the appearance of things in favor of an abstract recreation of the feeling it evoked, or perhaps surface detail.

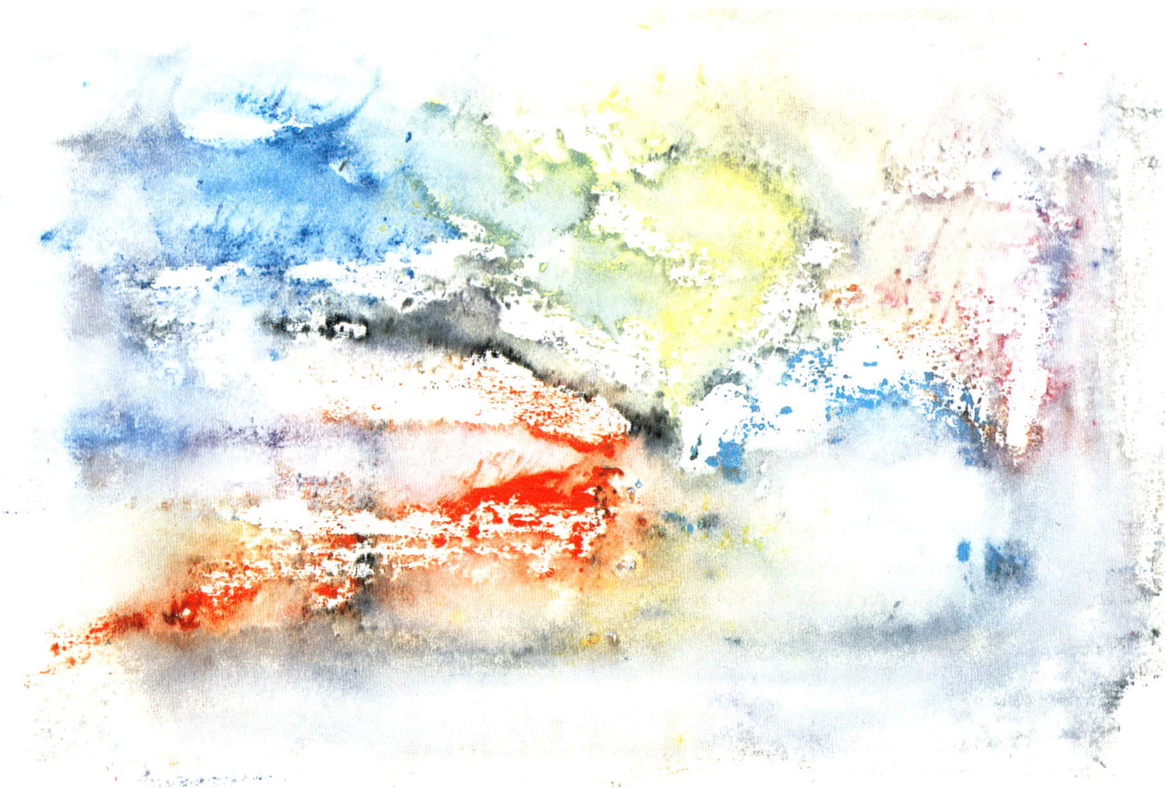

LEFT
Red and Blue Winter
Using just a few blots and sprinkles of pigment, subjects and themes may be suggested by the 'accidental' stains, and possibly emphasized by working into the surface.

BELOW
Experimental monoprint, using ink and colored pencil pigment.

RIGHT
Devayani Khakhria
Mithlin Piece

Imagination

The wonderful thing about the imagination, for me, lies in its ability to suggest all sorts of possibilities, especially in picture-making. These ideas seem to come as a gift from our minds, or even from dreams, without necessarily any reference to the world of reality; all we need to do is to sensitize ourselves to the potential.

Children seem to have no trouble with the idea that a box can be a house, or a cardboard tube a rocket ship. This is the essence of play, and it has something to do with the appearance of things. This shape or that form suggests another, richer, possibility. As we become adults, this playfulness gets a little stiffer and less rich. Some artists, however, manage to invent whole worlds through their use of materials, and we can also loosen up these imaginative skills through the use of colored pencils.

Look through the range of visual tests produced in the earlier sections. Some of these images may remind you of something; with awareness and a little manipulation, the suggestion can be brought out. In the examples shown here, some aspect of the materials has been used to evoke other pictorial ideas. Try some experimenting for yourself. Other ideas can come from qualities shown in actual objects. These can be drawn, collected and transformed into something quite magical.

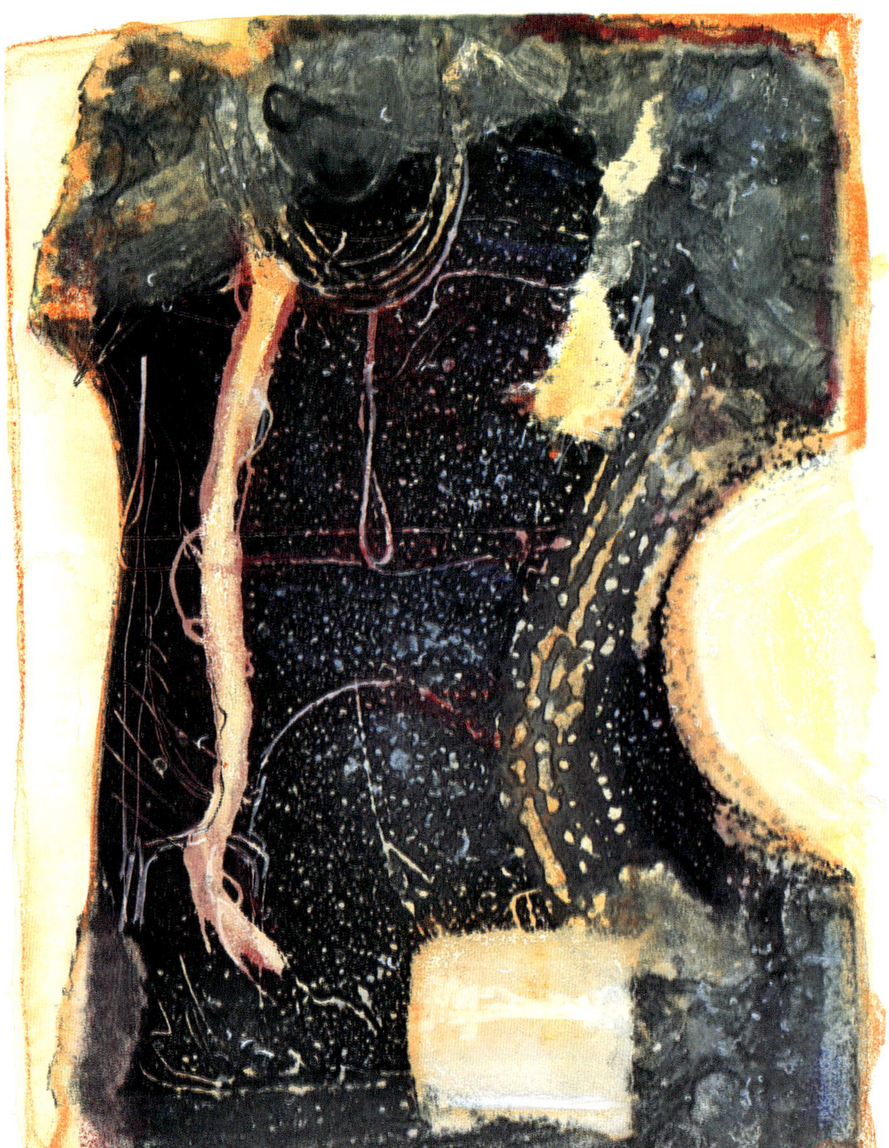

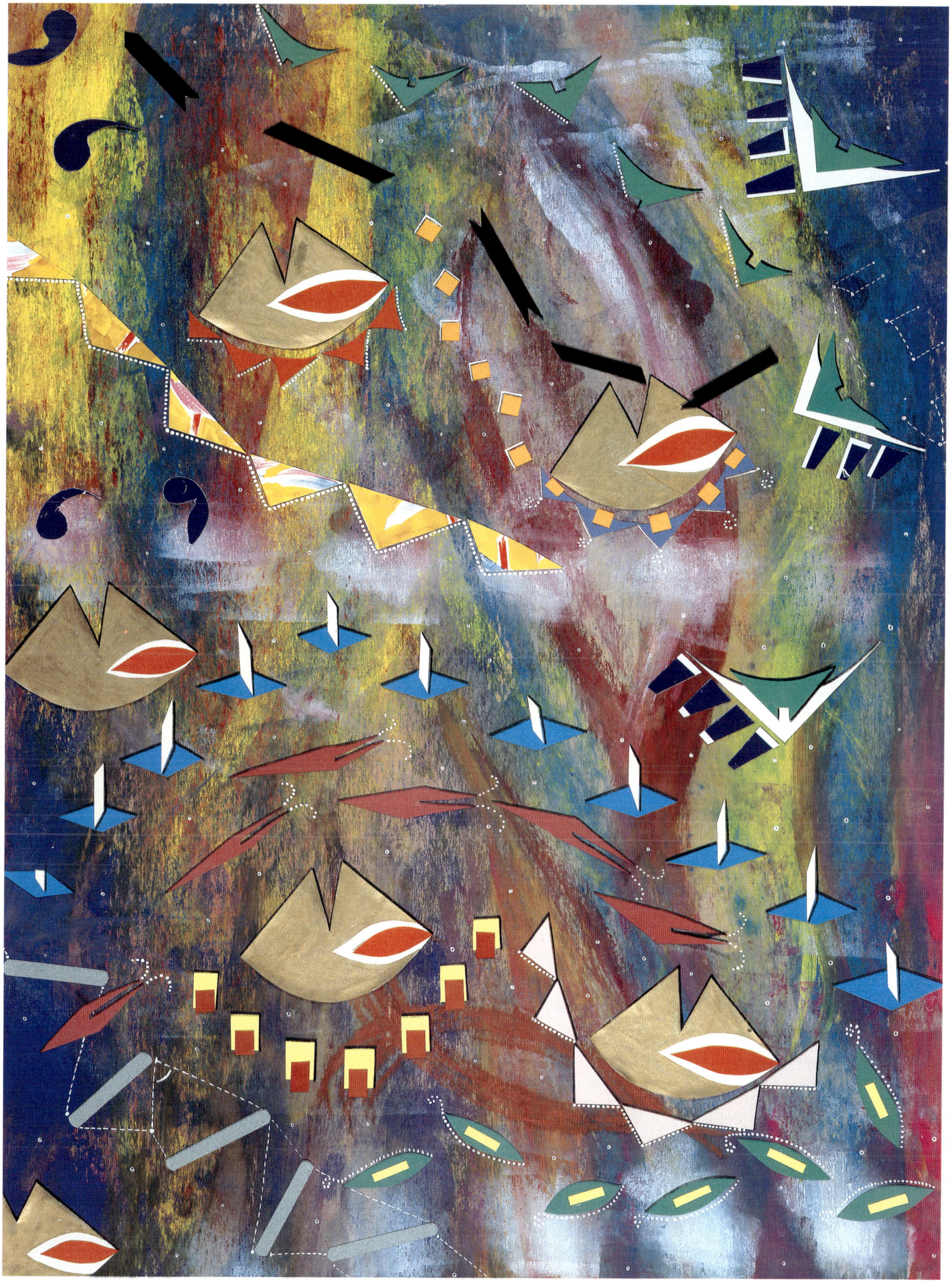

Using a Sketchbook

No matter what your personal interest, some method of collecting ideas and possibilities is really necessary. Even artists who work in the abstract, or entirely from visual memory, usually have some form of sketchbook. Colored pencils are ideal for this, as they are both extremely portable and very broad in their range of mark-making. I do not wish to imply that we should all carry a great leather-bound sketchbook full of impressive drawing. What you need is a small sketch-cum-notebook in which you can write and sketch ideas in a sort of shorthand. In the examples shown, the artists probably had no direct ideas what the sketches might turn into, they are simply a record of what interested them at the time.

The other side of this collecting approach is that, when you are interested in some aspect of making pictures, you will find all sorts of pictorial references in magazines and newspapers. Grab these too; my 'sketchbook' has turned into a garden shed full of collected pictures, photographs and sketched ideas.

Below is the sort of general advice given to art students on sketchbooks, no matter what your special interest.

- Carry a small sketchbook with you to record things of interest.
- Date your sketches and notes and write them up at once; treat your book as a visual diary.
- Keep a larger supply of paper for more developed work.
- Extend your collecting to photographs, pictures collected from the media, and objects themselves.
- Be fully aware of your surroundings; record mood, sounds, smells, light, etc. Cultivate all your senses.
- Do not be strategic in your drawing by only collecting the easy pieces. It is in the challenge of what you find difficult that you will make progress. Be led by your interest.
- Ideas will arise from your general interest. Work them through as sketches.
- Keep building up your understanding of the materials; bench-test them in the sketchbook.
- Seek to balance your choice and use of materials with your pictorial needs.
- Look at artist's sketchbooks, past and present, especially the work of those with whom you share an interest.

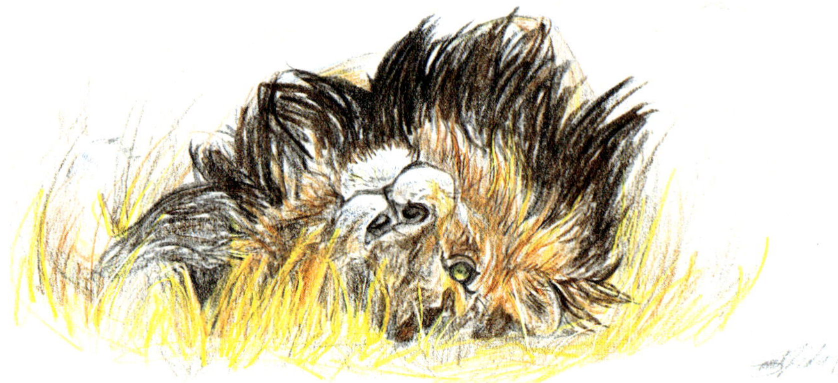

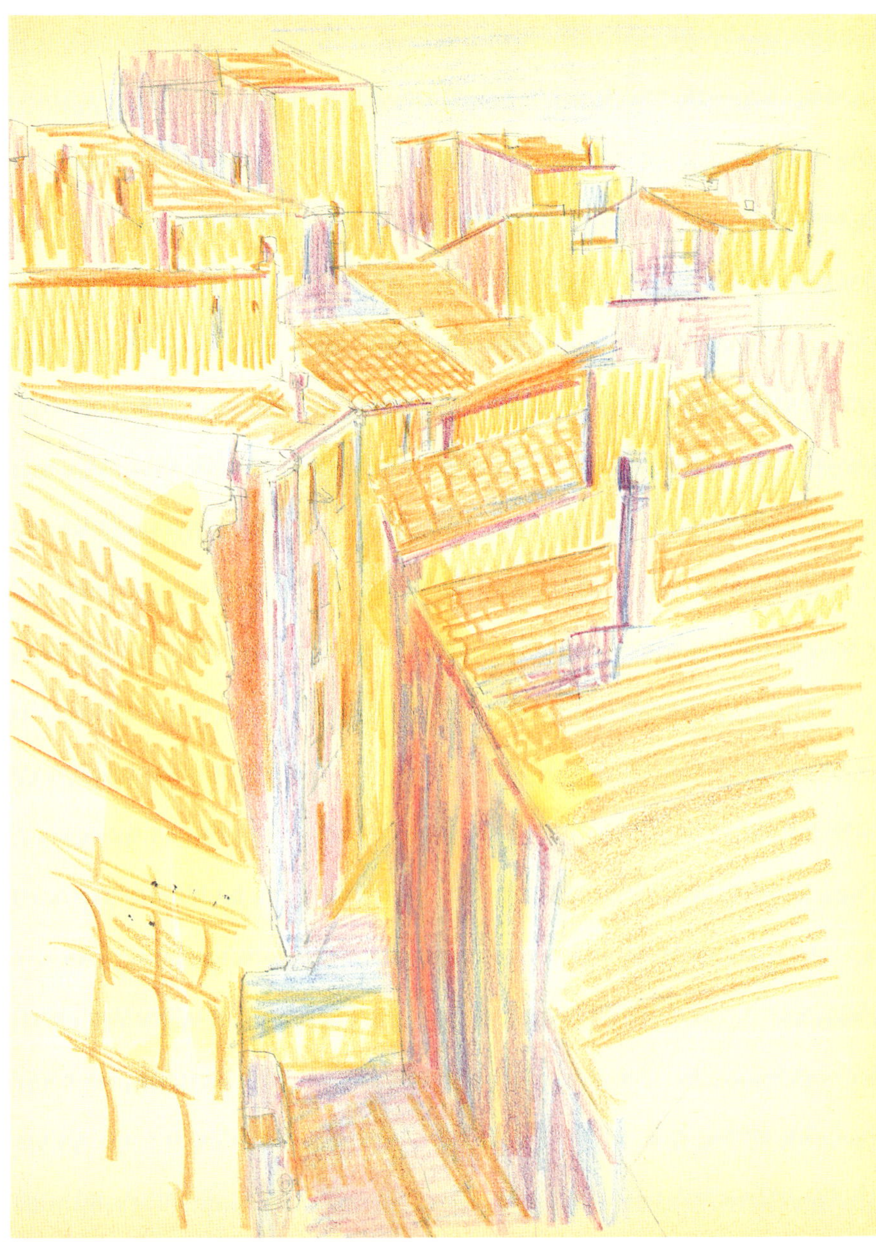

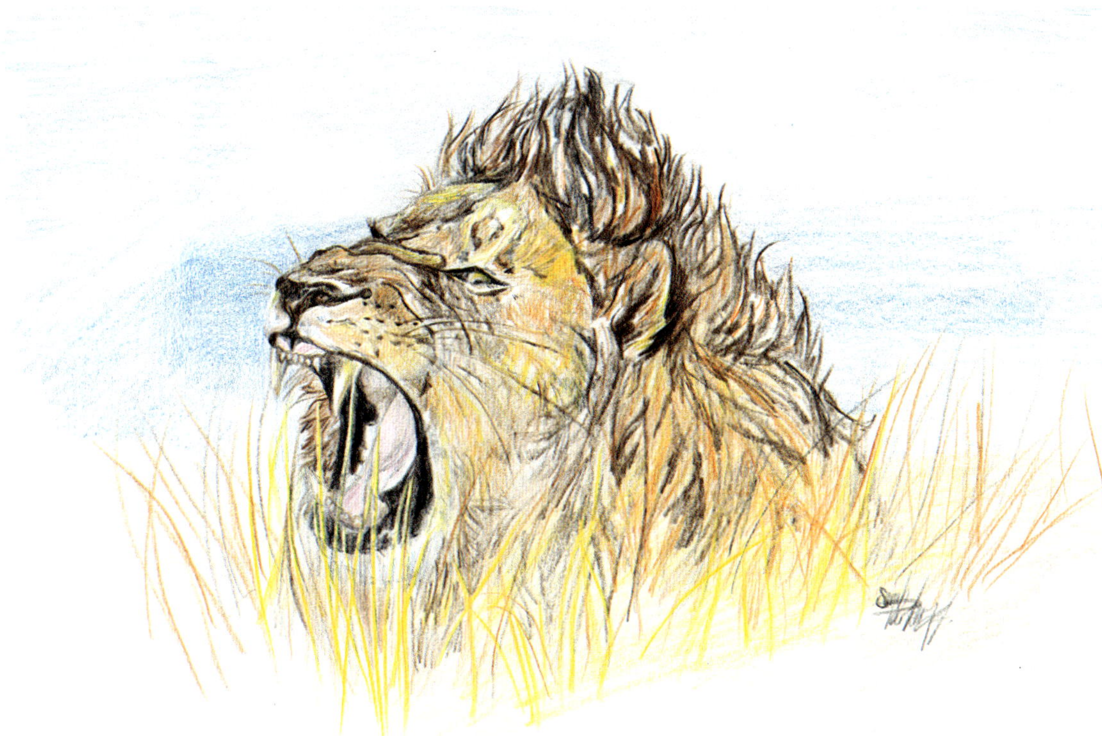

FAR LEFT
Sarah Parker
Sketchbook study of a Lion.
This artist makes detailed wildlife studies; colored pencils provide a swift and convenient sketching material.

FAR LEFT BELOW
Sketchbook study made in northern Spain.

LEFT
Sarah Parker
Sketchbook study

BELOW LEFT
Sketchbook study

BELOW AND BOTTOM
Ivy Pether
Sketchbook studies
Simple and effective preliminary paintings and drawings made using color pencils as a watercolor resource.

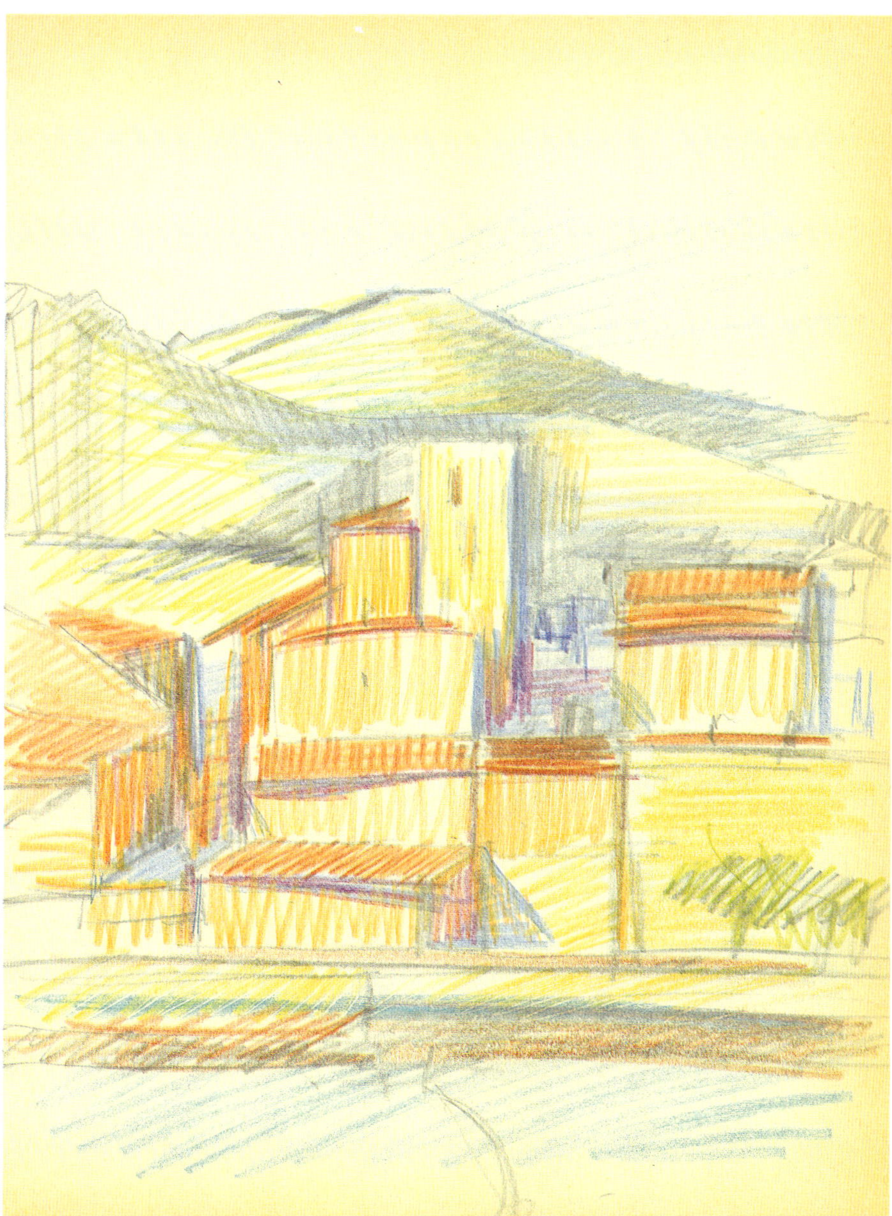

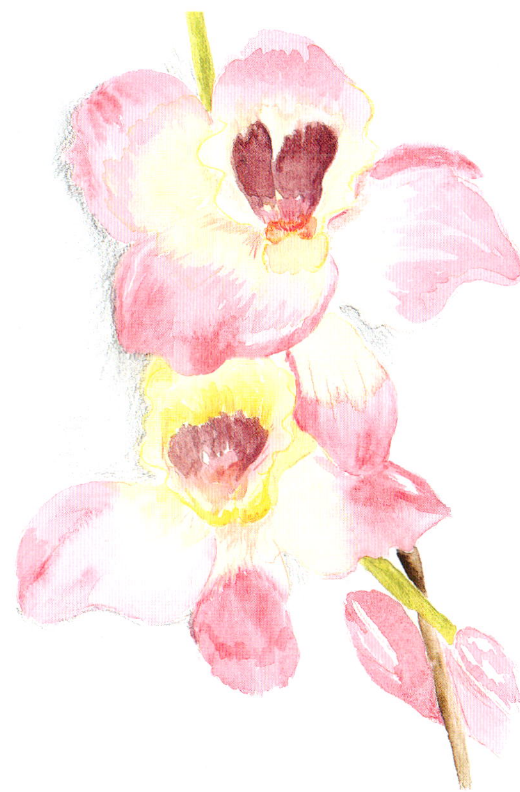

7. Landscape

Although landscape elements appear in both classical Greek and Roman art, landscape painting as a separate theme probably first appeared in China during the Tang Dynasty (618-906 AD). A tradition of landscape drawing developed in the East that was based on visual memory. A view was observed, and after meditation back at the studio, a simplified and idealized view was created.

The observed and directly painted landscape comes much later. From the early fifteenth century, Renaissance art began to include delicate and detailed imaginary landscapes as a background element, as an evocation of mood and place, but it was the Northern European artists, such as the Dutch masters of the sixteenth/seventeenth centuries, who brought the landscape to our

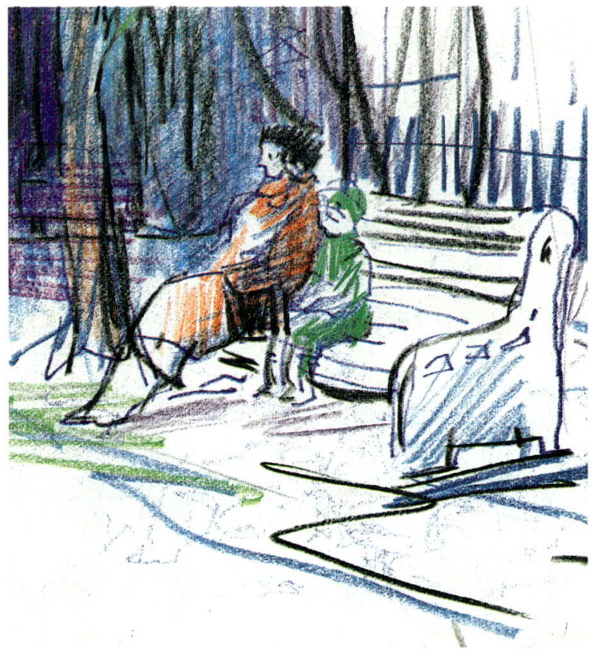

LEFT (DETAIL) AND BELOW
Madeleine Baker
St Anne's Church, Wandsworth
A simple and direct drawing where the role of color is to add atmosphere and space.

RIGHT AND FAR RIGHT
Oliver McLarnon
These sketches made with soluble color rehearse most of the themes that will be taken up as a finished painting.

BELOW RIGHT
The Louvre Pyramid
This is a worked version of an earlier detailed sketch, and uses both the dry and wet qualities of color pencils.

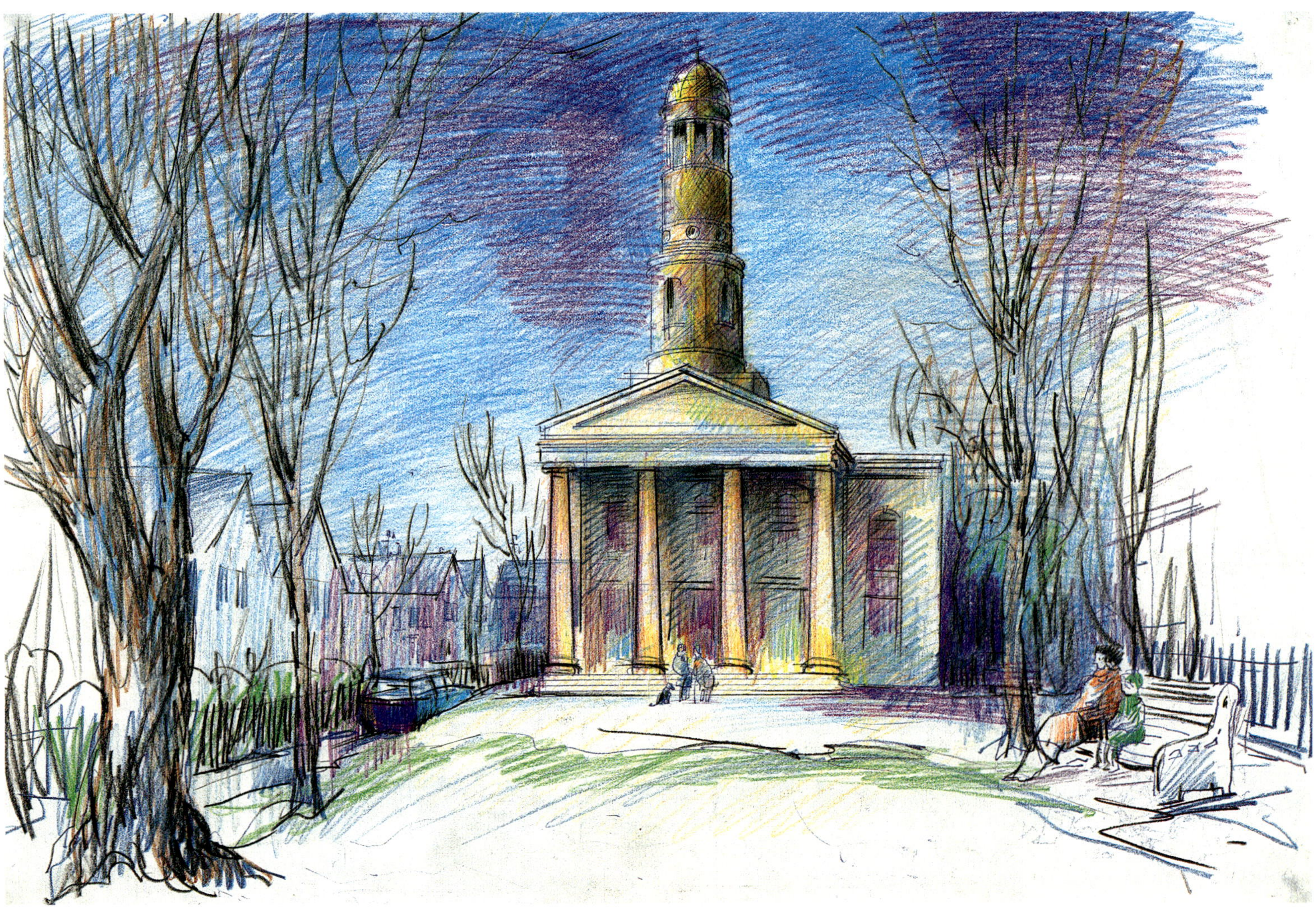

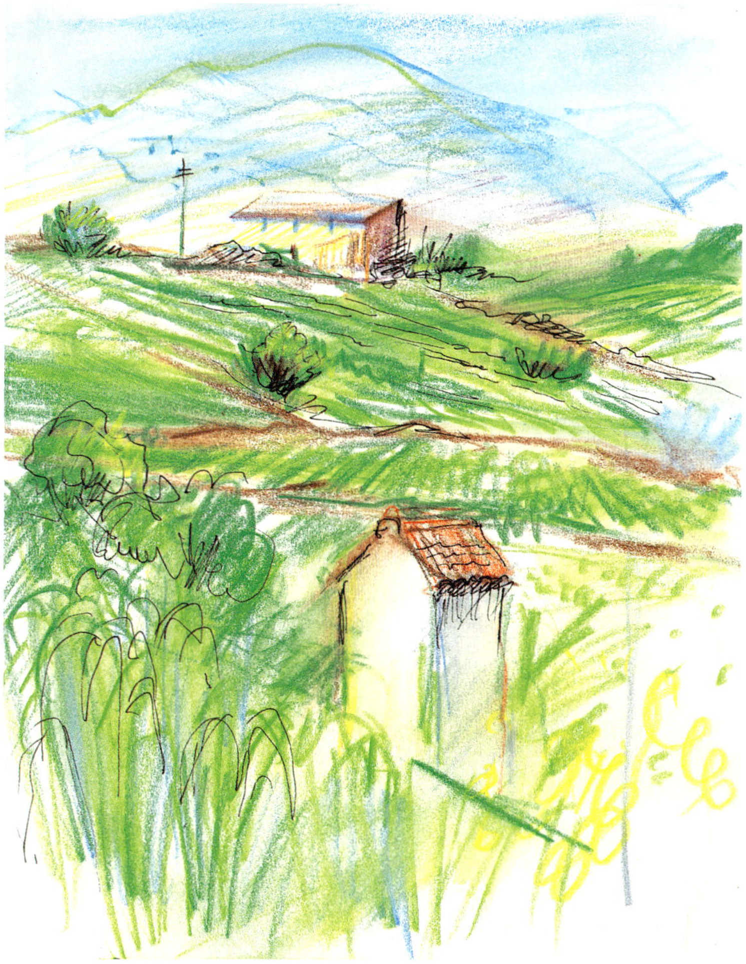

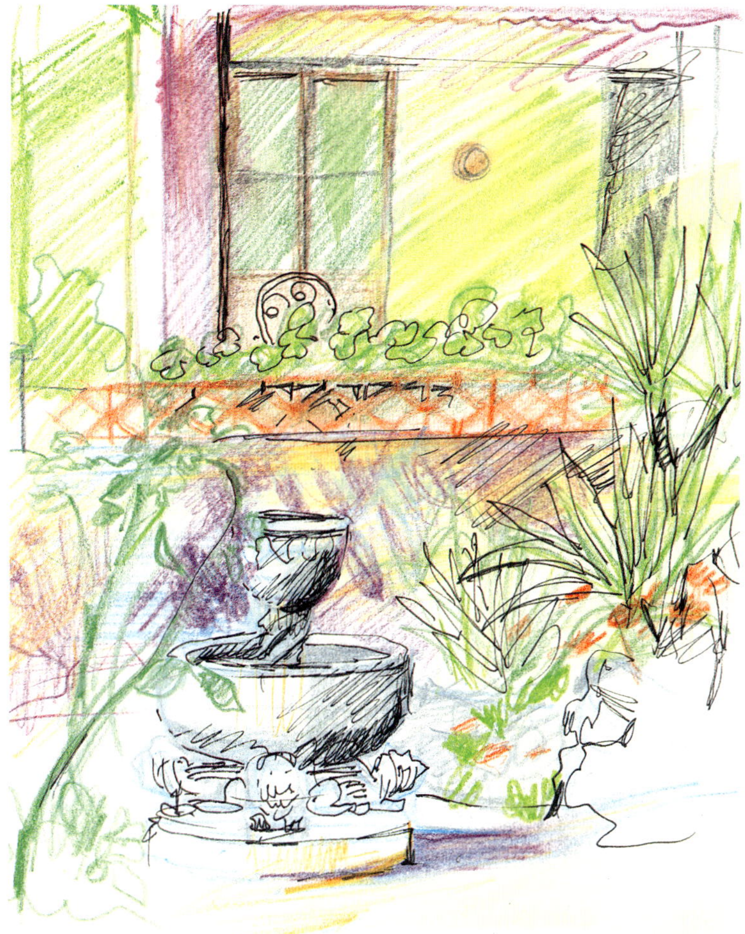

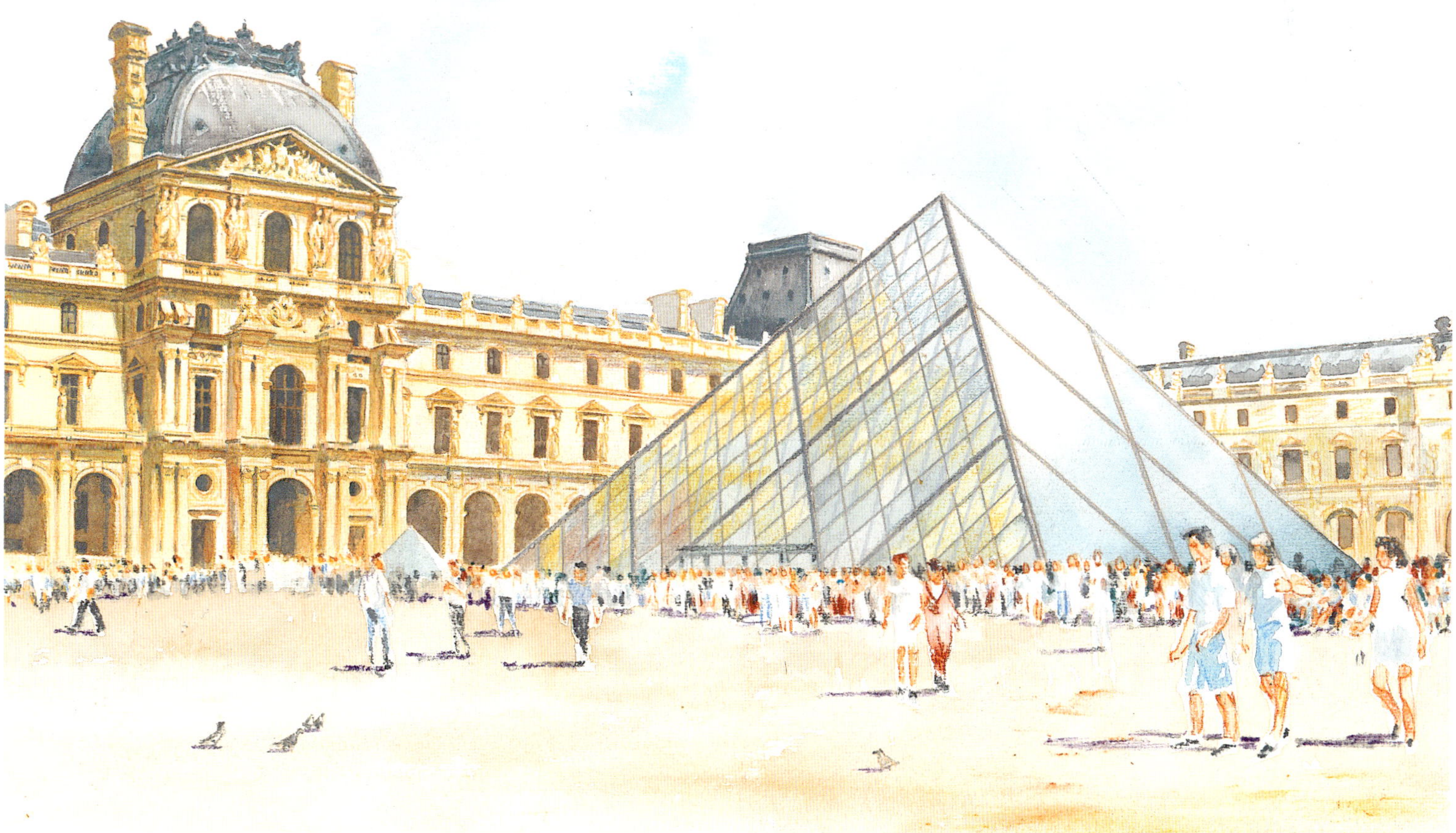

attention as a subject in its own right. While Dutch paintings were essentially representative and naturalistic, the French classicists Poussin and Claude created idealized evocations of a golden age. With the easily portable materials of the nineteenth century, from which our color pencils derive, artists began to travel widely in search of fresh inspiration and to record the landscape, albeit with a deeply romantic eye.

Because they are so easy to carry, colored pencils are an ideal material for working in the landscape. If you are interested in images from the landscape, a few points and directions are listed below.

- Make use of small sketches.
- There are many ways to interpret landscape. You might focus on color, space, structure, perspective, scale, elements that evoke mood.
- You might try a simplification of what you see: complex forms replaced by simple related structures.
- You might try to evoke the feeling of place in a decorative or abstract way, using sketches done on site.
- Remember that your picture is a graphic version of what you see.
- Look at the work of other artists who work in a similar way.

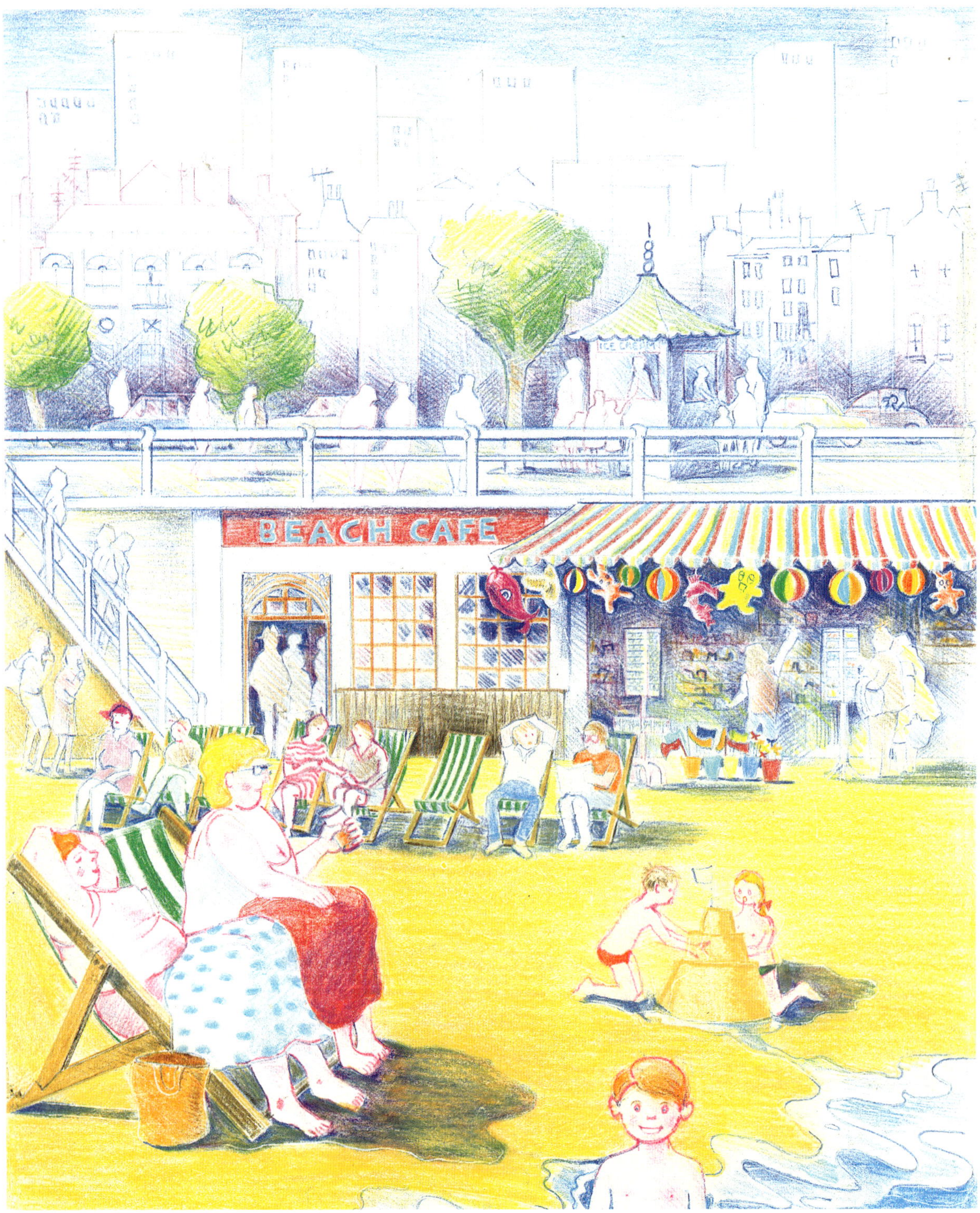

LEFT
Madeleine Baker
Beach Scene
A humorous picture, using bright color to describe the scene and the feel of the place. Distance and space are indicated with some selective open drawing in blue.

RIGHT ABOVE
Winter Wood
This piece evokes the subject using the gentle contrast between pale pink-gray and blue-gray.

RIGHT BELOW
Cornish Coast
Space, scale, and atmosphere is indicated by working color into the paper with a damp cloth. The tones are then worked into with pencils.

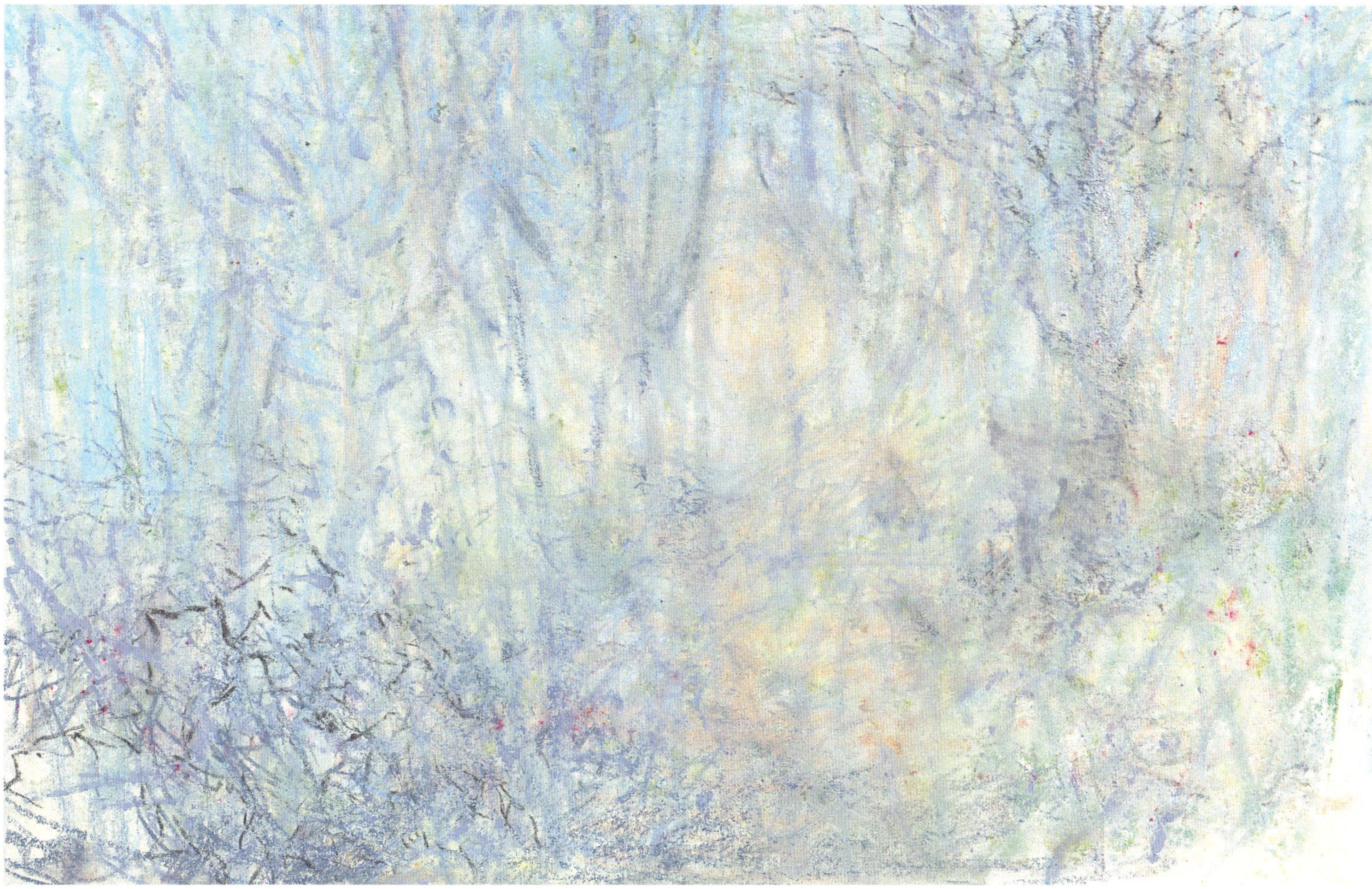

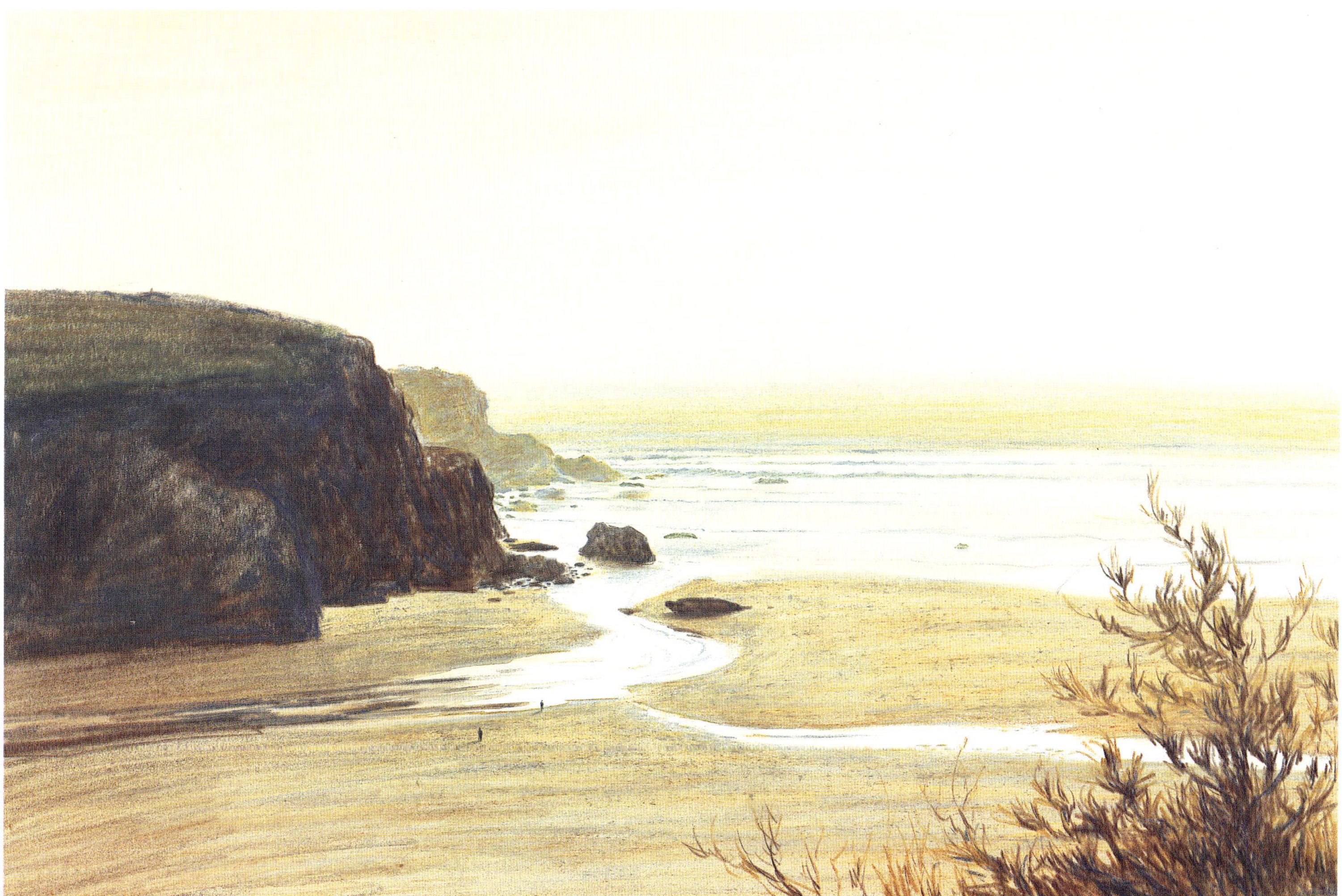

8. Figure and Portrait

The matchstick men of prehistoric cave-painting, still found in some bush cultures, and always a characteristic of children's art, is where figure drawing starts. From these beginnings, civilizations produced their own ideas of the human figure. The depiction of the figure was often coded or schematized, rather than drawn from observation, but remember this was done from custom, and not necessarily from an absence of visual skill. Artists could load a schematized figure with all sorts of other information, in a way that corresponds to writing.

The first views of the human figure that seem in any way realistic arose in Egypt, and more impressively in the Aegian civilizations of the Mediterranean. Even when further developed by the Greeks, the figure was idealized, and the interest was in pursuing an image based on 'perfect' human proportions.

Early Christianity reacted against the depiction and visual celebration of the physical body. Once again the flattened schematized figure was preferred. The change between this medieval approach and what is now termed Renaissance art can be easily seen in the work of the great artist and draftsman Albrecht Dürer. Here we encounter drawings of people who look both human and believable, although the general

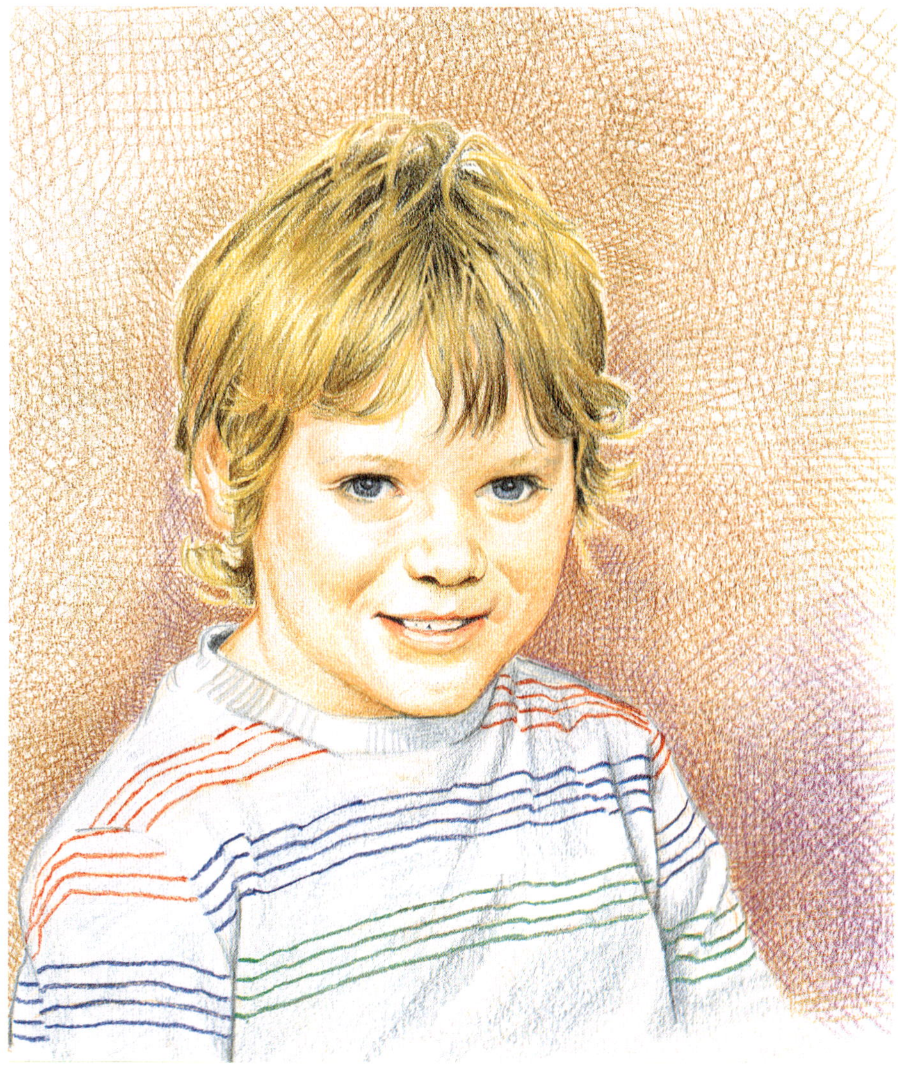

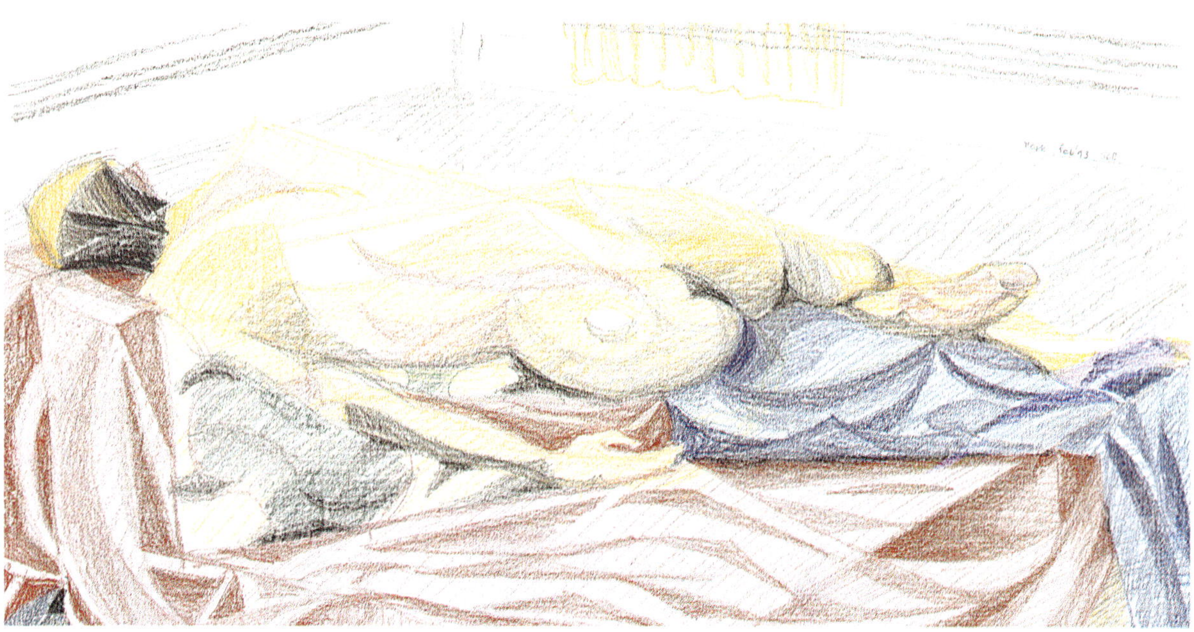

ABOVE
A traditional drawing, using a pale-colored paper as a base, with simple cross-hatching and shading.

LEFT
Sandy Brown
Figure Drawing
Here the figure is constructed with simple contours, using local color.

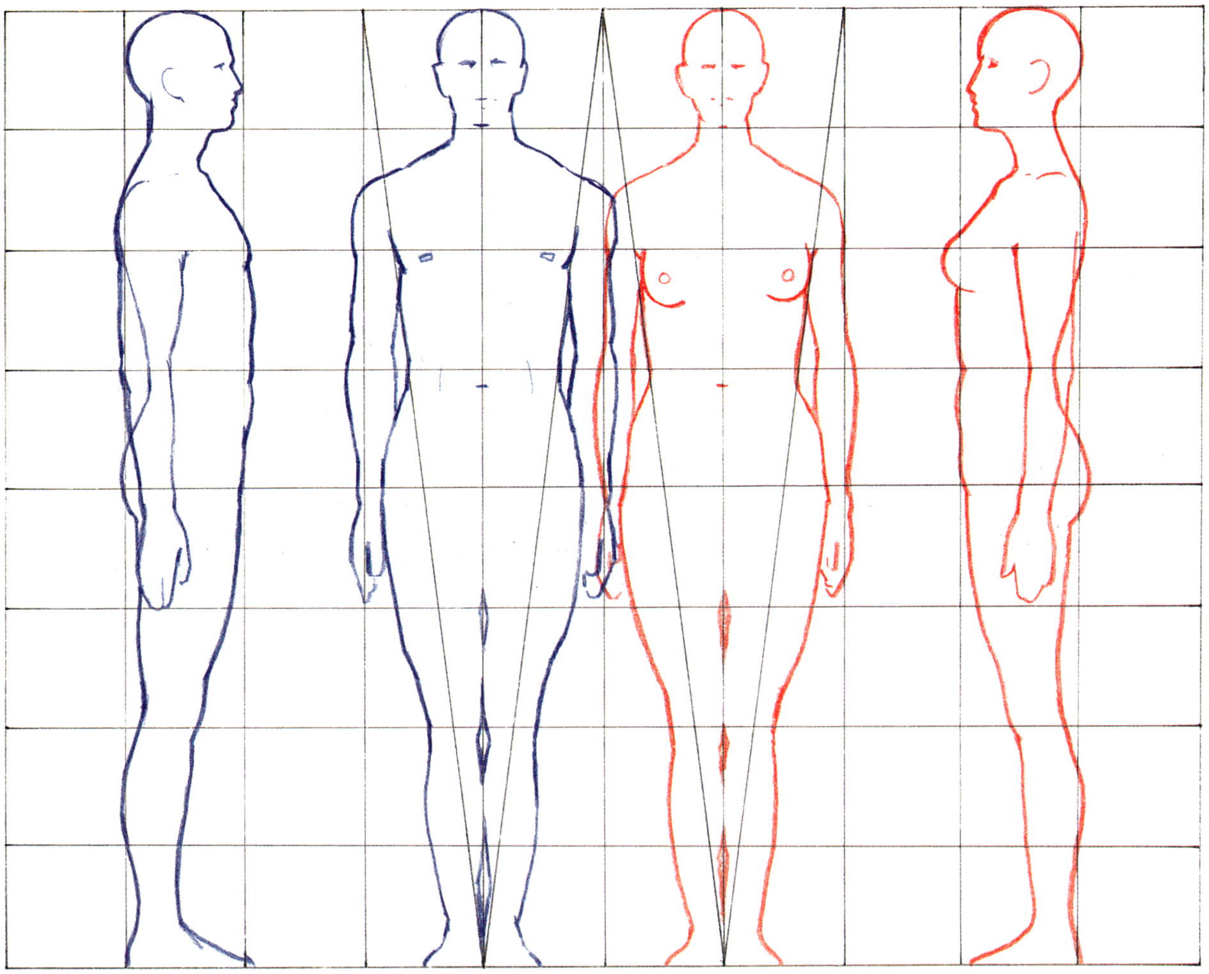

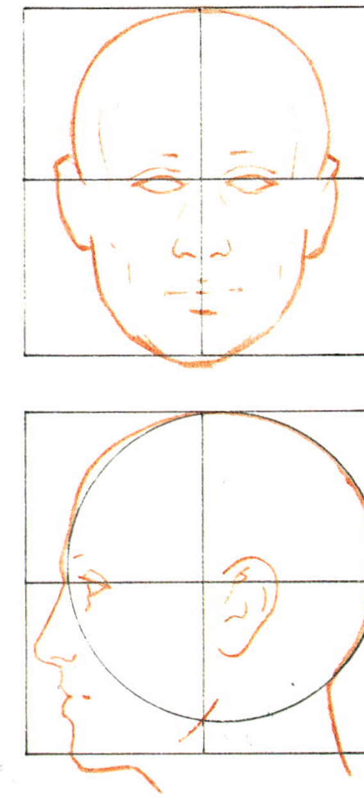

ABOVE AND ABOVE LEFT
The generalized proportions of the head and body.

BELOW
Figure Drawing
This drawing was begun in a simple pale-gray wash which described the surrounding space. The rest of the pose was articulated with progressively darker pigment and flesh color as a highlight.

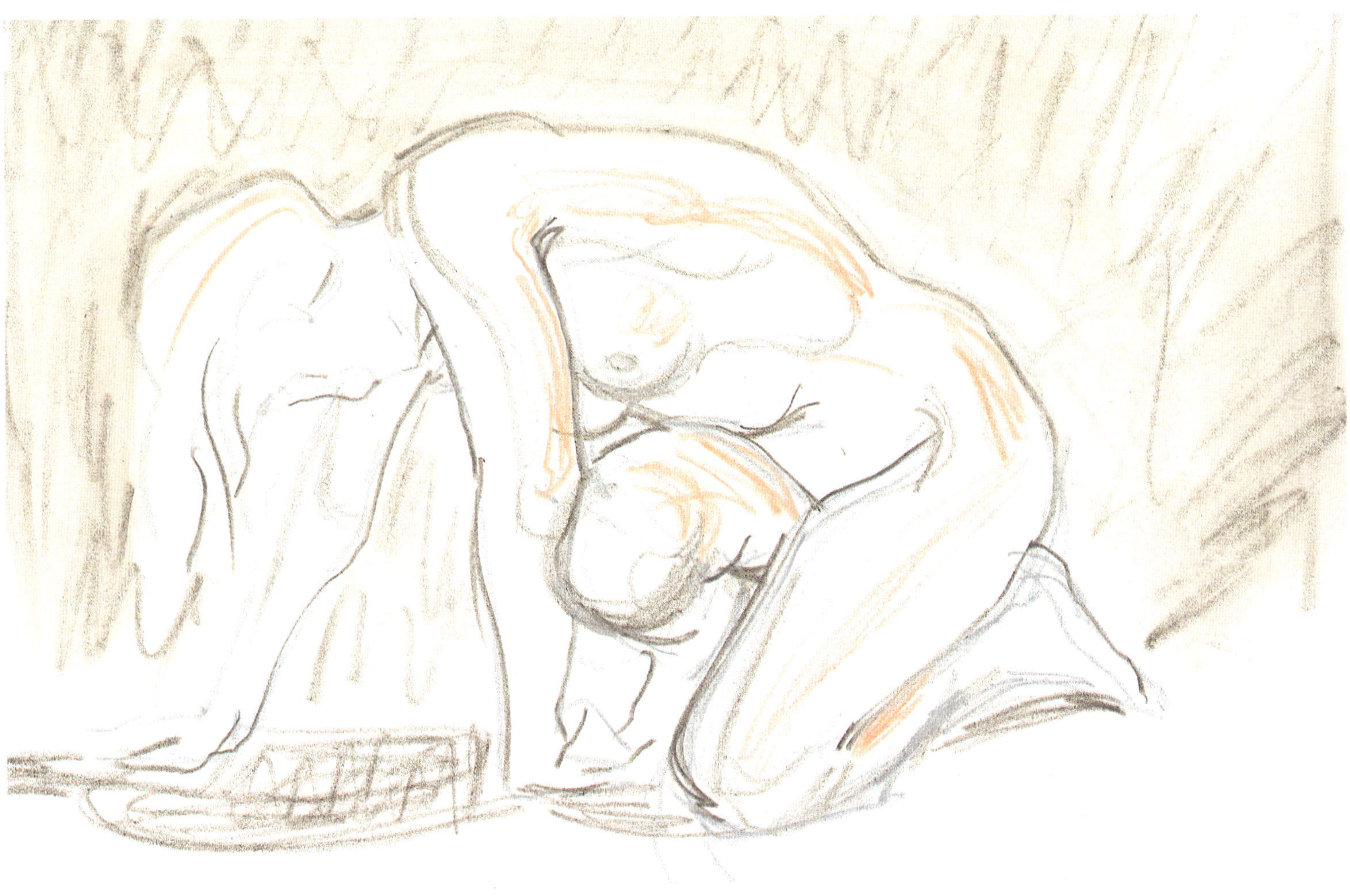

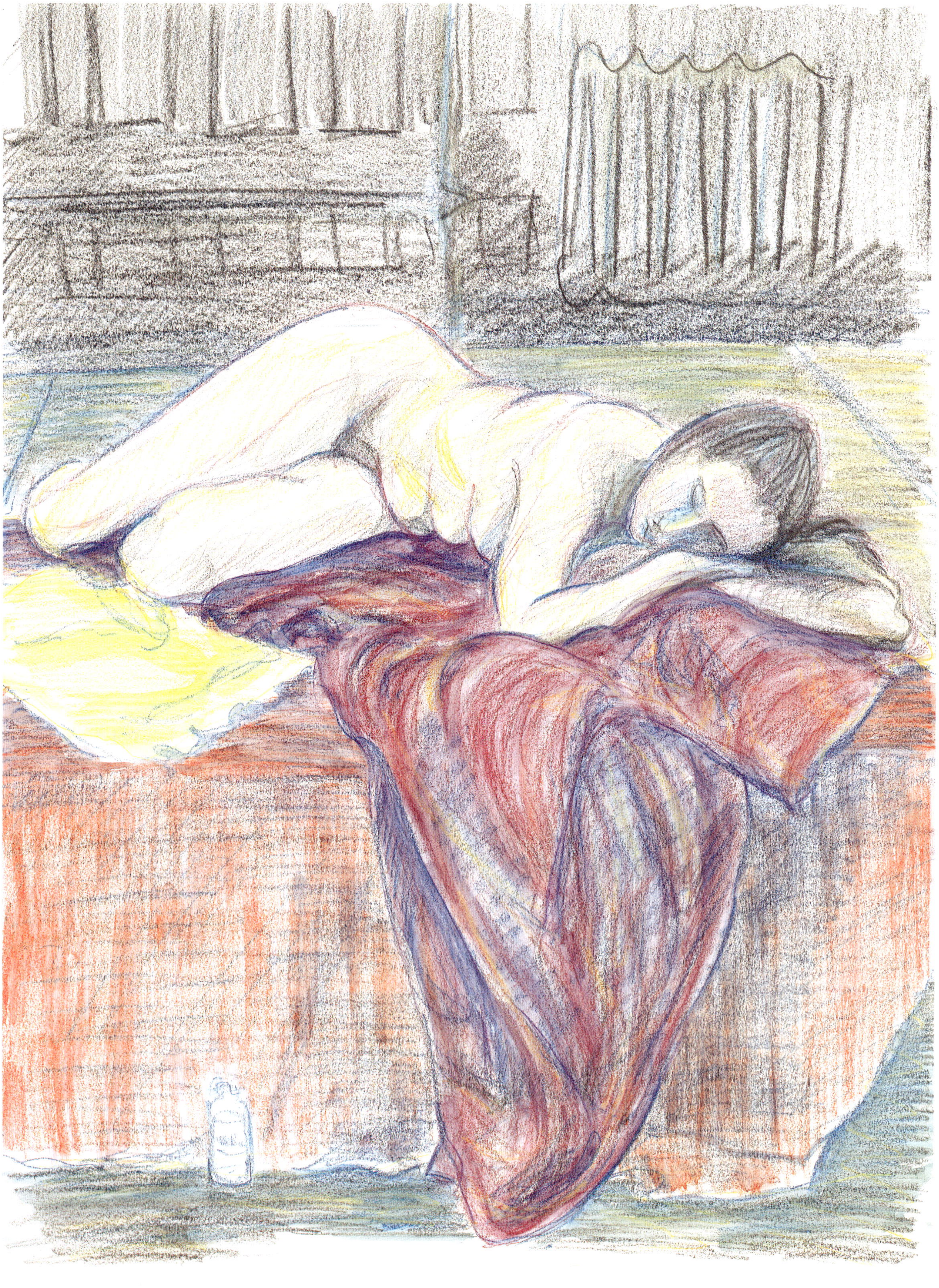

trend in Renaissance art looked to a reinvention of idealized figures.

For us, whether we are looking for ideal beauty, or just ways of drawing the figure as we see it, it is helpful to borrow some of the old ideas of proportion to avoid the mistakes we all make when false memory and observation collide. I have included a view of the generalized proportions of the human figure and head. This is only a guide; few of us match these ideal proportions. Some figure work has also been shown using the processes described earlier.

Because of their importance and familiarity, figures and faces can be seen and recognized as such even in the most distorted and dismantled views, which can give the artist the chance to load all sorts of other meanings and elements onto the figure. Below are a few guidelines for figure and portrait drawing.

- Because we are human ourselves, we are extremely critical of figure drawing.
- The problems are many: proportion, recognition, play of form, light, color.
- Choose first a simple statement of the pose.
- Pose your subject with clear intentions, control the light and surrounding area.
- Move around the pose, see its place, space and weight.
- Choose your position carefully. Try a

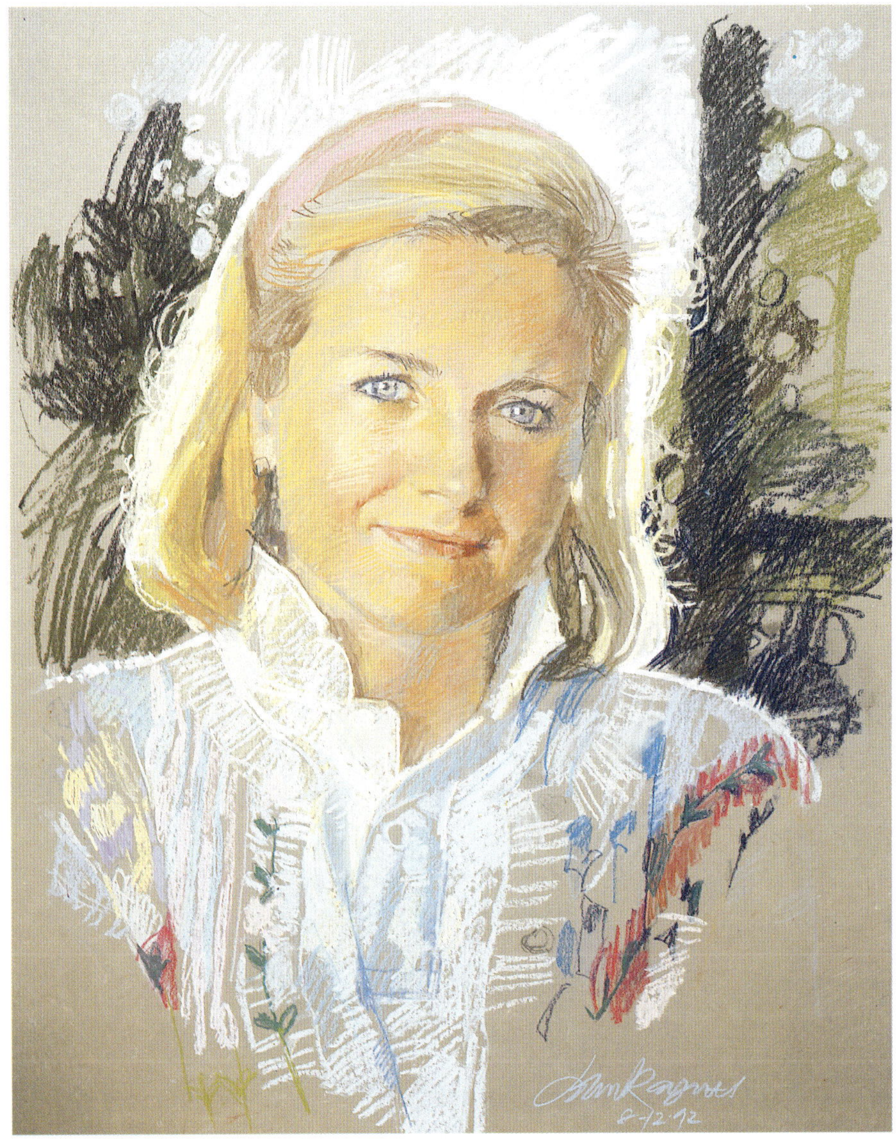

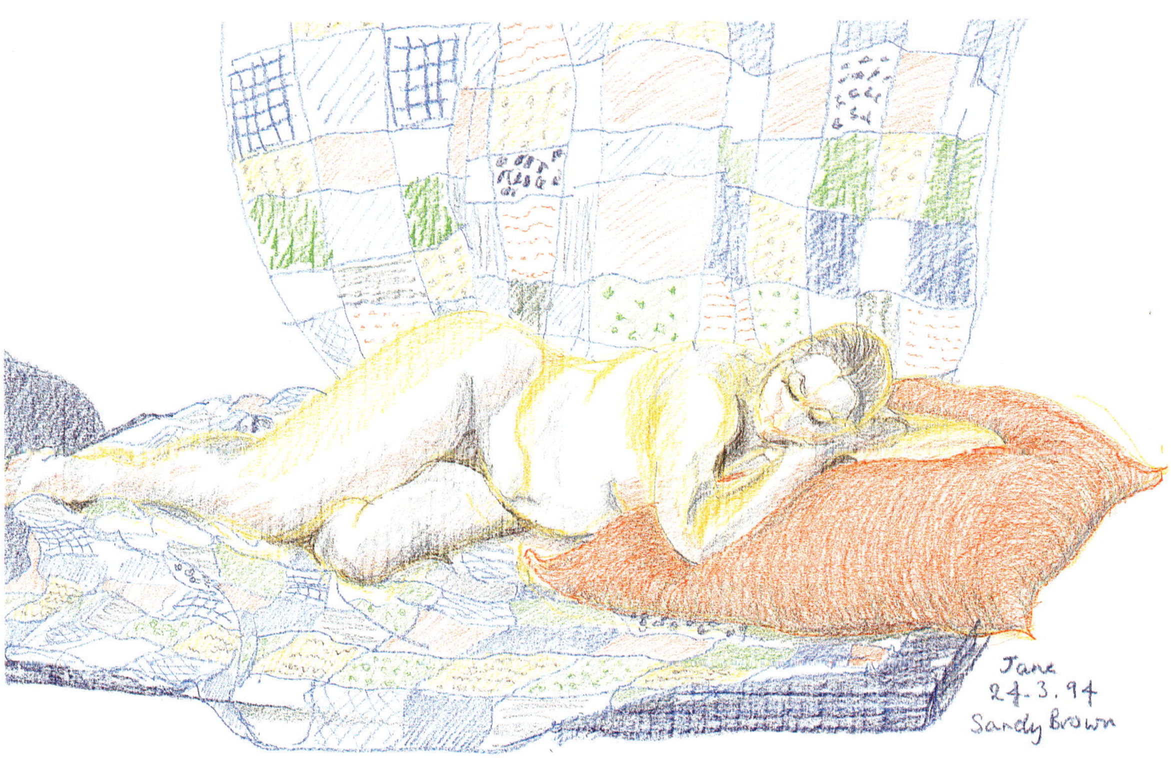

FAR LEFT AND LEFT
Two figure drawings where the artist is experimenting with ways of seeing the figure. In one (far left), the model is almost isolated by concentrations of tone and color; in the other (near left), a delightful use of open pattern and color both encloses and complements the model.

ABOVE
John Raynes
Portrait Study
All sorts of technical skills are on display here, from the minimal early marks to the focused overlaid work on the head.

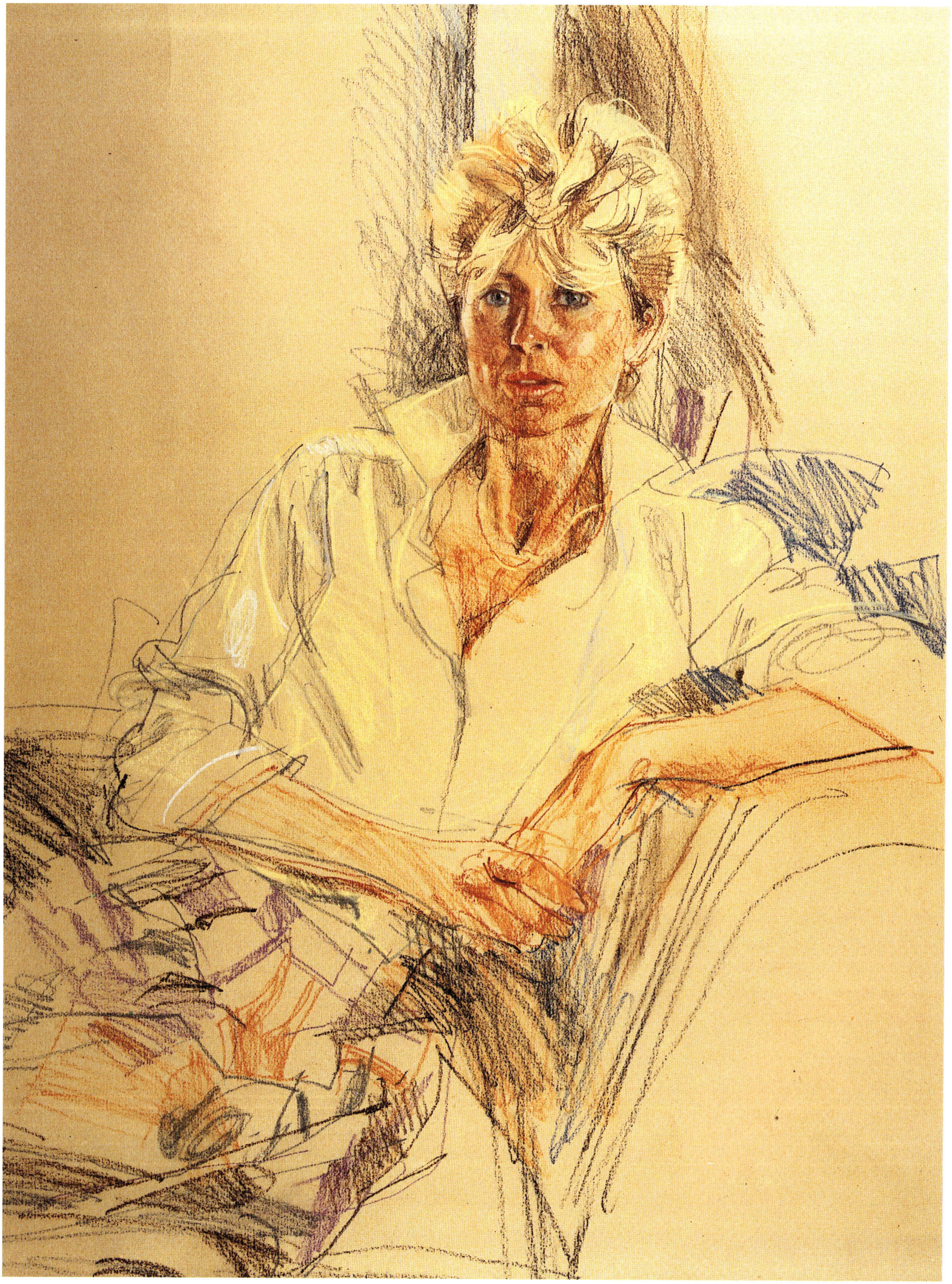

small provisional sketch, try a rectangular viewer, see it as a whole composition.
- Start faintly, build toward a finished view.
- Look for references: vertical, horizontal, angles of limbs, features, spine.
- Check proportions, measured sighting.
- Strengthen tone and color when you are confident of the pose.
- Look at the model more than at the drawing.
- Look at other artists' solutions to similar problems.
- Because of the many problems, figure drawing is a superb artistic training.
- If possible, attend a figure drawing class; we learn well from one another.

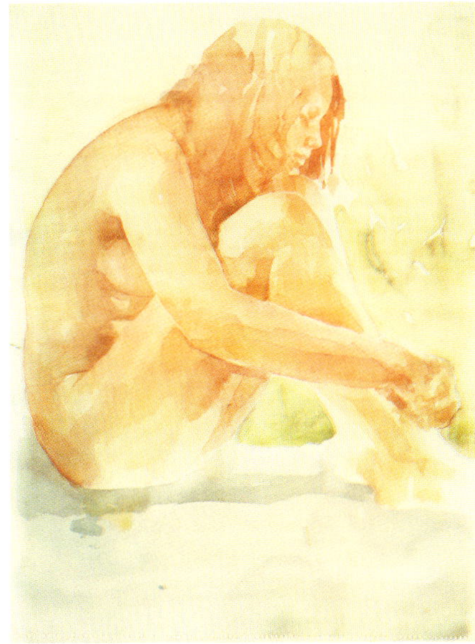

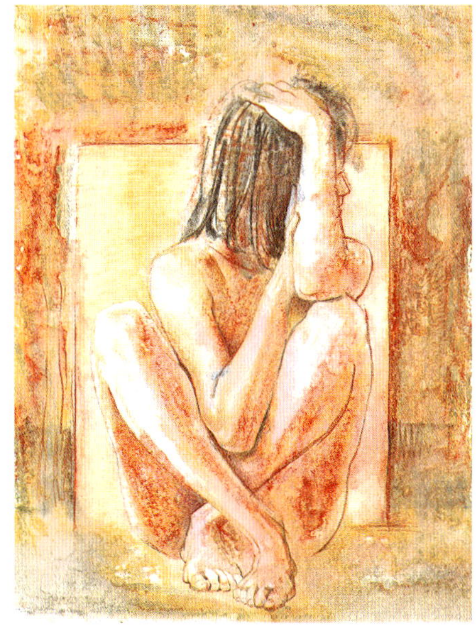

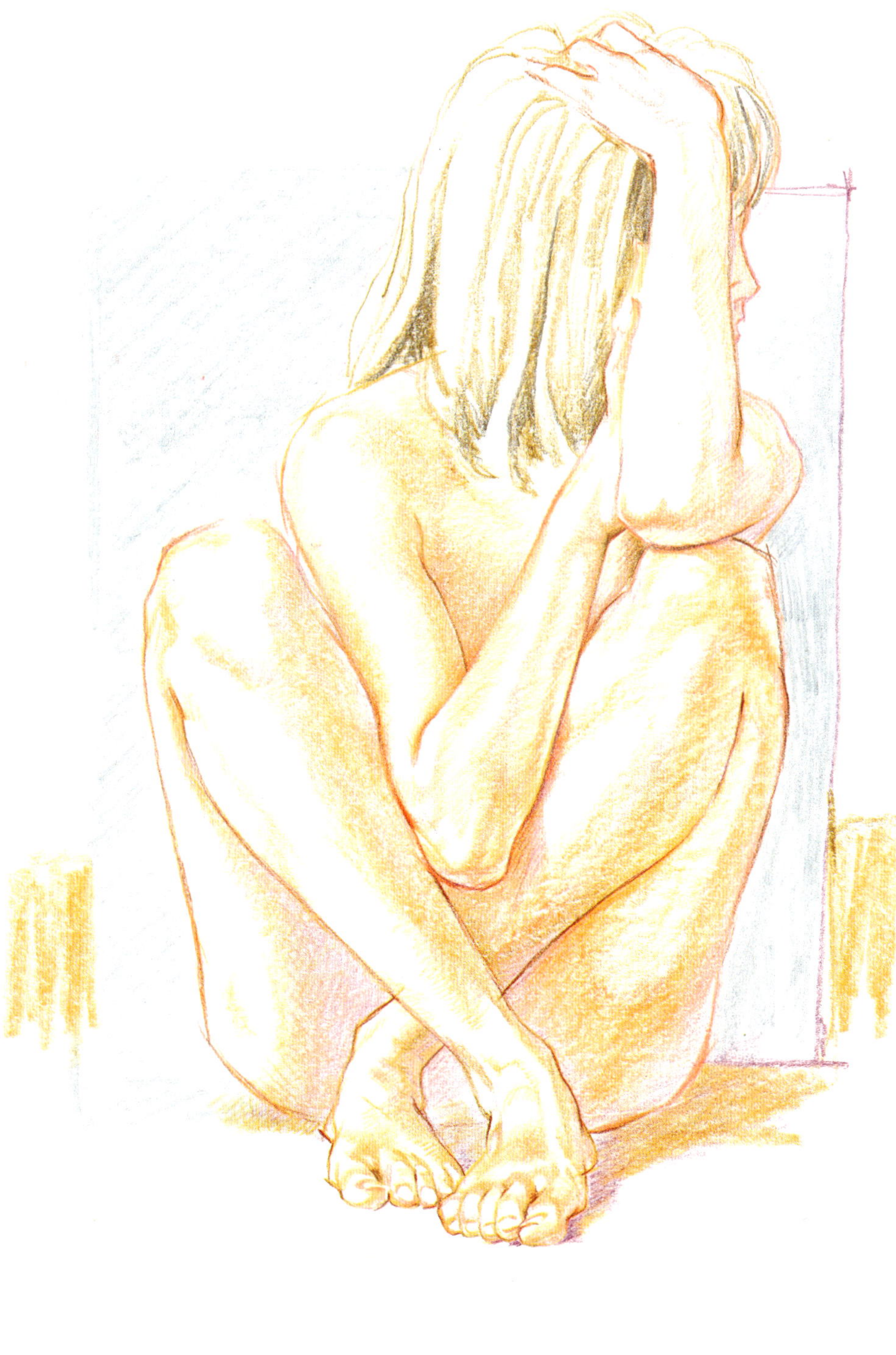

FAR LEFT
John Raynes
Portrait Study
A vigorous and dynamic drawing, with most of the work consisting of open, energetic line. We can see the whole process exposed; the first marks are as visible as the last.

ABOVE LEFT
Figure Drawing
This is really a traditional watercolor, where the pencil pigment has been scraped and dissolved. The starting point was a very pale red line in soluble pencil.

ABOVE
Surface Print
Once the basic drawing (left) is understood, color and tecture can be manipulated by printing pigment from another piece of paper, using damp surfaces and a hairdryer. This can then be drawn into.

LEFT
Figure Drawing
Here the real descriptive mark is made by a cutting line, started faintly in red, and worked into with darker violet and burnt sienna. The flesh and other tones sketch in form and color.

8. Natural Forms

Objects and collections of things have a fascination all their own. From Renaissance art, where an artist might display his technical wizardry by depicting a bowl of fruit that is practically edible, to the Dutch masters who used still-lifes as subjects and even as commentary on their lives, the delight in the depiction and visual understanding of a real object is with us still.

To gain a visual understanding of a natural form or a made object, I recommend some preliminary structural drawings as outlined above (page 73). In this way, you can get an understanding of the underlying structure both on the page and in your head. This is really necessary if you are attempting a closely observed drawing. The following are guidelines for drawing a still life.

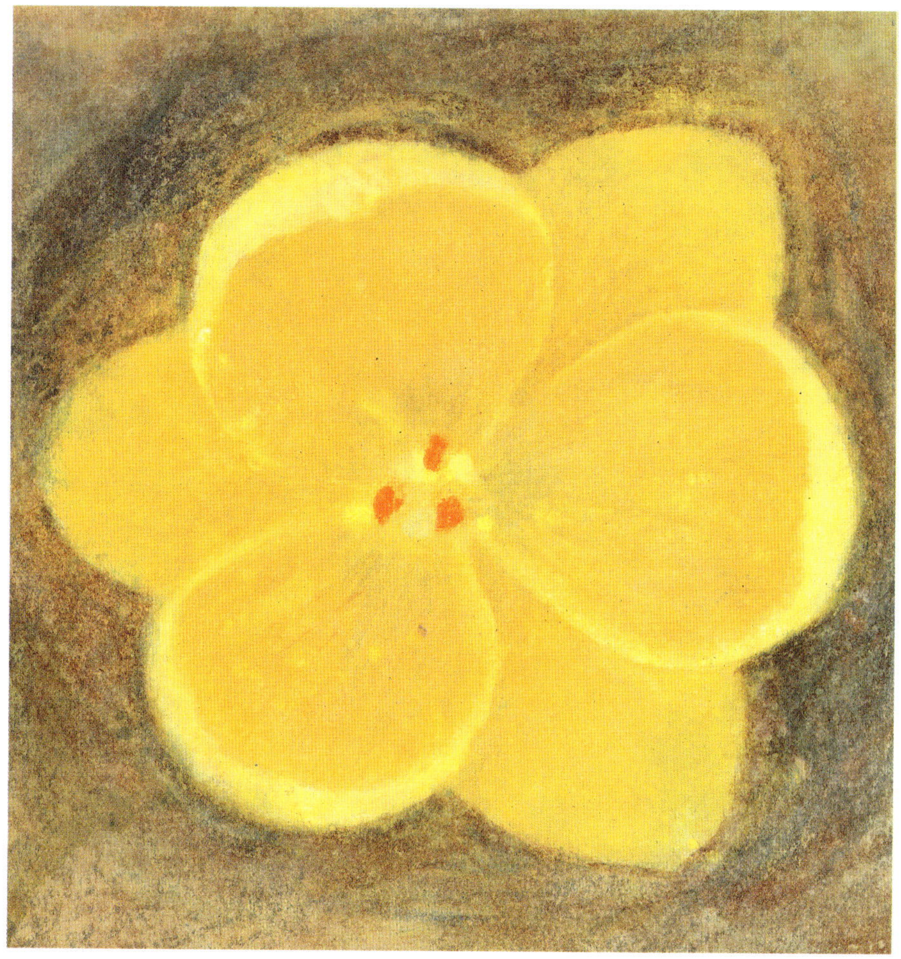

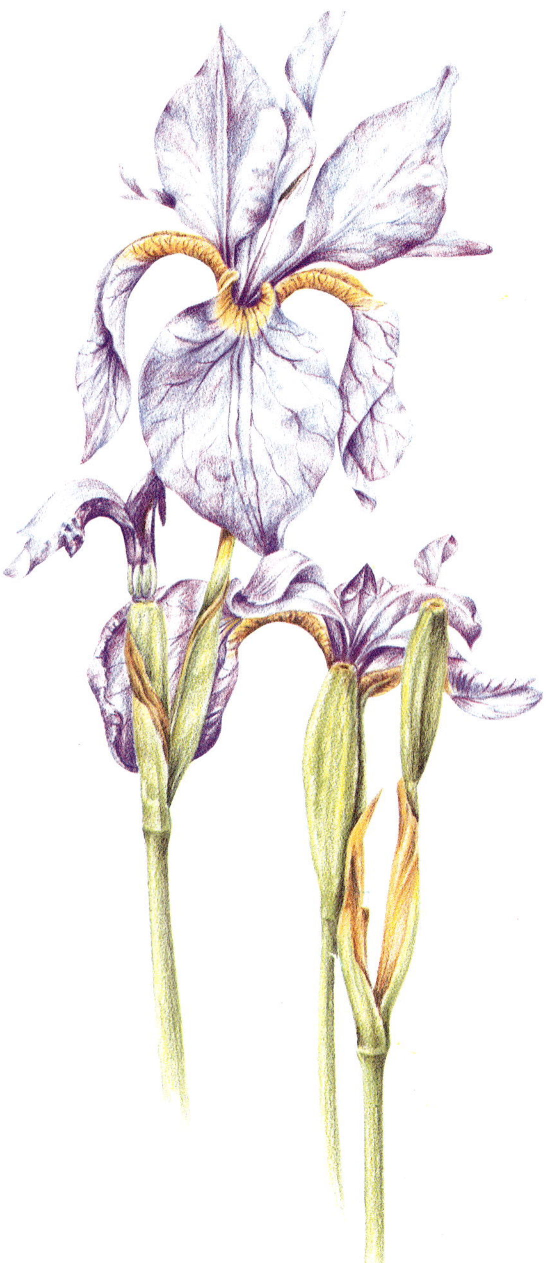

- We are surrounded by a vast array of natural and made objects. The most humble weed or item of rubbish can become a real challenge to the artist.
- The way you select and place objects in their real space is the first act of composition.
- Through preliminary sketching, try and understand the structure, shape, color and texture of your objects.
- In the same way, understand the spatial relationships within the object.
- These considerations can spark off more imaginative ideas and compositions.
- Look at other artists' work.

ABOVE
This piece is printed whole, using soft pigment drawn onto a separate piece of paper and ironed onto the artwork with a domestic iron. This produces a surface with a lovely saturated feel and gives a subtle ambiguity about the edges.

LEFT
Jane Bennett
Irises
This exquisite rendering of natural forms uses just the texture of the paper and the traditional skills of the botanical illustrator.

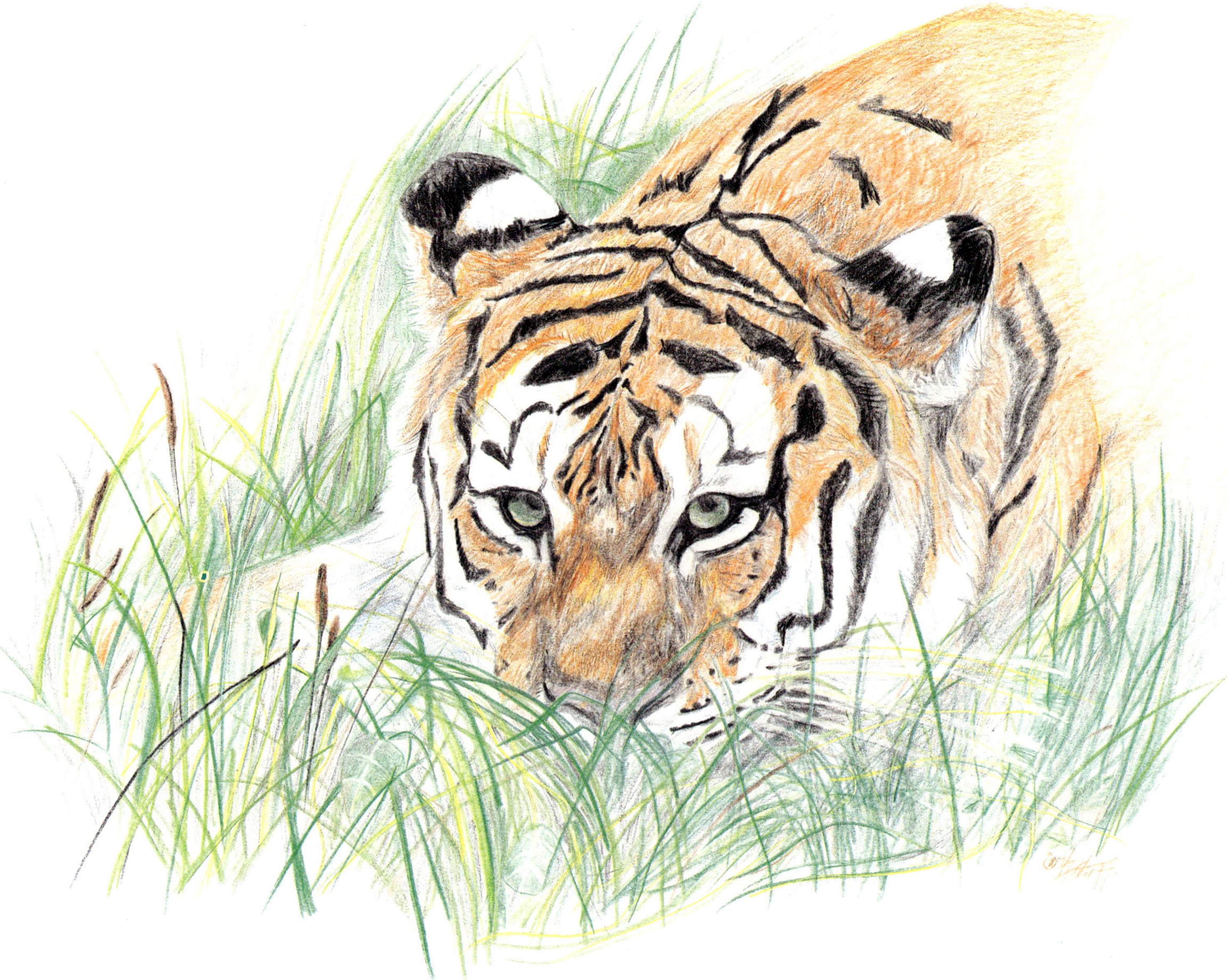

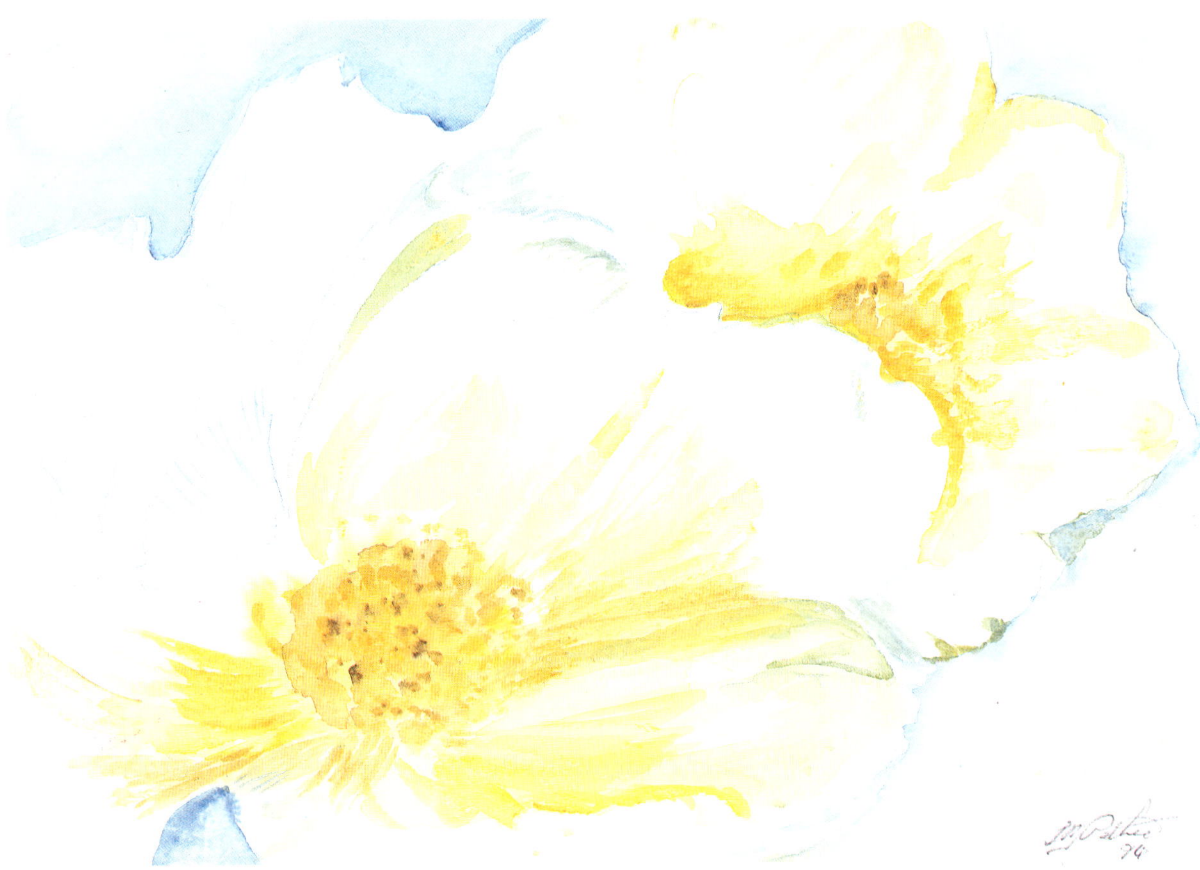

ABOVE
Sarah Parker
Tiger
This is a closely-observed and fully-realized drawing using traditional color pencils. To achieve this degree of realism, as with botanical studies, requires close proximity, preliminary drawings and, often, photographic reference.

LEFT
Ivy Pether
Flower Painting
This delightful expression of a flower is not observed as a botanical illustration, but rather freshly treated almost as a landscape. Three soluble colors were used as watercolor.

10. Criticism and Self-Appraisal

Other people may want to judge your work by all sorts of different criteria, from the 'I don't know about art but I know what I like' brigade, to people who want to hijack particular artistic values for some political or prejudicial agenda. Art history is packed with different movements, schools and styles, which can bewilder both professional and amateur artists. The key to your own confidence and development lies in a clear understanding of your own likes and dislikes, and what you are trying to do.

In his book entitled *The Story of Art*, Professor Sir Ernst Gombrich starts his introduction 'On Art and Artists' with the statement: 'There really is no such thing as Art. There are only artists.' In this marvelous book, the author takes us through the story of art in a language that is informative without resorting to jargon or condescension. I recommend this book to anyone who wants a thorough introduction to the subject. It is clear from his opening statement that art is what people make, and that Art with a capital A has no real existence except in the terms of the people at the top of various cultures, who seek to define it.

So where does that leave us? How are we to judge our own work? And how can we judge others' work? Firstly and simply, by preference, in the same way as you might judge a meal or a drink - I like this, I don't like that. This is a perfectly respectable first approach; in fact it is infinitely preferable to trying to like something because somehow we think we should.

However, to stay with this approach does not get us very far, and for those who may wish to further their understanding of their own and others' work, there are some useful questions we might ask when we consider any piece of art. I have set these out below as a sort of model, and although they are worded to address other artists' work, they can equally well relate to your own. It can be much more difficult to criticize your own work, and artists often go to great lengths in attempting to assess and rank their finished pieces.

Some people find it useful to display the piece for a while. Some parts of the drawing may be found wanting after you have lived with it for a while. An opposite approach is to hide the work and then look at it afresh, as if it was not yours. If it is a question of composition or drawing, it may help to look at it in a mirror, where these elements will appear reversed. If some parts of picture-making are intuitive, we can only improve by informed self-criticism and practice.

In the model below, some of the questions may obviously be quite inappropriate to the particular work in question, and few pieces will respond to all these categories. However, in general terms this is a useful exercise for assessing your work.

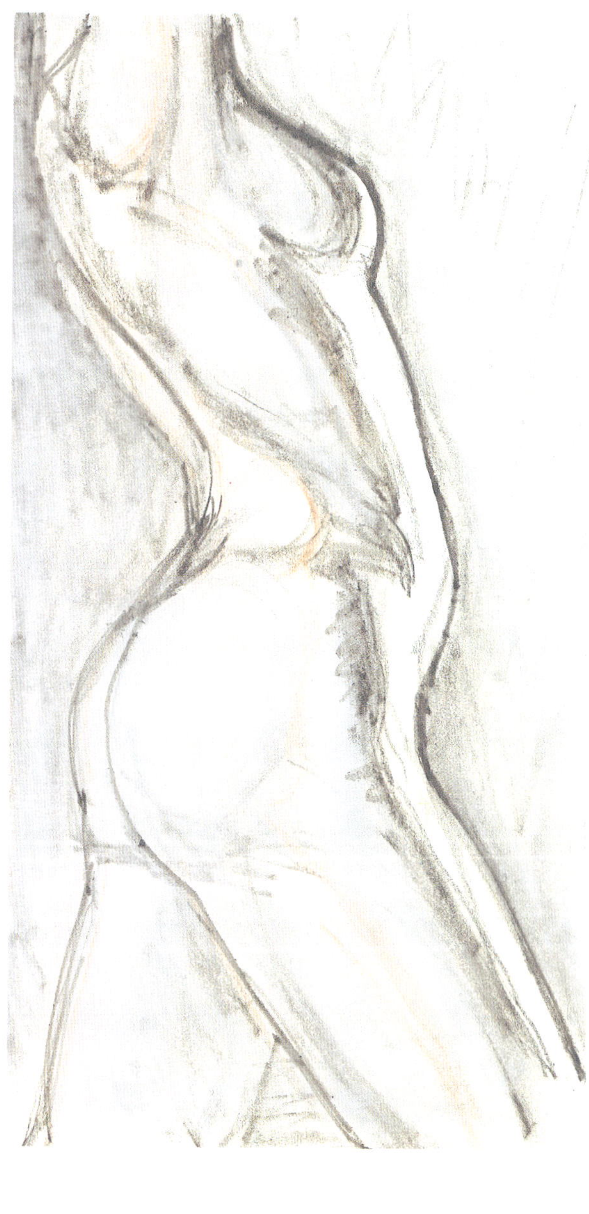

LEFT
Figure Drawing
Using the same method as the drawing on page 71, this piece was more successful in its earlier stage. The clean, white area of highlight is supposed to do all the work.

Assessing

- What does it feel like? How am I affected by the artwork; what response does it provoke? What is it that affects me? Is it simply expertise and skill? Is the work soothing or disturbing? Does it evoke feelings about nature or life? Can I recognize any emotions?
- What is it about? What is the subject of this drawing? Do I think the subject is important or secondary? Is the subject carrying a message of some personal concern to the artist? Do I think the subject was remembered or drawn from life? Is it a symbol for something else? Has it been distorted?
- What is it like? How are the elements arranged? What is the format and is it sympathetic with the subject? Is there one dominant shape or lots of inter-relating shapes? Does it work as a whole or only in parts?
- How was it made? What was it made with (in our case colored pencils)? What was the process and is it visible? Might there have been preliminary sketches? Was this speedily made or did it evolve over a long period? What variety of skills does the artist display?
- What is its background? What is the story behind this piece? How might others attempt a similar subject? Does this work belong to some school or style of art from which I might learn?

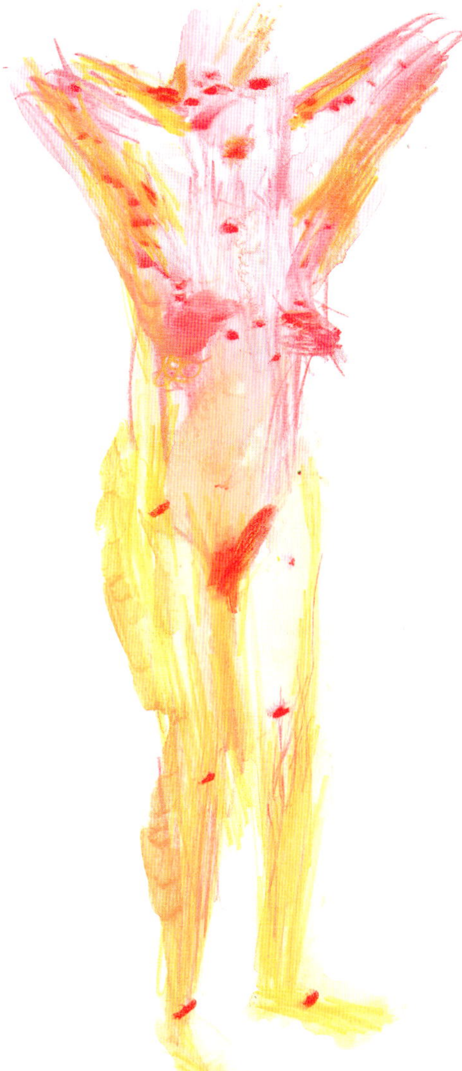

LEFT
Barbara Nicholls
Figure Drawing
A spontaneous and expressive reinvention of a figure. The pencil travels swiftly over the surface, and suggests a figure when the pink and orange marks are united with a wet brush.

BELOW
John Raynes
Figure Drawing
Technical confidence allows the artist to display the sensuous nature of silk, skin and hair with what appears to be a dynamic and effortless open line.

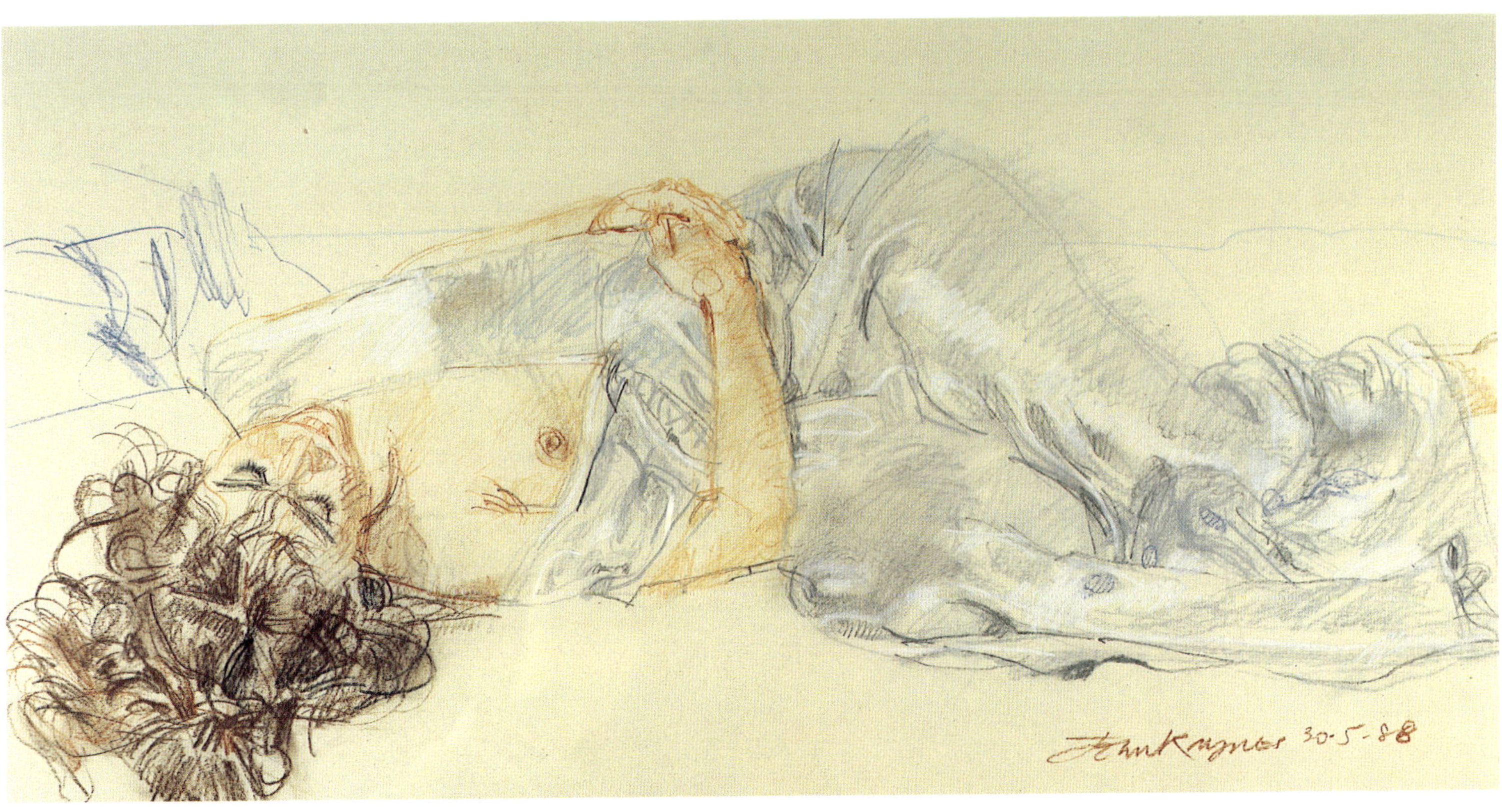

Index

Titles of drawings are italicized
Page numbers in bold italics indicate illustrations

Acknowledgments
The publisher would like to thank designer David Eldred, production manager Simon Shelmerdine and editor Jessica Hodge. We should also like to thank the following individuals, agencies and institutions for supply additional illustrative material.

Ashmolean Museum, Oxford: page 10
Baker, Madeleine: pages 2-3, 18 top, 30 top, 55 top, 66 both, 68
Bennett, Jane: page 76 left
Brown, Sandy: pages 28 top, 70 bottom, 72
Khakhria, Devayani: pages 4, 9, 34-35, 43, 52 bottom, 63
McLarnon, Oliver: pages 17 top right, 22 bottom, 67 top left and right
Metropolitan Museum of Art, NY: page 54 top (Gift of Felix M Warburg 1918, 18.58.3)
Musée d'Orsay, photo courtesy of RMNS: page 48 top
Nicholls, Barbara: 28 bottom, 42 top left, 79 top
Parker, Sarah: pages 1, 64 top, 65 top, 77 top
Pether, Ivy: page 42 bottom, 65, 77 left
Pether, Sophie: page 48 left
Raynes, John: pages 7, 21, 27, 41, 73 top, 74, 79 bottom
San Diego Museum of Art, CA: page 14 bottom
Tate Gallery, London: page 12/13
Windsor Castle, Royal Library c 1995 Her Majesty the Queen: page 11